The Blessings of Weekly Communion

THE BLESSINGS OF WEEKLY COMMUNION

Kenneth W. Wieting

CONCORDIA PUBLISHING HOUSE · SAINT LOUIS

Published by Concordia Publishing House
3558 S. Jefferson Ave., St. Louis, Missouri 63118-3968
1-800-325-3040 • www.cph.org

Library of Congress Cataloging-in-Publication Data
Wieting, Kenneth W.
      The blessings of weekly communion / Kenneth W. Wieting.
         p. cm.
      Includes bibliographical references.
      ISBN 0-7586-0614-1
      1. Lord's Supper—Frequency of communion. 2. Lord's Supper—
Lutheran Church—Missouri Synod. I. Title.
      BX8073.W48   2006
      264'.041322036—dc22

                                                            2006004881

1 2 3 4 5 6 7 8 9 10   15 14 13 12 11 10 09 08 07 06

To all laymen and laywomen whose scriptural questions may help others understand God's saving treasures.

Contents

Abbreviations

AC	Augsburg Confession
Ap	Apology of the Augsburg Confession
FC	Formula of Concord
K-W	Kolb, Robert, and Timothy J. Wengert. *The Book of Concord*. Translated by Charles Arand et al. Minneapolis: Augsburg Fortress, 2000.
LC	Large Catechism
LCMS	The Lutheran Church—Missouri Synod
LW	Luther, Martin. *Luther's Works*. American Edition. General editors Jaroslav Pelikan and Helmut T. Lehmann. 56 vols. St. Louis: Concordia; Philadelphia: Muhlenberg and Fortress, 1955–1986.
SA	Smalcald Articles
SC	Small Catechism
SD	Solid Declaration

Preface

It was a simple question: "Pastor, if the Lord's Supper is everything that Scripture and the catechism say it is, why don't we have the opportunity to receive it when we come for worship each week?" I had conducted the same pastoral visit with this young man and his wife that I had with numerous families, but I had never been asked this question before. At that time I had spent four years as a pastor in the LCMS, but the thought had never occurred to me.

My initial reaction was that he was asking the wrong question. I remember saying something about our schedule of offering Communion on the first and third Sundays of the month. I told him I would investigate the reasons for our practice and give him an answer in a week or two. It would be easy. I would come back and explain why it was good that members were only offered the Sacrament once or twice each month. Surely I could justify our practice.

That was more than eighteen years ago. Finding an answer to that simple question led to a great deal of study and also to the recovery of every Sunday Communion in that congregation and in the one I now serve. It has also led to a great deal of conversation about weekly Communion with pastors and laypeople in the decade and a half since that interview.

I wanted to understand more completely the place of this treasure in the Divine Service. The pursuit of that fuller understanding led me also to see how much is connected to this Gospel gift. The reason for this book is to share scriptural, confessional, and historical insights with you concerning Holy Communion and its presence in weekly worship. It is also to share issues related to the Lord's Supper—some theological, some practical, some raised by pastors, some raised by laypeople, some raised by personal study. For example, weekly Communion has an intimate connection with worthy preparation, with closed Communion, with the sermon, with the liturgy, and even with the pastoral office. On the other hand, weekly Communion may also have an intimate connection with such practical matters as church architecture, the service of the altar guild, and the length and times of the worship service. It is my hope that these pages will enlighten you concerning the treasure of weekly Communion and will encourage its recovery in our midst.

I would like to thank Mr. Matt Renner of Trinity Lutheran Church, Wautoma, Wisconsin, for his "simple" question. He was hearing the Word of God more deeply than his pastor when he asked about the opportunity to receive this gift in weekly worship. The members of Trinity, Wautoma, and Grace, Hancock, Wisconsin, gave a great deal of support and encouragement in the initial years of study. The members of Luther Memorial Chapel, Shorewood, Wisconsin, have provided hundreds of hours to facilitate the survey conducted throughout the LCMS, which is referenced herein. They also provided critical feedback during the writing process. Their kind understanding and ongoing congregational support of this study has been essential for its completion. The vicars they so willingly support have also been helpful in this endeavor.

I desire also to convey my sincere appreciation to two anonymous donors who provided the thousands of dollars needed for the survey. I thank my dear wife, Barbara, for the love and understanding she shows each day. As Scripture says, "He who finds a wife finds a good thing, and obtains favor from the LORD" (Proverbs 18:22). My children, Hannah, Luke, Ben, and Mark, are gifts from God that have enriched my life. God's undeserved Fourth Petition gifts through my wife and children; through my parents, Norbert and Lillian; through a brother and sister; and through Aunt Bertha have been instrumental in advancing this study.

Finally, let me thank professors, teachers, editors, and my fellow pastors. Dissertation advice, weekly sermon studies, continuing education classes, personal conversations, presentations, papers, courses, and books by professors of both the Fort Wayne and St. Louis seminaries and Concordia University Wisconsin have all helped shape this study. As we cover up our pastors with robes in the Divine Service in part to emphasize their office and not their person, so I thank all of you not by name but as gifts of Christ to teach and serve His church. To Him, Christ our Lord, who with the Father and the Holy Spirit is one God, be honor and glory now and forever. Amen.

Introduction

The use of the phrase "weekly Communion" here suggests the recovery of the celebration of the Lord's Supper in each Divine Service. If a congregation has three regular weekly services in which the appointed readings for that Sunday of the church year are read (e.g., one service on Saturday and two on Sunday), worshipers at each service would be given the opportunity to commune. A congregational member would then not have to adopt an irregular time of weekly worship to find the Lord's Supper or be denied the opportunity altogether. This is not meant to belittle services for morning or evening prayer offered on the days of the week or even early or late on Sundays. God grant that individual and corporate prayer (Matins, Vespers, Morning and Evening Prayer) increase among us. However, if there is a regular weekly service intended for a portion of the membership (because of shift work, size of congregation, preference for worship time, etc.), then encouragement is also given to offer the Lord's Supper. If that weekly service is the regular time to gather with Christ and His church to receive the gift of Christ's Word, members would then not be denied the opportunity to receive also the gift of His holy body and holy blood.

This thought is not the normal perspective for most congregations of the LCMS, as later chapters will discuss. Although each congregation has its unique circumstances, such as pastoral vacancies, multipoint parishes, scheduling problems, and the like, the scriptural, confessional, and historical matters presented here will suggest the opportunity to receive the Lord's Supper as the starting point for our thoughts regarding the regular weekly worship for God's people.

Encouraging Signs

During the past fifteen years, we have seen increased recognition of the treasure God's people receive in the weekly Eucharist. Note, for example, this explanation found in the 1991 edition of *Luther's Small Catechism with Explanation*: "In the New Testament, the Sacrament was a regular and major feature of congregational worship, not an occasional extra (Acts 2:42; 20:7; 1 Cor. 11:20, 33). In Reformation times our churches celebrated the Sacrament 'every Sunday and on other festivals' (Apology XXIV 1)."[1] Similarly, Norbert Mueller and George Kraus, in their 1991 *Pastoral Theology*, state: "The heritage of 18th- and 19th-century German Pietism notwithstanding, the Lord's Supper should be offered each Lord's Day to those who hunger for Christ's body and blood and who are prepared to receive it. The fact that some of those present do not wish to receive should not prevent others from receiving."[2] And in 1995, the LCMS in convention adopted Resolution 2-08A, "To Encourage Every Sunday Communion," with these final words:

> *WHEREAS,* Our Synod's 1983 CTCR document on the Lord's Supper (p.28) and our Synod's 1986 translation of Luther's Catechism both remind us that the Scriptures place the Lord's Supper at the center of worship (Acts 2:42; 20:7; I Cor. 11:20, 33), and not as an appendage or an occasional extra; therefore be it

> *Resolved,* That the Lutheran Church—Missouri Synod in convention encourage its pastors and congregations to study the scriptural, confessional, and historical witness to every Sunday communion with a view to recovering the opportunity for receiving the Lord's Supper each Lord's Day.[3]

A 1998 booklet from the LCMS Commission on Worship says: "Because God's Word and Sacraments do not exist in a vacuum the liturgy serves to provide a structure through which these gifts are delivered to the congregation. Since earliest times, that structure has exhibited two basic patterns, one for daily prayer in morning and evening and the other for the *regular, weekly celebration of the Lord's Supper.*"[4]

David Schoessow, in a 1998 article in *Concordia Journal* concerning Communion frequency, writes: "By offering the opportunity, the church at least does its part. Each individual decides for himself or herself when to commune. A pastor or council doesn't decide for everyone else."[5] And former LCMS President A. L. Barry stated in his 2000 pamphlet *What about the Sacrament of the Altar*:

> We receive the Lord's Supper often because of how much we need what the Lord gives in His Supper. We dare never make a law about how often an individual "should" or "must" receive the Lord's Supper. But this is a separate question from how frequently Holy Communion is offered in our congregations. Our Lutheran Confessions make it clear that the Lord's Supper is offered every Lord's Day and on other days when there are communicants present (AC XXIV.34 and Ap. XXIV.1).[6]

These and other encouraging signs highlight what Scripture and the Lutheran Confessions express so clearly. From the beginning and through centuries of church history, the weekly gathering of God's people centered on a single serving of two holy treasures: Word and Sacrament. Some of that scriptural and confessional witness will be presented in chapter 1.

Before moving on to that chapter, however, two initial thoughts are offered here. One relates to the place of the sermon when weekly Communion is recovered. This concern has been frequently voiced by pastors and laity who have a deep care for the preached Word. Such concern should not be ignored in a time and culture such as ours. The Word of God is under attack. That is why this concern is addressed in these opening pages. The other thought addressed in this introduction has to do with the true presence of the living Christ in the Divine Service to serve us. Understanding His presence *for us* is foundational to understanding what follows in this book and ultimately what takes place in the Divine Service. This thought has been crucial for me and has also helped others understand more readily what follows.

Recovering Weekly Communion Does not Elevate the Sacrament over the Sermon

For most of the 155-year history of the LCMS, the vast majority of its congregations has not celebrated the Lord's Supper in each regular weekly service. Although chapters 5 and 6 will touch on this history more fully, a brief historical introduction might be in order. In the early 1900s, it was normal to celebrate Communion four times a year. In the 1950s and 1960s, monthly Communion was the prevalent practice. By the end of the twentieth century, most LCMS congregations were offering the Lord's Supper two weeks of the month. Thus the trend has been to increase the frequency of the celebration of the Sacrament.

Nevertheless, these statistics indicate a significant absence among us of the Lord's Supper in the Sunday service. Over time the occasional offering of the Sacrament came to be viewed as normal. Most of the laity and pastors have lived their entire lives without every Sunday Communion. From this historical perspective, some people falsely assume that those who advocate every Sunday Communion are attempting to elevate the Sacrament over the sermon—not so. We should take the place and promise of the Sacrament seriously because we take seriously the promise of the Word of God concerning the Sacrament. To recover every Sunday Communion in no way makes the sermon less central. Rather, it heightens the wondrous truth that He who is present to teach us His holy Word is also present to feed us with His true body and true blood.

Word and Sacrament are not separate entities that compete with each other in importance. Rather, Word and Sacrament are the single serving of two holy treasures bestowed by the risen Christ as He comes into the midst of His gathered church. They are not liturgy-dividing competitors but life-giving complements. Subsequent chapters will more fully express the intimate connection of Word and Sacrament in weekly worship.

The presence of this concern—Sacrament over sermon— may sometimes prevent one from hearing the full witness to weekly Communion. In a similar way, the absence of the following understanding may also hinder a full consideration of subsequent related thoughts.

An Impoverishing Omission

The heart and center of this book will not be rightly understood unless the true presence of the living Christ in the Divine Service is also understood. This presence is not simply His omnipresence—His presence everywhere—but His saving presence, His presence in the concrete means by which He has promised to give us forgiveness and life. This is not Jesus in the air, whom we must try to contact through spiritual achievement. This is not Jesus in our hearts, whom we control with our feelings. This is Jesus who comes to us from the outside in the specific, humble ways He has chosen to make our hearts new. For example, the Offertory from Psalm 51 looks forward to Holy Communion with this anticipation: "Create in me a clean heart, O God." This is the true bodily presence of Jesus as He comes in the Lord's Supper.

We cannot overemphasize the negative effect of this omission in understanding worship. In one of his best-known books, C. S. Lewis collects a series of letters written by the devil Screwtape to Wormwood, his nephew and apprentice. In this forum, Lewis is able to provide unique insight into the human condition. In one letter, Screwtape tells Wormwood that human beings are always worried about devils putting things in their minds; however, devils do their best work when they keep things out.[7] If Satan can keep the invisible yet true presence of the risen God-man out of mind in the Divine Service, he can easily marginalize and misshape weekly worship. As Richard Eyer explains:

> If worship were not God at work among us, the idea of "going to church" for any other reason would personally lead me to find other things to do on a Sunday morning. The cult of joggers and cyclists I pass on the way to church might tempt me to join them . . . but there is only one place to find God at work in our lives the way He is in the liturgy of the Divine Service—offering healing at the core of life.[8]

While God is present everywhere, He cannot be found everywhere as the God of love and mercy. This is what Luther referred to as His "presence for us," something significantly different from His omnipresence.[9] Luther explained it this way: "Because it is one thing if God is present, and another if he is present for you. He is there for you when he adds his Word and binds himself, saying, 'Here you are to find me.' Now when you have the Word, you can grasp and have him with certainty and say, 'Here I have thee, according to thy Word.' "[10]

We see this presence of God *for us* in specific ways and specific places in the Old Testament. Moses knew that God was everywhere. But if he had been asked, "Is God in any specific place at any specific time to bring His saving Word to bear for His people?" his answer would have been a resounding *yes*: "Yes, God is in this burning bush. Here God came and called to me and said, 'I AM WHO I AM' (Exodus 3:14). The ground of His presence is so holy He commanded me to take off my shoes." The people of Israel during the exodus and wilderness wanderings knew that God was everywhere. But if they were asked, "Has God promised to be present in any special place to bless you?" the answer would have been a resounding *yes*: "Yes, God is in the tabernacle over the ark of the covenant for us, that is, to dwell among us and forgive us. God is in the Holy of Holies *for us.* Likewise, God is present in the pillar of cloud and the pillar of fire."

The New Testament witness is the same. The God who is everywhere came down to locate Himself somewhere *for us.* The fullness of the Godhead (Colossians 2:9) dwelt in the womb of Mary bodily *for us.* At the annunciation, Mary was told by the angel, "The Holy Spirit will come upon you, and the power of the Highest will overshadow you; therefore, also, that Holy One who is to be born will be called the Son of God" (Luke 1:35). The Greek word translated as *overshadow* is the same word used in the Greek translation of the Old Testament to describe the cloud covering the tabernacle, or tent of meeting, as the glory of the Lord filled it (Exodus 40:34–38). In other words, as God's presence was in the tabernacle, so God's presence was in the body of Jesus in the womb of Mary. This was where He located Himself in the months before Jesus' birth. The God who is everywhere was there in Mary's womb *for us*, that is, to redeem us from sin and death. That is why He took on flesh and blood (Hebrews 2:9, 14–18).

While God's dwelling place *for us* is no longer the womb of Mary, God's dwelling place *for us* is and will always be the body of

Jesus. Doubting Thomas certainly knew that God was every-where, but if he had been asked if God was in any specific place to bless him, his answer would have been a resounding *yes*. In fact, as he touched the crucifixion marks of the risen Christ, Thomas did say *yes* by exclaiming, "My Lord and my God!" (John 20:28).

God grant that we also magnify God's presence *for us* sin-ners. The center of human history is Christ's service to the world on the cross. The center of our current life is Christ's ongoing presence among His gathered people in Word and Sacrament. The reason His Church gathers together in worship each week is because the risen Christ comes to teach and feed His people. What He did visibly in the forty days between His resurrection and ascension He now does invisibly until His second coming.

In the midst of two or three gathered in His name, Christ is present today *for us* (Matthew 18:20). He comes *for us*, not to be served but to serve (Matthew 20:28). What He began to do and teach before He was taken up into heaven (Acts 1:2) He contin-ues to do and teach *for us*. Therefore what happens each week in the Divine Service is a matter of life and death because the Lord comes to bring life to us dying sinners. Harold Senkbeil writes: "[Jesus is] embodied life. Life in person in a world full of death."[11]

God bestowed new life on us in Holy Baptism. He now comes to feed and nourish us. We cannot go back to the cross, but because the risen and ascended Christ possesses all the authority of God's right hand, He can and does bring the fruits of the cross to us. The Confessions put it this way: "[I]n the Lord's Supper the body and blood of Christ are truly and substantially present and are truly offered with those things that are seen, bread and wine. Moreover, we are talking about the presence of the living Christ, for we know that death no longer has dominion over him [Rom. 6:9]."[12] Holy Communion is not a meal remem-bering a dead man. It is a meal hosted by the living God-man, who once was dead but now comes to give us life. The personal, redeeming Christ is present *for us* in this Sacrament. This is Immanuel, God with us.

This is why nothing in all the world even comes close to the importance of gathering each week in the presence of the risen Christ to receive His gifts and respond in prayer and praise. The Word made flesh is present to teach us through His Word. The Word made flesh is present to feed us with His body and blood. This is where God, who is everywhere, is present *for us* to bring forgiveness, life, and salvation directly to us.

Understanding Christ's true bodily presence in the Lord's Supper to serve us sinners is vital to understanding worship. Without this understanding, the mystery of the liturgy will seem strange and irrelevant rather than strangely fitting and eternally relevant. Without this understanding, much of what has been handed down to us may seem stiff and formal. Without this understanding, worship may be viewed as an experimental thing that we must make lively rather than that by which Jesus comes to give us life. Without this understanding, we may miss the reverent acknowledgment of the hidden presence of the King of kings.

It is no accident that our liturgy leads us to begin the Divine Service "In the Name of the Father and of the Son and of the Holy Spirit" instead of "We make our beginning in the name of . . ." Here we are not addressing one another and telling ourselves what we are going to do. We are not the chief doers in the service. Instead, "[t]his is an invocation. We are not merely reminding ourselves that the God whom we worship is Father, Son, and Holy Spirit. We are asking the one true God to be in our midst and to fill our hearts as we offer him our worship and praise."[13] God Himself is addressed as His holy name is invoked, and the people say "Amen," that is, "Yes, it is so." He who put His name on us in Holy Baptism and gave us new life comes to feed and nourish that new life in us. He is here in our midst *for us.* Amen.

It is also no accident that the rubrics of the liturgy for nearly two thousand years have led the pastor to say, "The Lord be with you," immediately before Holy Communion. The word *you* is plural, meaning "you all," and does not refer to the individual. Here the heavenly Bridegroom unites in love with His bride, the church. This pastoral greeting is in essence a blessing that speaks the foundational truth of the Divine Service: Christ comes *for us* in the words and actions that are taking place. And Christ's bride responds, "And with your spirit." The individual personality of the man standing before them is not important. The response "And with your spirit" gives verbal recognition to the truth that the greeting is from the Lord Himself, spoken through His called servant.[14] God's Word does what it says, even as the pastor says, "The Lord be with you."

Martin Luther summarized the heart of the Divine Service in his hymn "Here Is the Tenfold Sure Command." The fourth stanza focuses on the Third Commandment:

> And celebrate the worship day
> That peace may fill your home and pray,
> And put aside the work you do,
> So that God may work in you.
> Have mercy, Lord![15]

As we put aside the work we do so God may work in us, why would we want to preclude the risen Christ from working in us also with the heavenly food of His body and blood? What more can the risen Lord do for us than give us this blessed rest, refreshment, and release as He comes under the very roof of our mouths to feed and forgive us? As will be shown, the presence of the Lord's Supper in weekly worship is central in the scriptural, historical, and confessional witness.

Brief Outline

In chapter 1, we will examine some foundational thoughts concerning the Words of Institution and some scriptural and confessional texts. In chapter 2, we will focus on the Lord's Supper in the early church. Chapter 3 will discuss the celebration of the Sacrament during the Middle Ages. In chapter 4, we look at the wondrous recovery of the proper celebration of the Lord's Supper by Luther and the reformers, along with the resistance that this recovery encountered. Chapters 5 and 6 discuss the modern era and the Lord's Supper in the LCMS today. In chapter 7, there is a description of some of the beautiful treasures that come to us with this heavenly food, treasures that may too easily be overlooked. Then chapter 8 addresses issues closely related to the Lord's Supper, such as the sermon, the liturgy, and the practice of closed Communion. The final chapter looks briefly at confessing Christ and His Word and receiving His Word and Sacrament as the center of life in the future.

Discussion Questions

1. Discuss the difference between God's omnipresence and His promised presence to serve us in the Divine Service. Is this widely understood in Christendom? Why or why not.

2. Read Luther's quote on page 18. Is the distinction that Luther taught concerning Christ's "presence for us" a distinction you were taught "from your youth"? Is it a distinction that is understood in American Christianity? Discuss.

3. List some of the places that God revealed Himself or promised to be present for His Old Testament people. Discuss.

4. Can we return to the cross? As the Lutheran Confessions attest, where can we encounter the presence of the living Christ?

5. How has lack of understanding the true presence of the living Christ to serve us contributed to the experimentation with worship in our day?

6. Discuss the differences between the pastor saying "In the name of the Father and of the Son and of the Holy Spirit" or "We begin in the name of the ...."

7. Discuss the fourth stanza of Luther's hymn "Here Is the Tenfold Sure Command" (page 22). What are we to put aside? What is it that God does?

Now I plead with you, brethren, by the name of our Lord Jesus Christ, that you all speak the same thing, and that there be no divisions among you, but that you be perfectly joined together in the same mind and in the same judgment. (1 Corinthians 1:10)

снартек оne

Foundational Thoughts

The Words of Institution

In the miracle of the ages, God became man and dwelt among us. In a miracle of love that reaches down through the ages to us, the God-man Jesus Christ gave His true body and true blood as heavenly food. He did it at Passover as the sacrificial Lamb of God (1 Corinthians 5:7). He did it on the night of His betrayal before the day of His crucifixion for the sin of the world. On that night Jesus spoke deliberately and carefully. According to the Solid Declaration of the Formula of Concord:

> This reliable, almighty Lord, our creator and redeemer Jesus Christ, spoke these words, which established and instituted the Supper, concerning the bread that he had consecrated and distributed, "Take and eat, this is my body which is given for you," and concerning the chalice or wine, "This is my blood of the New Testament, which

is poured out for you for the forgiveness of sins" [Matt. 26:26–28; Mark 14:24; Luke 22:19–20].[1]

[A]ll three evangelists [Matt. 26[:26]; Mark 14[:22]; Luke 22[:19]) and St. Paul, who after Christ's ascension received the same account (1 Cor. 11[:25]), were in complete agreement. With the same words and syllables they repeated these clear, simple, certain, reliable words of Christ, "This is my body," in just the same way, referring to the bread that they had blessed and distributed, without any interpretation or alteration.[2]

This foundation of the spoken word of Christ is essential in understanding the central place of Holy Communion in the worship of the church. The Lord's Supper is not something that we do. Rather, the Lord's Supper is something the risen Christ comes to do in the midst of His gathered people. As He does so, "the chief thing is God's Word and ordinance or command. It was not dreamed up or invented by some mere human being but was instituted by Christ without anyone's counsel or deliberation."[3]

In the Gospel accounts and in 1 Corinthians, there is no word present that could be translated as *symbolizes* or *represents*. There is no indication that the words of Christ are picture language. Rather, God's Word clearly teaches that in the Lord's Supper the bread and wine are a participation (communion) in the body and blood of Christ (1 Corinthians 10:16). It clearly teaches that those who misuse the Sacrament sin against Christ's body and blood (1 Corinthians 11:27, 29). Neither the bread is imaginary nor is Christ's body. "According to Jesus' words, *the bread is his body*. This is not a parabolic or metaphorical use of language. 'Is' [*estin* in the Greek] means 'is.' The giving of his body with the bread is just as real as the giving of his body into death on the cross."[4] Nineteenth-century theologian Charles Porterfield Krauth writes: "We believe that the bread is there on the evidence of the senses; we believe that Christ's body is there on the evidence of the Word."[5]

The same is true for the blood. Krauth writes: "In Matthew and Mark the predicate is, My blood; the blood of the New Covenant; the blood which is shed for the remission of sins. In Luke and Paul, the predicate is: The New Covenant in my blood. The blood constitutes the Covenant, the Covenant is constituted in the blood."[6] (See Matthew 26:27–28; Mark 14:23–24; Luke 22:20; 1 Corinthians 11:25.) Neither the wine (cup) is imaginary nor is the blood. The "blood of the new testament" in Matthew and Mark is identical to the "new testament of the blood" in Luke and Paul. According to Krauth, "[t]hat which we drink in the Supper is the shed blood of Christ and that shed blood is the New Covenant, because the covenant is in the blood and with the blood."[7]

From the Words of Institution recorded by the evangelists and St. Paul, Dr. Luther expressed this gift in the Small Catechism:

> What is the Sacrament of the Altar?
>
> It is the true body and blood of our Lord Jesus Christ under the bread and wine, instituted by Christ Himself for us Christians to eat and to drink.
>
> Where is this written?
>
> The holy Evangelists Matthew, Mark, Luke, and St. Paul write: Our Lord Jesus Christ, on the night when He was betrayed, took bread, and when He had given thanks, He broke it and gave it to the disciples and said: "Take, eat; this is My body, which is given for you. This do in remembrance of Me." In the same way also He took the cup after supper, and when He had given thanks, He gave it to them, saying, "Drink of it, all of you; this cup is the new testament in My blood, which is shed for you for the forgiveness of sins. This do, as often as you drink it, in remembrance of Me."[8]

Luther said that everything in the Sacrament of the Altar "is established from the words Christ used to institute it. So everyone who wishes to be a Christian and to go to the sacrament should know them."[9] Emphasizing that the greatest thing in the Sacrament is God's Word, Luther pointedly asks and answers, "Do you think God cares so much about our faith and conduct that he would permit them to affect his ordinance? No, all temporal things remain as God has created and ordered them, regardless of how we treat them. This must always be emphasized, for thus we can thoroughly refute all the babbling of the seditious spirits who, contrary to the Word of God, regard the sacraments as something that we do."[10]

The New Testament of Christ's Body and Blood Is the Sum and Substance of the Gospel

Most recent Bible translations use the word *covenant* instead of *testament* in the texts wherein Jesus instituted the Lord's Supper. Both are possible translations, but as Robert Kolb observes:

> If the word is understood as covenant, it must be understood as the kind of covenant that is given by the king to his vassals. The king offers; the king imposes. The covenant is his gift to vassals who have no claim on his protection and rule. Christ's Supper is likewise pure gift. . . . Thus, it is better to think of the Lord's Supper as a last will and testament. Here Jesus bestows all his blessings, the blessing of forgiveness and new life, the blessing of his presence, upon his people.[11]

Early in his battle against Rome, Luther used the translation *testament* in its legal sense as his chief weapon.[12] The Lord's Supper was being treated as a sacrifice, a work of man to appease God, not as God's free gift to His church. Luther stressed that the Lord's Supper was Christ's last will and testament by which He bequeathed to us all blessings. Citing Christ's words "this is the cup of the new testament" (Luke 22:20; 1 Corinthians 11:25), Luther wrote: "Not every vow is called a testament, but only a last irrevocable will of one who is about to die, whereby he bequeaths his goods, allotted and assigned to be distributed to whom he will. Just as St. Paul says to the Hebrews [9:16–17] that a testament must be made operative by death."[13] This new testament, said Luther, depended totally on the Words of Institution.

> Everything depends on these words. Every Christian should and must know them and hold them fast. He must never let anyone take them away from him by any other kind of teaching, even though it were an angel from heaven [Gal. 1:8]. They are words of life and of salvation, so that whoever believes in them has all his sins forgiven through that faith; he is a child of life and has overcome death and hell. Language cannot express how great and mighty these words are, for they are the sum and substance of the whole gospel.[14]

This inheritance of Christ's testament is inexhaustible. This sum and substance of the whole Gospel is continually given out where He is present to give it out. Because He is ascended to God's right hand, Jesus has the authority to come and bestow this inheritance of forgiveness and life and salvation. So the Lutheran Confessions attest:

> For the true and almighty words of Jesus Christ, which he spoke in the first institution of the Supper, were not only effective in the first Supper; they remain so. They retain their validity and power and are still effective, so that in all places in which the Supper is observed according to Christ's institution and his words are used, the body and blood of Christ are truly present, distributed and received on the basis of the power and might of the very same words that Christ spoke in the first Supper. . . . Christ himself exercises his power through the spoken words.[15]

That this was understood since the earliest years of the LCMS is expressed clearly by its first president, C. F. W. Walther: "The Son of God Himself is repeating the once spoken words of institution through the mouth of the minister and thereby hallows, consecrates and blesses the bread and wine so that they are the means of distributing His body and blood."[16]

Luther explained in a simple and straightforward way the clarity of Christ's words.

> If these words are not clear, I do not know how to speak German. Would I not understand, if someone were to place a roll before me and say: "Take, eat, this is white bread"? Or again, "Take and drink, this is a glass of wine"? Therefore, when Christ says: "Take, eat, this is my body," even a child will understand perfectly well that he is speaking of that which he is offering. . . . These words are quite clear and explicit . . . . For this reason we stick closely to the words and close our eyes and senses, because everyone knows what "this is my body" means, especially when he adds "given for you." We know what Christ's body is, namely that which was born of Mary, suffered, died, and rose again.[17]

This presence of the living Christ depends on His words, not our faith. Here, in His promised gift, He is present *for us*. Therefore His presence is so certain that all communicants receive the body and blood in the Sacrament whether or not they believe.[18] Not all receive the forgiveness, life, and salvation offered there, for only through faith can we receive the blessings offered with Christ's body and blood.[19] But all who partake of the Lord's Supper receive the very body and blood of the risen Christ, even those who sin against it (1 Corinthians 11:27).

This is part of the basis for the loving practice of closed Communion. It is also a truth that is offensive to our natural human reason and religious feelings. The human heart does not care for mysteries that go beyond its control and beyond the mind's ability to discern. How can it be that the true body and true blood of Jesus Christ are received by all who partake—whether they believe it or not? But this is the unshakable nature of the inheritance Jesus gives in the new testament of His body and blood. When the living Christ comes into the midst of His gathered congregation today and names or calls "This is My body" and "This is My blood," it is not a matter that human speculation can change. Luther says it clearly: "This is his Word, when he says, 'This is my body,' just as he says in Genesis [1:3], 'Let there be light,' and there is light. My friend, it is God who names or calls, and what he names immediately comes into existence, as Psalm 33[:9] says, 'He spoke, and it came to be.' "[20]

In the Large Catechism, Luther summarizes it this way:

> With this Word you can strengthen your conscience and declare: "Let a hundred thousand devils, with all the fanatics, come forward and say, 'How can bread and wine be Christ's body and blood?' etc. Still I know that all the spirits and scholars put together have less wisdom than the divine Majesty has in his littlest finger. Here is Christ's word: 'Take, eat, this is my body.' 'Drink of this, all of you, this is the New Testament in my blood,' etc. Here we shall take our stand and see who dares to instruct Christ and alter what he has spoken. It is true, indeed, that if you take the Word away from the elements or view them apart from the Word, you have nothing but ordinary bread and wine. But if the words remain, as is right and necessary, then by virtue of them the elements are truly the body and blood of Christ. For as Christ's lips speak and say, so it is; he cannot lie or deceive."[21]

What His lips offer is, as Luther said, the sum and substance of the Gospel or, as Krauth says, the heart of the Gospel. Krauth writes: "Christ is the centre of the system and the Supper is the centre of Christ's revelation of Himself. The glory and the mystery of the incarnation combine there as they combine nowhere else. Communion with Christ is that by which we live, and the Supper is 'the communion.' "[22]

In giving this precious gift, Jesus did not make a new law commanding its daily or weekly observance. Yet at first there was a daily and then weekly use of Holy Communion. This is so because what Jesus gave to His church is the inviting and absolving Gospel, not the insistent and accusing Law. The Lord's Supper is a gift of life and love to be received, not a requirement to be fulfilled.

The Lord's Supper after Pentecost

Now we will look at how that gift was received by the church after Pentecost. Luke extends his narrative in the Acts of the Apostles to include the ongoing activity of the Lord through His sent ones by the power of the Spirit.[23] Therefore Luke and Acts will be used for a discussion of Acts 2:42 and Table fellowship with Jesus as it relates to the Lord's Supper. A few additional thoughts related to the presence of the Lord's Supper in 1 Corinthians and in the first three chapters of Revelation are then considered.

Acts 2:42—The Gifts of the Holy Spirit

> And they were continually devoting themselves to the apostles' teaching and to the fellowship, to the breaking of bread and to the prayers. (Acts 2:42)[24]

There is no better place to look at the place of the Lord's Supper in the life of Christ's church than to look at what followed the pouring out of the Holy Spirit at Pentecost. St. Luke's first summary description of the church in Acts 2:42 included persistent and faithful devotion to the preaching of God's Word (the apostles' teaching or doctrine) and equally persistent and faithful devotion to the Lord's Supper (the breaking of the bread).

The breaking of bread here denotes something more than the ordinary partaking of food together; the regular observance of the Lord's Supper is undoubtedly indicated.[25] The celebration of the Sacrament may be called "the breaking of the bread."[26] While the phrase may be used of an ordinary meal, the *Concordia Self-Study Bible* clarifies that the Lord's Supper is indicated in both Acts 2:42 and Acts 20:7.[27] Commenting on Acts 2:42, Martin Franzmann speaks of a life of fellowship at the Table of the Lord (breaking of bread).[28] Similarly, the explanation in the Small Catechism lists the breaking of bread in Acts 2:42 as one of the names for the Sacrament of the Altar.[29] Such use is in agreement with the Lutheran Confessions. They speak against using the phrase "the breaking of bread" as Rome did to limit the laity to receiving only one kind (the body and not the blood of Christ). Instead, naming only the one element includes the other. But the Confessions also state no serious objections to understanding such passages as Acts 2:42, 46; Acts 20:7; and Luke 24:35 as referring to the Lord's Supper.[30] Howard Marshall states that the elements in Acts 2:42 are preferably seen as what characterized a Christian gathering in the early church. Their fellowship or holding of a common religious experience included the breaking of bread, which is Luke's term for what Paul calls the Lord's Supper.[31] Lenski sees here a brief description of the religious life of the first Christian congregation. "The prayers" he sees as the entire service of worship, not merely the praying. He adds that "Luke . . . characterizes the celebration of the Lord's Supper by use of the expression that was common at that time: 'breaking the bread.'"[32]

The Holy Spirit led the baptized to continue steadfastly in the teaching of the apostles. In that teaching God fed them the new life He had given them in Holy Baptism. The devotion of the baptized to the apostles' doctrine was not one choice among many, but it was the very means by which the Holy Spirit continued to bring Christ to them. Likewise, the Holy Spirit led them to continue steadfastly in the Lord's Supper with devotion equal to their commitment to God's holy Word. It wasn't a new law. Nor was it one choice among many. Rather, like the apostles' doctrine, the breaking of the bread was the very means by which the Holy Spirit continued to bring Christ to the baptized. In that eating, God fed the new life He had gifted them with in Holy Baptism.

At the heart of the early Christians' fellowship with God and with one another was this treasure of Word and Sacrament. "The prayers" to which they were devoted were not divorced from the ordered prayers and liturgy of the synagogue or of the temple. It is also possible that "the prayers" were drawn from "the Prayer" that Jesus Himself taught, that is, the Lord's Prayer. Yet "the prayers" to which they were devoted flowed from and framed the receiving of the new testament, the risen Christ's gift of Word and Sacrament. It can also be expressed this way:

> Not only was that first Christian congregation in Jerusalem devoted to the apostles' doctrine and breaking of bread; we also read that they were "devoted to the prayers," as St. Luke puts it in the plural. It's not just that these early Christians were accustomed to pray, but they were accustomed to pray in a certain way, with certain prescribed prayers; in other words, they had a liturgy.
>
> This may come as a shock for some who think that early Christians gathered for worship generally in free-form settings, with each person praying as the spirit moved him. But we have to remember that Christianity didn't arrive in a vacuum. God built His New Testament church squarely on the foundation of the Old Testament.[33]

There is another gathering for worship described in the Acts of the Apostles that bears witness to this same order of Word and Sacrament. The church at Troas gathered together on a Sunday (Acts 20:7–11). The portrayal of this gathering helps us see the church's ongoing devotion to the breaking of the bread begun at Pentecost. The description begins: "And on the first day of the week, when we were gathered together to break bread . . ." (Acts 20:7). This was not a service, however, which included only the Lord's Supper and excluded the apostles' doctrine. The context also describes a word of teaching delivered by the apostle Paul himself. The clear indication is that the joining of the apostle's doctrine and the breaking of the bread continued on the first day of the week.

Steadfast Devotion to the Breaking of Bread and Table Fellowship with Jesus[34]

The Gospel according to Luke and the Acts of the Apostles were conceived as one work and were meant to be read sequentially.[35] In fact, the title *The Acts of the Apostles* does not belong to the original document but was added only after the two volumes were separated.[36] Luke and Acts show how the crucified and risen Christ continued His work through the apostles. Luke clearly states that he ordered his writing of the Gospel and Acts for the purpose of teaching us (Luke 1:1–4). A point of teaching that has direct connection to the Lord's Supper is Jesus' table fellowship with sinners.

Luke and Acts show us that devotion to the breaking of bread and eating with Jesus on the Easter side of the open tomb is related to Jesus' table fellowship with sinners, especially during His three years of visible public ministry as recorded in Luke's Gospel. Jesus came to restore that intimate fellowship with God that we sinners lost in the fall. Concerning the meals in Luke and Acts, "[t]he presence of Jesus at the meal makes this table fellowship different from all other meals. It is a meal with God! *Not every meal is the Lord's Supper, but each is a supper with the Lord, and each relates to his cross and resurrection."*[37]

In St. Luke's first book, we see Jesus at table fellowship in many situations in which His body and blood were not yet the food and drink. However, He was present to bless. When He ate with Levi (Matthew), the Pharisees grumbled because Jesus ate with tax collectors and sinners. To this Jesus responded, "Those who are well have no need of a physician, but those who are sick. I have not come to call the righteous, but sinners, to repentance" (Luke 5:30–32). Jesus' table fellowship brings to sinners the medicine of the Great Physician. "Jesus pronounces no absolution upon Levi . . . but Jesus' presence with Levi at table and Levi's banquet for Jesus imply that Levi's old way of life was a thing of the past and his new life had begun. Subsequently he is among those following Jesus."[38]

When Jesus miraculously fed the five thousand, distributing the food through the hands of His disciples, twelve baskets of leftover fragments were taken up (Luke 9:10–17). The one through whom all things were created miraculously provided table fellowship in overflowing abundance so all were filled, yet more remained than what first was present. Immediately following this miracle, Luke records Peter's confession of Jesus as the "Christ of God" (Luke 9:20). According to Just, "Peter's reaction indicates that Luke considers this feeding to be a messianic miracle, a confirmation that Jesus is *the* prophet of Deut 18:15. He feeds his people with the eternal bread of life at his table fellowship of teaching and eating."[39]

When He was the guest of Zacchaeus, Jesus said, "Salvation has come to your house today" and "the Son of Man has come to save that which was lost" (Luke 19:9–10). In offering Zacchaeus table fellowship with Himself, Jesus offered him eternal salvation.

It is also in Luke that we hear from the lips of one who sat at table with Jesus, "Blessed is he who shall eat bread in the kingdom of God!" (Luke 14:15). The Greek word for *blessed* is the opposite of *woe* or *being cursed*. It is a state of being that only God can give, and it means that one is fortunate in the highest degree. In other words, God can give us nothing more or beyond table fellowship with Himself in the kingdom of God. And the wonderful thing is that Jesus invites those who cannot repay Him— the poor, the maimed, the lame, the blind—to dine with Him (Luke 14:12–13).

Jesus, in opposition to the Pharisees with whom He was eating, had just taught that the Sabbath Day did not preclude God's healing gifts (Luke 14:3). He then described proper conduct when invited to a wedding feast, that is, taking the lowest place so the one who invited you may exalt you by inviting you to a more prestigious place (Luke 14:7–11). He bracketed the saying "Blessed is everyone who shall eat bread in the kingdom of God" by clearly teaching that such fellowship does not belong to the Pharisees but with humble, repentant, believing sinners.[40]

Jesus' table fellowship with sinners ascended to new heights on Maundy Thursday in the Upper Room. There He took over the Passover of the old covenant and gave the new covenant of His very body and very blood in the Lord's Supper (Luke 22:14–20). While He is still living, the Lamb of God offers for food the very redemption price He will hand over for the sins of the world in His death. He then goes forth to finish our redemption on the cross.

The first postresurrection meal of the risen Christ occurs at Emmaus, where He is recognized in the breaking of the bread (Luke 24:30–35). According to Just, "[t]he Emmaus meal is unique since in the breaking of the bread, Jesus is *for the first time* recognized as the crucified and risen Messiah."[41] The Emmaus meal is the first celebration of the new covenant and the event at which the order is clearly established: teaching before eating, Word before meal. In Acts this same concern of teaching and eating will be present in the Table fellowship of the church (Acts 1:1–4; 2:42). Luke's summary statement for the entire Emmaus meal in Luke 24:35—"the things he taught on the road and how he was known to them in the breaking of the bread"—lays the foundation for early Christian worship.[42]

After years of teaching and table fellowship, after His suffering and sacrificial death, Jesus is physically present and teaching His followers after His resurrection. But He chooses to reveal Himself in the breaking of bread that followed His teaching. The disciples' hearts were burning as He taught them from the Old Testament Scriptures of His suffering and death and His gift of forgiveness. But they did not know Jesus until the breaking of the bread (Luke 21:31, 35). Only then did Jesus cease to be visible to them.

With the crucifixion and resurrection of Jesus, the table fellowship of Jesus has been transformed. He no longer reclines at table as He did during His earthly ministry, for He is now present with His church in a new way. The presence and disappearance of Jesus at the Emmaus meal helps prepare the church to understand that Jesus will be present yet unseen at the church's eucharistic meals. Emmaus is the transitional meal between the preresurrection meals of Jesus' earthly ministry, including the Last Supper in which He physically and visibly ate with His disciples, and the church's continuing celebrations of the Lord's Supper in which Jesus is present in flesh and blood yet unseen. The church, like the Emmaus disciples, is to recognize with the opened eyes of faith that Jesus is truly present in the breaking of the bread (Acts 2:42, 46; 20:7).[43]

After Pentecost the Holy Spirit carried out His Christ-confessing and Christ-revealing work through the apostles' doctrine and the Lord's Supper (Acts 2:42). Christ's presence in this gift (Word and Sacrament) formed and fed the believers' fellowship. Christ's presence in this gift (Word and Sacrament) framed and fueled their prayers. Christ's presence in this gift (Word and Sacrament) was and is the very life of the church. His promised presence in His Supper isn't a spiritual presence but a true bodily presence. In giving the Lord's Supper, "Christ deliberately took His vocabulary from the divinely instituted sacrificial cultus, which He would consummate in His bloody death (see Dt 12:27). Body and blood can only mean the body and blood of a sacrificial victim, separated in death. Although such vocabulary is a stumbling block to Jews and folly to Greeks, it is received as truthful discourse by believers."[44]

To speak now of Table fellowship with Jesus is therefore to speak of the presence of the living Christ, the God-man, to serve us His body and blood, the same body and blood once for all sacrificed on the cross. The words used by Jesus in giving the new testament are straightforward. They were clearly understood and accepted by the early church, for "while they differed among themselves over other articles of faith, the ancient Fathers were virtually unanimous in avowing the real presence."[45] The real presence of our Savior's body and blood is closely related to the opportunity provided to receive this gift in regular weekly worship. As will be shown later, the initial decline in the weekly celebration of the Sacrament was directly related to changes in teaching the real presence.[46] As the phrase "real presence" is used here, it means that the body of Jesus is in fact in the bread and the blood of Jesus is in fact in the wine for us Christians to eat and drink. That is, "*through the sacramental bread and wine there is direct and oral reception of the Lord's crucified and glorified body and blood.*"[47]

To speak of Table fellowship with Jesus is also to acknowledge with Luther that in Holy Communion Jesus is all in all. Luther wrote: "We know, however, that it is the Lord's Supper, in name and in reality, not the supper of Christians. For the Lord not only instituted it, but also prepares and gives it himself, and is himself cook, butler, food, and drink."[48] Or as a modern-day Lutheran theologian stated it: "In the Lord's Supper Jesus approaches us as the banquet speaker and the meal itself; He is chef as well as entrée."[49]

In other words, the question is not whether the true, risen, living Christ is present or whether His body and blood sacrificed on the cross are present. Both are true. The risen Lord is not a ghost but has flesh and bones (Luke 24:37–39). He is God and man, not a disembodied spirit. He is the one who comes invisibly into the midst of His gathered people to teach them His holy Word and to feed them His true body and true blood. He is the host of a Table fellowship with heavenly food that only He can offer. The reason His church gathers together each week is because He comes to serve them.

What earthly sight cannot observe, the eyes of faith can perceive and receive for the forgiveness of sins, life, and salvation. What is unseen but eternal (2 Corinthians 4:16–18) includes the presence of Christ with His church in Word and Meal. Now it is a forgiving foretaste of the feast to come and the place where heaven touches earth. Then, in heaven, it will be the eternal fulfillment of all God's promises to His church on earth.

Those promises are found already in the Old Testament in ways that clearly speak of God's presence with His people in a feast that He prepares, a feast of the finest of wines and the choicest of food, a feast flowing from His defeat of death (Isaiah 25:6–9). On the day of His mighty resurrection from the dead, the conquering Lamb of God taught concerning Himself from all the Old Testament Scriptures (Luke 24:27, 44). Their witness clearly and repeatedly communicates God's saving and forgiving presence with His people in the context of meals.

There was the Passover meal as God rescued His people from bondage in Egypt. If God had not promised to turn aside His wrath because of the blood of a lamb, if He had not been with the Israelites in that eating, their lot would have been death, not life (Exodus 12). It was a feast to be repeated through all generations, the Lord's Passover, a service to be kept annually (Exodus 12:25). Down through the centuries, as the youngest child asked, "What is the meaning of this service?" the parents would respond in the present tense, "This is the night of our deliverance." This was no ordinary meal, for God was with His people with saving power. However, the Passover pointed to the greater feast to come.

After the exodus, as the children of Israel were gathered before Mount Sinai, Moses sprinkled the blood on the people and there was a meal. We read that Moses and company "beheld God, and ate and drank" (Exodus 24:9–11 ESV). This was no ordinary meal, for God was with the Israelites. However, the sacrifices that preceded this meal pointed to the greater feast to come.

The meals connected with the Old Testament sacrifices— the sin, guilt, and peace offerings—also give clear witness of table fellowship with God. Consider, for example, the peace offering. This sacrifice was not offered to make peace with God; rather, it was offered in acknowledgment that peace had been given by God. As Daniel Brege said, "[t]his final sacrifice was particularly associated with a meal of thanksgiving and praise. Having received forgiveness in the sin offering, the peace offering was obviously sacrificed *after* peace with God was already a recognized reality."[50]

The two major emphases of the peace offering were eating and rejoicing (Deuteronomy 27:7). Both the priests and the laity ate holy portions. A portion was also burned upon the altar and described as "food, an offering by fire to the Lord" (Leviticus 3:11). Thus "like no other sacrificial rite, the peace offering communicated an all inclusive form of communion between God and man."[51] The holy meal in which the holy meat from the peace offering was eaten united the Israelites as a holy people with their holy God—God gave this holy meat back to His guests to eat. Like the servants of a king in the ancient world, they ate the meat that came from God's table, the meat from the altar. They ate and drank in God's presence (cf. Exodus 24:11; 1 Chronicles 29:22).[52]

We could continue with the meals that accompanied the other sacrifices and the meals that accompanied the giving of all God's covenants to the people. These meals were joined to the highest points of God's saving revelation and forgiving presence. In these meals He had intimate communion, table fellowship, with His people to give them rescue and release and redemption. Yet each of these meals pointed to a greater feast to come.

Then God came in the flesh. The one through whom all things were created (John 1; Colossians 1), the one who accompanied Israel in the exodus (1 Corinthians 10:4), the one who gave Moses the Ten Commandments, the one whom those accompanying Moses saw on Mount Sinai (Exodus 24)[53] came in the flesh. One with the Father and the Holy Spirit, the preincarnate Christ had been present at meals with God's people throughout the Old Testament. But now, born of the Virgin Mary, He took His first meals in the flesh by nursing at His mother's breast. The one who had table fellowship with His people in the Old Testament had taken on flesh and blood to give us a new Table fellowship, that is, the new testament of His body and blood for us Christians to eat and drink.

There is nothing more central to God's reconciliation and presence with His people then His presence in Word and Meal with them. Man brought about division and barriers by grabbing forbidden food from the tree (Genesis 3). But God has torn down those walls by the sacrifice of His Son on the tree of the cross. The redemption is so final and the rescue is so complete that God now prepares a feast of the richest of foods and the finest of wines (Isaiah 25:6–9). The redemption is so final and the rescue is so complete that "[t]he holy Supper with the body and blood of Jesus Christ is the new Tree of Life, which stood in Paradise, which Christ has now again planted in His kingdom of Grace."[54]

Death has been swallowed up in victory, and the crucified and risen Christ now gives us His body and blood for the forgiveness of sins. This is no ordinary food but the very bread of life. Remember again Luke's inclusion of the beatitude "Blessed is everyone who will eat bread in the kingdom of God!" (Luke 14:15 ESV). Remember also Jesus' words in the Upper Room: "I will no longer eat of it until it is fulfilled in the kingdom of God" (Luke 22:16) and "I will not drink of the fruit of the vine until the kingdom of God comes" (Luke 22:18). Both verses indicate that Jesus will again eat and drink with His disciples in the kingdom of God.[55]

The kingdom of God has come to earth in the person of Jesus Christ. Where He is, there the kingdom is in our midst (Luke 17:21). The Greek word here is plural, meaning "among you" or "in your midst." This means that the eating and drinking that Jesus spoke of on the night of His betrayal is no longer just a future event. It means that already now we have Table fellowship with Jesus in His kingdom as the risen Christ brings to us the fruits of His sacrificial death on the cross.

Jesus came into His kingdom through His suffering, death, and resurrection. He said to His disciples, "I bestow upon you a kingdom, just as My Father bestowed [past tense, meaning it has been done] one upon Me" (Luke 22:29). He said to the thief on the cross, "Today you will be with Me in Paradise" (Luke 23:43). In other words, by His death and resurrection Jesus has been given the kingdom. Arthur Just states:

> Thus the church's eating and drinking of the Supper, from Easter to the parousia [Jesus' second coming], is an act of table fellowship celebrating that the kingdom of God *has* come. The Supper is the OT Passover transformed and "fulfilled in the kingdom of God" ([Luke]

22:16). Jesus did eat with his disciples after the resurrection. The first meal of Jesus with disciples after he comes into his kingdom in his resurrection is the Emmaus meal. . . . [T]he Emmaus meal is a connecting bridge between the Last Supper and the continuing table fellowship of Jesus with his disciples described by Luke in Acts. *But it is in the church's celebrations of the Lord's Supper that the fulfillment of Jesus' two words of promise comes.*[56]

The wedding banquet at the end of time is yet to come in all its fullness (Luke 14:15–24). But already the risen Christ comes into our midst with heavenly food. Already the Bridegroom comes to His bride with abundant provision of peace with God, anticipating the eternal pleasure He has prepared for her at God's right hand. Already God has reestablished Table fellowship with us as a foretaste of the feast to come.

The Sacrament at Corinth

What St. Paul taught the Corinthians concerning the Lord's Supper was in perfect harmony with Jesus' Words of Institution at the Last Supper and with the Holy Spirit's leading after Pentecost. Several of our names for the Sacrament come from St. Paul's first letter to the believers at Corinth. The name Holy Communion is derived from 1 Corinthians 10:16–17. The phrase "the table of the Lord" comes from 1 Corinthians 10:21. The name Lord's Supper is drawn from 1 Corinthians 11:20.

> The cup of blessing which we bless, is it not the communion of the blood of Christ? The bread which we break, is it not the communion of the body of Christ? (1 Corinthians 10:16)

> Therefore when you come together in one place it is not to eat the Lord's Supper. (1 Corinthians 11:20)

The problem that St. Paul addressed in 1 Corinthians 11:20 was that when the believers gathered together, it was no longer to eat the Lord's Supper. Although the Sacrament was celebrated, it had become a secondary thing. This the apostle condemns.[57] The term used in this Scripture passage for gathering together is a technical term for the coming together of the Christian congregation especially to administer the Lord's Supper.[58]

The context at Corinth indicates that when the church came together to celebrate Holy Communion, a shared meal also took place. The people's misuse of that meal at Corinth in conjunction with Holy Communion called forth St. Paul's sharp rebuke. The Corinthian Christians were destroying the holy character of the Supper by their selfishness and individualism. It was no longer the Lord's Supper that was the highlight of their gatherings. Rather, each person's chief interest had become "his own supper."[59]

Around AD 55, about two decades after the Last Supper on Maundy Thursday, Paul wrote, "I received from the Lord that which I also delivered to you" (1 Corinthians 11:23). Some see the words *receive* and *deliver* as technical terms that indicate oral teaching passed on from the apostles to St. Paul.[60] Others hold that just as St. Paul received the Gospel itself directly from Christ through a revelation (Galatians 1:12), so also He received the Lord's Supper by a similar direct revelation.[61] Another opinion is that the liturgy of the Lord's Supper is the most likely means by which St. Paul received this gift from the risen Christ.[62]

What is absolutely clear, however, is that the gift Jesus gave in the Upper Room is the same gift Paul had received from the Lord, and what the Holy Spirit led the Jewish church to receive at Pentecost is exactly what Paul was also delivering to the Gentile church at Corinth. When the Lord's people gathered together for worship, the Lord's Supper was the norm. Their gathering was to be for eating the Sacred Meal (1 Corinthians 11:20), and when abuses altered that purpose, Paul wrote to correct the matter. Lindemann writes: "It is significant that the Apostle did not propose the discontinuation of the regular celebration of the Lord's Supper because there was so little appreciation. Rather, he insisted that the abuses be corrected and the Lord's Supper restored to the place our Lord intended for it in the worship of His people."[63]

Revelation 1–3 and the Lord's Supper

As a final scriptural text in these brief foundational thoughts, I would invite you to consider the first three chapters of the Book of Revelation. As the seven letters written to the seven churches in these chapters are widely understood to be God's Word for the church of all time, an interesting question is whether the seven letters also bear witness to the Lord's Supper for the church of all time.

The apostle John was not on the island of Patmos by choice. He had been exiled there because he was proclaiming the apostles' doctrine. He had been sent to the island "for the word of God and for the testimony of Jesus Christ" (Revelation 1:9). Imprisoned there, John was in the Spirit on the Lord's Day when the glorified Christ gave him words to write to the seven churches (Revelation 1:10). This was certainly the day when John would normally be preaching the apostles' doctrine to the gatherings of the church in Asia Minor. In keeping with the witness of Scripture concerning the serving of Word and Sacrament in weekly worship, it was also the day when the Lord's Supper would be administered after the teaching was completed.

However, an emperor's persecution and miles of water now separated John from the churches gathered for worship. Is it not fitting, therefore, that on the Lord's Day, He who was dead and is alive forevermore, He who holds the key of Hades and of death, the glorified Christ, commands John to write instead of speak? The apostles' doctrine must continue to be heard in the church.

Indeed, it still is heard today through the written word of John and the other apostles, which is the basis for the proclamation of the Word of God from the pulpit.

Each of the seven letters found in the first three chapters of Revelation was written to a particular church and was relevant to that church's specific situation. However, each letter was to be received—as part of the one Book of Revelation—by all seven churches. The seven letters to seven particular churches are also Sacred Scripture and as such are addressed to all churches and to all Christians until the end of time.[64] Would it not seem strange if there were no mention of the Sacrament in this revelation to the churches? Would it not be strange if on the Lord's Day (Revelation 1:10) there was no proclamation of the Lord's Supper (1 Corinthians 11:20), no mention of a meal taken with the Lord?

Perhaps it is anything but coincidence that when the teaching on the Lord's Day is done, that is, when the last of the seven letters to the seven churches is concluded, there is an invitation to a meal taken with the Lord: "Behold, I stand at the door and knock. If anyone hears My voice and opens the door I will come in to him and dine with him, and he with Me" (Revelation 3:20).

This is not an invitation for unbelievers to open the door of their heart to Jesus (decision theology) as it is often conveyed in our time. As man is dead in sin (Ephesians 2:1–5) and as faith is a gift of God, not man's doing (Ephesians 2:8–9), unbelievers cannot open the door of their hearts to Jesus. Although this thought is prevalent in modern Christianity, it is a serious misunderstanding and an expression that does not come from God's Word. While often sincerely expressed, it falsely assigns to man that work which only the Holy Spirit can do: giving the new life of faith to those dead in sin.

This text that depicts Jesus standing at the door and knocking deals not with unbelievers but with believers. It deals with the church's reception of Christ now and her readiness for His second coming (Matthew 24:31–33; Luke 12:35–37; James 5:9). This text is written on the Lord's Day (Revelation 1:10) and issues an invitation to banquet with Christ (Revelation 3:20), to have Table fellowship with Him. Gaylin Schmeling expresses it this way in a short devotion on Revelation 3:20:

> Our condition by nature was so terrible that we could not even open the door of our hearts to our gracious Lord. His invitation fell on deaf ears that were dead in sin. As Jesus once called Lazarus forth from the grave, so he through his almighty voice in Word and Baptism called us forth alive. Faith in the Savior was worked in our hearts, and we were given new spiritual life.

> Now the doors are open wide to him, and he comes in and eats with us and we with him. This intimate relationship with the Savior occurs in the Holy Supper, where we indeed have a meal with him, receiving his life-giving body and blood.[65]

Gordon Lathrop points out that "[t]he letters to the seven churches can be regarded as substitutes, necessary under duress, for personally coming into the assembly. It is not surprising for us to find, then, at the very end of these Sunday addresses to assemblies, an invitation to eat the meal with Christ (Rev. 3:20)."[66]

As the glorified Christ gave John words to write to the church on the Lord's Day, He included words of invitation to dine with Him. The very meal He gives us here on earth proclaims His final knocking at the door in His second coming (1 Corinthians 11:27). The very meal He gives us here on earth bestows His true body and true blood for the remission of sins (Matthew 26:26–28) and to prepare us for His final coming. As chapter 7 will discuss, the Lord's Supper has a close connection with the Lord's second coming. As the next chapter shows, the risen Christ continued to come into the midst of His gathered people each Lord's Day to teach them and feed them with the treasure of His Word and Sacrament.

Discussion Questions

1. Is the Lord's Supper something we do? Discuss. How can we refute those who regard the Sacrament as something we do?
2. Read Luther's statement about the Words of Institution on page 29. He said that they are "the sum and . . ."
3. Read C. F. W. Walther's statement about the Words of Institution on page 30. Who did Walther say is repeating the words through the mouth of the minister? Discuss.
4. Does everyone who partakes of Holy Communion receive the body and blood of Christ whether they believe it or not? Why or why not? Does everyone receive forgiveness of sins whether they believe it or not? Discuss.
5. Why did the early church practice weekly Communion? Was it commanded by Christ? Discuss.
6. How might the word *devoted* be understood in Acts 2:42? What is at the heart of the church's fellowship as expressed in Acts 2:42?
7. In the Lord's Supper, Jesus is all in all. As Luther said, He "is himself cook, butler, _____ and _____." Robert Kolb, a contemporary Lutheran theologian, said that Jesus is "the banquet _____ and the _____ itself. He is _____ as well as _____." Discuss these two quotes in light of the paragraph that follows them on page 40.
8. What did C. F. W. Walther say is the new tree of life planted in God's kingdom of grace? Discuss.
9. Arthur Just states that the church's eating and drinking of the Supper from Easter to Jesus' second coming is an act of Table fellowship, celebrating that the _____ has come. Discuss.
10. What problem did St. Paul address in 1 Corinthians 11:20? What was the norm when the Lord's people gathered together

for worship? Did St. Paul propose discontinuing the regular celebrations of the Lord's Supper? Discuss.

11. In Revelation 3:20, when Jesus bids people to open the door so we may dine with Him, is He speaking to believers or unbelievers? In view of the discussion of the seven letters to the seven churches as God's Word to the church of all time, what message would Jesus' Lord's Day invitation to a meal with Him have for His church?

One generation shall praise Your works to another,
And shall declare Your mighty acts. (Psalm 145:4)

chapter two

The Sacrament
in the Early Church

When I first began to answer the question about why we didn't
have the opportunity to commune in regular weekly worship, I
could find nothing in Scripture or the Lutheran Confessions that
spoke against it. In fact, I found just the opposite. I then sought
to answer questions about when and why regular weekly Communion was lost. That led to some study of what has happened
throughout church history. If weekly Communion was there at
the beginning, what happened and why? If weekly Communion
was confessed and the recovery of it was sought in the Reformation, what happened and why?

The following five chapters seek to describe general conditions and points of interest in different periods of history and
their relationship to both the opportunity to commune and the
actual reception of Communion by the laity. These chapters are

not an exhaustive treatment of this history, but they are a statement of some of my discoveries in this endeavor. Occasionally, information is also provided in a period of history that may not seem directly related to the frequency of Communion, but this information will help anchor the discussion of that time period and will apply to questions of worship and Communion in general. For example, this chapter includes a description of the persecution the church suffered in the third century, the origin of Holy Week services in the fourth century, and a brief mention of Eastern practice in the fifth century. First, however, we will look at the importance of church history to Martin Luther and to the other reformers.

The Lord's Supper has never enjoyed a golden age wherein its presence and practice were without opposition and perfectly understood and received. The church, with its strong, Spirit-led devotion to Word and Sacrament (Acts 2:42), quickly came under attack. Following Stephen's stoning, a general persecution broke out (Acts 7). Soon, however, one of the original persecutors, St. Paul, was extolling the proper place of the Sacrament in the life of the church. Even his encouragement was by way of correcting those who were abusing the Sacrament in the church at Corinth (1 Corinthians 10–11).

In the centuries that followed, the place of the Sacrament in the worship of the church was sometimes challenged from within the church and sometimes from without. The history of the church nevertheless gives clear witness concerning the weekly presence of Christ with His people in Word and Sacrament. This history holds great value for our faith and life today, even as it did for Luther and the reformers.

Church History Mattered to Luther

The place of the Lord's Supper from the time of the apostles until the time of the Reformation was of great importance to Luther and the reformers. It was never the intention of the reformers to break away from or begin a new confession within the church. Rather, it was their desire to recall the church to the faith once delivered to the saints. Tragic abuses and false teachings (private Masses, the Mass as man's sacrifice, indulgences) had crept in, and Luther sought to remove these abuses while retaining what was true and good.

To do this, Luther returned to the writings of the apostles. But he also drew upon the works of the fathers, who recorded the life and worship of the early church. Fred Lindemann writes: "When [Luther] reunited the word and sacraments and revived the Holy Communion as the standard of common worship, he was guided by the Scriptures, but surely he was greatly encouraged and strengthened by the knowledge that this was the way of worship from the very beginning and had proved itself in the experience of the centuries."[1]

Indeed, concerning the Lord's Supper, the Lutheran Confessions state clearly that no novelty had been introduced that did not exist in the early church. The Confessions reference Scripture and many writings of the fathers.[2] The Lutherans were not antihistorical nor did they put themselves above church history. Rather, they believed that God was also at work in church history wherein that history did not contradict God's Word. In this regard, there is a clear sense in the Augsburg Confession that the situation of the contemporary church—that is, the church in Luther's day—was far worse than it was in the early centuries. From the standpoint of reliable testimony to the catholicity of the church, or understanding its universal and eternal truths, the early period was viewed as unsurpassed by any other.[3]

In essential matters the Lutherans were in continuity with the Scriptures and the testimony of the ancient church. For example, concerning the use of both bread and wine in the Eucharist, the Augsburg Confession refers to Paul (1 Corinthians

11:20ff.), then goes on to say that "this usage continued in the church for a long time as can be demonstrated from history and the writings of the Fathers (AC XXII.4)."[4] Cyprian, Jerome, and even Pope Gelasius are referenced positively in the Augsburg Confession, for on this point their teaching and practice agreed with God's Word.

Therefore it is good for us to consider the historical witness to every Sunday Communion, for the Lutheran Church is legitimate heir to all that preceded it. Like us, the saints and fathers lived by the principle of *sola scriptura*. Of course we know that there were many abuses in the practice of the Sacrament, as well as centuries of misleading instruction concerning its purpose. But the history of the church also clearly demonstrates the presence of the Lord's Supper in its weekly worship.

The First Century (AD 1–100)

Lord, You have been our dwelling place throughout all generations. (Psalm 90:1 NIV)

All that we have considered from the Scriptures was occurring in this century. The Holy Spirit was poured out at Pentecost, Paul wrote to the church at Corinth concerning the Lord's Supper, and John wrote to the seven churches from his exile on the island of Patmos. While this occurred, the church's life centered on Word and Sacrament—the preaching of the apostles and the reception of the new testament of Christ's body and blood. The persecution of Christians also began in earnest in this century, first from the Jewish religious leaders. Soon, as John's exile to Patmos and Paul's imprisonments testify, the persecution widened in scope.

In AD 70, Jerusalem was besieged and the temple destroyed. The early center of Christian activity was now in ruins. Jesus' prophecy to His disciples as they admired the beautiful stones and adornment of the temple had come to pass: "The days will come in which not one stone shall be left upon another that shall not be thrown down" (Luke 21:5–6). Jesus' additional prophecy had also proven true: "Destroy this temple, and in three days I will raise it up" (John 2:19). Of course, He was speaking of the temple of His body (John 2:21). Even as the Jerusalem temple was destroyed, the temple of Jesus' crucified and risen body was present with His church scattered throughout the Mediterranean world. Whenever believers gathered in His name, the risen Christ, the God-man, came into their midst to teach them and feed them in Word and Sacrament. He came invisibly to give them His true body to eat and His true blood to drink for the forgiveness of their sins.

There is reason to believe that an early document of Syrian origin, the *Didache* or the *Teaching of the Twelve Apostles,* was present in this first century of the church. Some scholars suggest the *Didache* was present by AD 70,[5] but others suggest a date as early as the period AD 40 to AD 60.[6] This would mean that the *Didache* may well have been present even as the New Testament books were being written. Even if its writing were later in the century, it certainly reflects the practice that was in place in earlier decades.

The *Didache* is not a letter to a congregation or pastor, but it is an instruction manual that provides directions for different aspects of the church's life and teaching. It was intended for those desiring to be baptized. The *Didache* speaks about two ways: the way of death and the way of the teaching. It is the first picture outside the New Testament of how the church worshiped.

In chapter 14, the *Didache* briefly describes Sunday worship in this way: "On the Lord's day of the Lord come together, break bread, and hold the Eucharist, after confessing your transgressions."[7] It also bears witness to the practice of closed Communion[8] in chapter 9: "You must not let anyone eat or drink your

Eucharist except those baptized in the Lord's name. For in reference to this the Lord said, 'Do not give what is sacred to dogs.' "[9] The *Didache* is here quoting Matthew 7:6, and it must be remembered that to be baptized as an adult convert at that time required lengthy and rigorous instruction. Loving concern for the confession of the faith by those who communed was clearly in place, as seen from this early witness.

It is of great significance that the *Didache*, in its description of Sunday worship, puts the Lord's Supper at the center of worship. It does not specifically mention the preaching of the Word of God, but this would have been understood as the first course of the gathering, just as it is in Acts 20:7–11 or in Paul's rebuke of the Corinthian Christians: "Therefore when you come together in one place, it is not to eat the Lord's Supper" (1 Corinthians 11:20). When the Lord's Supper is spoken of as the heart of worship in the Scriptures and in the *Didache*, it means the full serving that the risen Christ brings to His gathered church—Word and Sacrament. As Paul Kretzmann observes:

> There were daily services with teaching of the Word and prayer . . . . And there were special services for the celebration of the Eucharist, usually on Sunday evenings, with the preaching of the Word, offering of prayer, oblation [presenting] of gifts, common meal, and the Holy Supper, in which the whole congregation took part, none but members being admitted [1 Corinthians 16:1–2; Acts 20:17; Revelation 1:10].[10]

The Second Century (AD 101–200)

"Do not think that I came to destroy the Law or the Prophets. I did not come to destroy but to fulfill." (Matthew 5:17)

As the first century ended and the second began, when the apostles had died or been martyred, their work was carried on by the apostolic fathers. The worship of those early Christians recalls synagogue worship and its reading of Scripture, Psalms, and prayer. The Jews called their worship by the Greek word *synaxis*, which comes from the same root word as *synagogue* and means "meeting."[11] The Christians took over this term and used it for a new meeting in the new creation: the weekly gathering to receive Word and Sacrament.

What is evident in the regular Lord's Day meetings of the scattered church is that these gatherings culminated in the Lord's Supper. Psalms and prayers and Scripture readings were present as they were in the synagogue meetings. But the new church now received the true presence of the living Christ, the God-man, in the preached Word and the Sacrament. A characteristic feature of Jesus' resurrection appearances was that they took place during a meal (Acts 10:41).[12] The certainty of the resurrection was the essential religious motive of the primitive Lord's Supper. Eucharistic meals were regarded as the continuation of the first Christian meals at Easter.[13]

This focus can be seen in the *First Apology* (defense) of Justin Martyr, written in the middle of the second century (ca. AD 150). This document was written to the Roman authorities to show that there was no subversive threat to the government in the faith and worship of Christians. That is, there was nothing about Christian faith and worship that should cause the state to persecute Christians. The *First Apology* describes worship in the church at Rome as a gathering on Sunday led by a "president" (one who presides). The worship began with readings from the apostles or the writings of the prophets "as long as time permits," continued with a sermon by the president, followed by congregational prayers, and culminated in the Eucharist.[14] There is no mention of a love feast at this time. The focus is clearly on the Sunday service that culminates in the Lord's Supper. Justin's testimony demonstrates that the main features of the eucharistic celebration were fixed as early as the second century.[15] Indeed, Justin described in writing the pattern of weekly worship that had been occuring through the years and was ingrained by midcentury. It is the same pattern of Word and Sacrament that we see in the church after Pentecost as recorded in Acts.

Sections 65–67 of the *First Apology* also give witness to the loving concern for pastoral care and closed Communion: "And this food is called among us the Eucharist, of which no one is allowed to partake but the man who believes the things which we teach are true, and who has been washed with the washing for the remission of sins, and for regeneration, and who is so living as Christ enjoined."[16] Here the loving practice of closed Communion demonstrates concern not only for unity of confession but also a godly life. Public, unrepentant sin did in fact preclude one from participation in the weekly opportunity to commune. The church discipline set forth in the Scriptures is clearly reflected here.

In this regard, it is important to recognize that forbidding the Sacrament to someone who is living in open sin is not what Jesus meant when He said, "Judge not, that you be not judged" (Matthew 7:1). Jesus was here speaking against judging hypocritically (Matthew 7:5) by trying to judge hidden motives of the heart. He was not setting aside the need to speak His word of truth in the face of continuous, public, unrepentant sin.

The weekly presence of Christ with His serving of Word and Sacrament determined the life of the church. There were no festivals or holidays that God commanded in the New Testament (see Matthew 12:1–8; Colossians 2:16–17; Galatians 4:9–11). In the second century, there was no church year as we know it today—only the festival of Easter seems to be observed, but this observance was not universal. The center of life for the Christians was clearly the weekly gathering to hear the preached Word and to receive the Sacrament of the Altar. They considered the Lord's

Day, with its live-giving Word and Sacrament, the eighth day, the day of the new creation.

The Third Century (AD 201–300)

"Therefore whoever confesses Me before men, him I will confess before My Father who is in heaven. But whoever denies Me before men, him I will also deny before My Father who is in heaven." (Matthew 10:32–33)

The church experienced specific periods of persecution at the beginning, middle, and end of the third century. The intervening decades saw relative peace, but the affliction during the years of active persecution was intense. Some specifics of these periods of persecution are here recounted to demonstrate that even amid severe trial, the presence of the risen Christ in Word and Sacrament each week was central to the lives of those persecuted. As will be shown, some faced martyrdom rather than give up the weekly gathering to receive Christ's gifts. These specifics are also recounted because the persecuted church of this century became the church of the powerful in the next century. That radical change also affected the reception of weekly Communion.

In AD 202, Emperor Septimius Severus (r. AD 193–211) issued a landmark edict in the history of persecutions. He followed a syncretistic policy (actions that recognized all gods) and decreed the death penalty for any who would convert to an exclusivist religion such as Christianity.[17] For the sake of the nation, the emperor felt it important that citizens would be willing to acknowledge also the gods of Rome. In other words, it was acceptable for someone to worship Jesus or to pray to Him as long as he or she gave a public witness that Jesus was one god among many. Thus Christians who would recognize pagan gods were tolerated by the state. Those followers of Christ who faithfully confessed Him both privately and publicly as the only Savior of mankind were not tolerated because such exclusivity was considered disruptive to national unity and strength.

It is important to note that what got the Christians in trouble was actually civic disloyalty, not the worship of Jesus Christ per se. In the Roman Empire of this time, Caesar was not "seen as a real god in the same league with Jupiter and Apollo. Caesar worship was a mere formality of civil religion. Nobody took it all that seriously. Except the Christians, of course, who paid the price for their refusal to make even token obeisance to Caesar."[18] Christians weren't being selfishly stubborn but lovingly faithful in their refusal to give a mixed witness. As a result, the state persecuted them.

Amid these persecutions, the weekly liturgy of the church confessed the bodily presence of the risen Christ in the Lord's Supper to feed and forgive His gathered people. Attendance at Holy Communion was closed because only baptized children and those adults who were fully instructed and baptized were allowed to partake. The Romans spread malicious rumors about these secret meetings, yet the church grew steadily as Christians confessed the faith in their homes and vocations and among their families despite suffering and persecution.

The centrality of the Sacrament in the weekly worship of the church in this century of periodic persecution is attested to by the *Apostolic Tradition*, which was compiled around the year AD 217.[19] Hippolytus said that he wrote to preserve the correct rites against "mindless innovators." His description of the Eucharist includes these details: only baptized and sufficiently instructed persons could participate, and the meal occurred as the usual climax of Sunday worship. Hippolytus also records the dialogue that preceded the celebration of the Lord's Supper:

> Bishop: The Lord be with you.
> People: And with your Spirit.
>
> Bishop: Lift up your hearts.
> People: We have them with the Lord.

Bishop: Let us give thanks [*eucharistia*] to the Lord.
People: It is right and proper.[20]

For Hippolytus there is no doubt that Christians are partaking of a resurrection meal, not participating in a wake for a departed hero.[21] Here we also see the treasure that we easily overlook in the liturgy, a treasure that has been handed down to us. These strange-sounding words confess the actual presence of the risen Christ. The living God-man is not visibly present, but He is present to feed believers His very body and His very blood and forgive them in His Supper. These are words that are not outdated today, for Jesus still comes into our midst *for us* in His Word and Sacrament. As He does so, His Word still does what it says.

The trial was extremely severe in AD 250. Emperor Decius believed that Christianity was weakening the Roman Empire and that a return to the old religion would make Rome great again. To stamp out the new religion (Christianity), Decius required that everyone in the empire receive a certificate from an official, witnessing that the person had sacrificed to the emperor.[22] At times, because of sympathetic local officials, it wasn't necessary for Christians to actually make the sacrifice of incense. Some officials simply gave Christians the certificate that stated they had made the sacrifice even if they hadn't actually done so. But the public witness of the certificate was still a denial of Jesus' sole-saving redemption. Decius, however, didn't want to make martyrs; he wanted to unite the country to fight the barbarians. Therefore he used public disapproval, ridicule, threats, imprisonment, and torture to brand Christians as criminals. He hoped that people would rather burn a pinch of incense to the emperor than suffer such ostracism.[23] Emperor Valerian (r. AD 253–260) followed a similar policy.

Because Decius's methods tried to avoid putting large numbers of Christians to death, those who stood firm through the assaults were given a new title of honor. They were called "confessors." Those who didn't stand firm in confessing Christ were known as the "lapsed."[24] For many years the church wrestled with the problem of whether to receive back into the fellowship those who had denied the faith and if so, how.

The centrality of the Sacrament amid these persecutions is seen in a letter Luther records from St. Cyprian (bishop of Carthage) to Cornelius (bishop of Rome) at the time of Decius's persecution. Both Cornelius and Cyprian died as martyrs in these midcentury persecutions. The letter expresses how Christians should be strengthened by the Sacrament for suffering in times of persecution. Cyprian's letter to Cornelius reads in part:

> [W]e must equip those whom we wish to be safe against the adversary with the armor of the Lord's food. For how shall we teach or incite them to shed their blood in confession of his name, if we deny them Christ's blood when they are about to fight? Or how can we make them fit for the cup of martyrdom, if we do not first admit them to drink in the church the cup of the Lord by the right of communion?[25]

In the third century, instruction in the faith (catechesis) generally lasted three years, yet there was large numerical growth in the Christian church.[26] This growth came not from revivals or evangelistic services; "[o]n the contrary, in the early church worship centered on communion and only baptized Christians were admitted to its celebration."[27] According to Gregory Dix, "[i]t was not that the church did not desire converts; she was ardently missionary to all who would hear, as Jews and pagans were quick to complain."[28] But such personal witness and even organized oral instruction were rigidly separated from worship. Those who were not already of the laity by Baptism and confirmation were invariably turned out before the prayers and the Lord's Supper.[29] That is, worship was for receiving God's gifts and for instruction in the faith. Worship was not shaped to make it attractive to unbelievers or the uninstructed.

It was the witness of Christians in their vocations—family settings, friendships, neighborhoods, kitchens, shops, and markets—and most especially the witness of their suffering and even martyrdom that won converts to the faith. Then as now, "[l]aypeople are especially positioned to reach people outside the church, by virtue of their secular vocation, which puts them in contact with people who would never darken the door of a church."[30] Then, as now, "[t]he Gospel is Holy Absolution for poor, miserable sinners, so gracious, so efficacious that the absolved ones long to share with other sinners that forgiveness which they themselves have received. (They will pray the Lord for more harvest-workers, they will pay for the sending out of such men, and they will urge their sons to obey Christ's call to ministry!)"[31] Then, as now, Christians will also humbly bear witness to the hope they have in Christ. Then, as now, persecutions will come where Christ is faithfully preached and confessed and His Sacraments faithfully administered and received. God will even use those persecutions for the spread of His Gospel.

The local congregations in the third century, as in the centuries before, were not huge operations. Justo Gonzalez notes that "[u]ntil Constantine's time, Christian worship had been relatively simple. At first Christians gathered to worship in private homes. Then they began to gather in cemeteries, such as the Roman catacombs. By the third century there were structures set aside for worship."[32] The rooms in these structures were fairly small, and there were no parish family centers, only the homes of the members. Ordinary people gathered in worship to receive God's strength to see them through the week. As they lived their daily lives, they bore witness with gentleness and respect to the living hope they had in Jesus Christ (1 Peter 3:15–16). That living hope came from their living Lord, who came to serve them the fruits of His death in Word and Sacrament in weekly worship.

This historical context helps us see that there was no tension between the church's worship and the church's mission. In a culture hostile to Christianity, much like our own, the baptized did not try to market worship or make it into something it was not. In a culture hostile to Christianity, bigger wasn't seen as better. With reverence, with loving concern for closed Communion, with central focus on the reception of the gifts of Christ and a clear confession of the faith, the early church was both ardently missionary and actively mindful of the doctrinal and sacramental fullness of the Gospel.[33]

Christian art, symbols, and decorations alluding to the Christian faith become obvious as Christians of this period developed their own cemeteries—the catacombs—and their own churches, such as the one in Dura-Europos. (This is the oldest church to be excavated—a private dwelling converted to a church before AD 256.)[34] Because Communion was the central act of worship, scenes and symbols referring to it are most often found. Sometimes what is depicted is the celebration itself or the Last Supper in the Upper Room. In other instances, there is simply a basket with fish and bread.[35] Early Christian art frequently represented the Lord's Supper under the form of a meal of fish.[36] This is not to say that fish were used instead of bread and wine. Rather, fish in the artwork were used to picture the presence of Jesus Christ, God's Son, Savior, in the Lord's Supper. For example, at the great church in Ravenna, Italy, which was built decades later, the Last Supper is depicted with Jesus and His disciples reclining around a table on which there are fish. The fish lying on the table symbolize Jesus Christ, the great ICHTHUS,[37] who is indeed present in the Holy Supper, for He promises to give us His body and blood under the form of bread and wine. As the five thousand received natural fish, so in the miracle of the Sacrament we receive the heavenly, living fish, Jesus Christ, partaking in all the blessings of salvation.[38]

Another early church witness to the central place of the liturgy of the Lord's Supper is the word *church* itself. There is broad understanding that this word did not first mean a building but the people who make up a church. What is not so widely known, however, is that even the people who make up the church are not the first or fullest understanding of the word *church*. Until the third century, the word *church* invariably meant not the building for Christian worship nor the individual Christians wherever they may be, but the solemn assembly for the liturgy (that is, the gathering around Word and Sacrament). It was then by extension from the gathering for worship that the word *church* also meant those who had a right to take part in that gathering.[39] In other words, the first meaning of the word *church* has to do with weekly Communion. It first meant the people as they actually gathered in the liturgy of Word and Sacrament for weekly worship. Its meaning then came to be applied to the Christian people who gathered for worship, even when they weren't gathered to receive Word and Sacrament. Later its meaning included the buildings in which this gathering took place.

The Fourth Century (AD 301–400)

If riches increase, Do not set your heart on them. (Psalm 62:10)

Give me neither poverty nor riches—Feed me with the food allotted to me. (Proverbs 30:8)

In AD 303, Galerius convinced Emperor Diocletian to issue a new edict against Christians. It was then ordered that Christians be removed from every government position and that all Christian buildings and books be destroyed.[40] There is clear indication in this edict that there were other homes and buildings than the one at Dura-Europos that had been converted for the purpose of the gathering of Christians in assemblies for Word and Sacrament.

There is also another clear secular witness that the central act of the Christians was gathering in their assemblies for weekly worship. In the edict of Galerius in AD 311 that ended this most severe of Roman persecutions of the church, we read: "Therefore, moved by our mercy to be benevolent towards all, it has seemed just to us to extend to them our pardon, and allow them to be Christians once again, and once again gather in their assemblies, as long as they do not interfere with public order."[41] Note the centrality of Christian assemblies in this edict. There is no indication that these weekly assemblies had changed from their purpose of receiving Word and Sacrament from the risen Christ. As alluded to here, they were understood even by the secular ruler to be at the center of the church's life. Therefore what was at stake when Galerius said we will "allow them to be Christians once again" was intimately connected to Christians being allowed to gather to receive Word and Sacrament. The primary meaning of the word *church* as noted previously seems to be clearly understood, even by the secular authorities.

The life-and-death importance of this weekly meeting with the crucified and risen Christ is witnessed to early in this century by Christians of North Africa. When they were accused of illegally gathering, they made this confession that contributed to their martyrdom: "We cannot be without the *dominicum*." *Dominicum* is translated as the "thing of the Lord," perhaps the Day of the Lord as the occasion for the Supper of the Lord. These North African Christians did not mean that they could not do without the day but that they could not be Christians and even live in any real sense without the assembly and its content—the risen Lord. Christians meet because of Christ's resurrection and around Christ's resurrection.[42]

Following the death of Galerius and two subsequent years of political and military turmoil, Constantine won military victory over the other claimants to the Roman throne. With his victory, the persecuted church became the tolerated church, then the favored church. After the death of Constantine, Christianity became the state religion of the Roman Empire. The Edict of Milan (AD 313) strengthened the edict of AD 311 by stating that not only should persecutions stop but also that churches, cemeteries, and other properties would be returned to the Christians.

Soon, with steady support from the state, the church was granted even more privilege. For example, Constantine gave the privileges formerly enjoyed by pagan priests to Christian ministers. The Christian Sunday was made a legal holiday and proclaimed a day of rest in AD 321. Christian bishops were permitted to travel like senators in government coaches. The holy books of the Christians, once given to the flames, were now bound in purple and inlaid with gold and jewels.[43] Larger spaces for worship were needed, and a program for building basilicas was initiated by Constantine.

In this century, the earliest festival of the Christian church was officially established. That annual celebration was Easter, and the Council of Nicaea in AD 325 settled the date as the first Sunday after the first full moon after the first day of spring (the vernal equinox).[44] The celebration of Christmas was fixed as December 25 a quarter of a century later in AD 354 by Pope Liberius.[45]

Thus in the first centuries of the church's history, the weekly gathering of Christ with His people in Word and Sacrament defined the church. Easter was being observed in the second century, but its date was not officially fixed until the fourth century. The festival of Christmas was first officially recognized also in this century.

This has great significance for the importance we assign to the weekly gathering for Word and Sacrament worship versus the importance we assign to gathering only for annual celebrations such as Christmas and Easter. Occasionally we refer to Sunday as a little Easter, which in one sense is absolutely right. On Sunday, the worship of the church on the Lord's Day is nothing but a continuation of the resurrection appearances of the risen Lord. He is no longer visible, but He is in the midst of His gathered people to teach them His holy Word and to feed them His body and blood once sacrificed on the cross. In another sense, this expression may be understood in a backward and harmful manner. If the reference is to Sunday as a littler, lesser copy of the annual observance of Easter, then it would be a false expression. In such a case, it would be more historically accurate to refer to Easter as a big Sunday. That is, Easter Sunday came to be observed with a specific focus and emphasis on the miracle of the resurrection. What must be kept in mind, however, is that our life in Christ doesn't flow from an annual remembrance with a little more celebration of one or two of Christ's mighty acts. Our life in Christ flows from Christ Himself, who comes into our midst each week to give us the new life of Easter morning. Instead of saying that Sunday is a little Easter, perhaps it would be better said that Sunday or weekly worship is the *continuation* of Easter. In the weekly Divine Service, Jesus comes *for us* to bring us life. It is not a mundane matter of going to church, but it is the magnificent moment of meeting with the risen Christ as His bride to receive His love. Just as Jesus continued to meet with His church visibly in the flesh in the first forty days after His resurrection, so now He continues to meet with us invisibly to teach us and to feed us.

In AD 325, an event occurred that was to affect the course of the church for centuries to come. Emperor Constantine called a council of all the church leaders at the city of Nicaea, which is near Constantinople in the modern nation of Turkey. The Council of Nicaea marked the first ecumenical or worldwide council of the church. Emperor Constantine wanted harmony in his empire.

Because the church had legal recognition and had become rich and powerful, it was a crucial factor in wider social and political harmony. According to Justo González, "[t]he Empire had a vested interest in the unity of the Church, which Constantine hoped would become the 'cement of the Empire.' Thus the state soon began to use its power to force theological agreement on Christians."[46]

One area of unrest was the theological dispute concerning the relationship of Christ and God. Arius held that Jesus was not true God, not eternal, not one with the Father. The error of his teaching attacked the very heart of the Christian faith. Athanasius of Alexandria was the chief advocate of the true teaching that Jesus Christ *was* God, equal with the Father and the Holy Spirit. This doctrinal struggle had and has far-reaching importance for the church's reception of and teaching about the Lord's Supper. Luther was not turned aside from the straightforward witness of Christ's Words of Institution chiefly because of who was speaking them. As Athanasius affirmed from the Scriptures, Jesus is true God and also true man in one person. The union of the divine and human natures in the flesh of Christ means that our limits of reason do not apply to the body and blood of the God-man. It is not too great a thing for the ascended Lord to be with His church just as He promised in this gift. Jesus' ascension is not to be understood as some sort of space travel, going from one place to another, but as His removal from the sight of the disciples and His liberation from the limitations of His humiliation. Because He is God and man in one person, Jesus' ascension does not contradict His promise to be with His church.[47] The mystery of His real presence in the Supper goes hand in hand with the mystery of the personal union of the divine and human natures in Christ.

The Council of Nicaea made an unambiguous confession that Jesus was true God and true man. The Arian view that Christ was a creature, not true God, was condemned. The Creed confessed that the Son was of one substance with the Father.[48] The Creed, now called the Nicene Creed, was not completed until some years later and was adopted at the Council of Constantinople in AD 381.[49] Nonetheless, it deserves the name Nicene because it expresses the clear doctrinal statement of the Council of Nicaea made already in AD 325. The proclamation of the truth defended and fostered by this council reaches through the centuries, even to the use of the Nicene Creed in our services today.

The Nicene Creed is normally recited in the Communion service. Its use in the liturgy since the sixth century has been a strong confession of the two natures of the God-man who is present in the Sacrament. This creedal statement was written against the false worship of the Arians. This heresy and related ones that redefine Jesus to fit the mind of man or the culture in which we live are always current. So also the Nicene Creed is always contemporary. Luther saw this creed as a confession of praise before the lordship of Christ.[50] It is a mark of catholic and orthodox identity and also a deeply evangelical summary of God's gift to us in Christ.[51]

But the Council of Nicaea also left another legacy that was not so positive for the church—the increased intermingling of the church and the world. The distinction between the church and the world that Nicene Christology preserved was, in fact, compromised by the very events that led up to the declaration of Nicaea.[52] With the conversion of the emperor, the reality of the church as a persecuted community, separate from the world, eroded tremendously. Pastors and laity began to find comfort in their popular place in society. According to Gonzalez, "[t]he rich and the powerful seemed to dominate the life of the church."[53] Especially during the fourth through seventh centuries, as the Christian faith spread into northern and western Europe, the actions of rulers in initiating, promoting, supporting, and often dictating to the church gradually accustomed leaders in both church and state to notions of establishment.[54] In AD 380 Emperor Theodosius recognized Christianity as the state religion. The temptation to forget that Jesus' kingdom is not of this world (John 18:36) had become an institutionalized temptation.

Safety and success can be fraught with spiritual danger. All of society began to claim a nominal Christianity. There was increased indiscriminate admission to Baptism and confirmation. Careful concern for instruction in the faith under the threat of persecution gave way to political approval and popular applause of the church as an institution. It had become economically advantageous, socially stylish, and politically patriotic to join the Christian church. Receiving Christ in the humble means of Word and Sacrament is not a popular or patriotic act, however. It is the act of faith drawing its life from the promised presence of the Lord *for us*.

The external statistical growth of the church in this period was accompanied by symptoms of serious spiritual sickness. Amid all the outward excitement and expansion and enrichment, an inward decline in lay Communion began to set in. According to one commentator, "[t]he decline in lay Communion is complained of already by Chrysostom in Antioch at the end of the fourth century, and from then on things move downhill."[55] Chrysostom complains that "[i]n vain do we stand before the altar; there is no one to partake."[56] A trend had started that was leading the church away from the steadfast devotion to Word and Sacrament in which the Holy Spirit had led the church after Pentecost. Another contributing factor to the decrease in reception of Holy Communion has been identified as the church's reaction to the Arian heresy. As the struggle waged over the divinity of Christ, church leaders emphasized Jesus' power and rights and His judgment of the living and the dead.[57]

These are correct emphases, but not exclusive ones. A one-sided stress of the Godhead of Christ led to novel language in respect to the Eucharist and fostered fear of receiving the Sacrament. The humanity of Christ, Christ's mediatorship which draws us to Him, receded into the shadows. The tremendous distance that separates us from God and the saints gained greater and greater power over the Christian mind despite the strong hold that traditional teaching had. It became customary to speak of the awesome Table of the Lord, so it was no wonder that people dared not approach. Where the upheavals in the structure of liturgical prayer were least violent, namely, in Rome, the ancient traditions of frequent Communion naturally connected with the celebration of the sacrifice continued the longest.[58]

Another hindrance to frequent Communion was the link between sacramental confession and the Lord's Supper. This barrier blossomed later in the Middle Ages as confession became increasingly a requirement for reception of the Sacrament. Related to this barrier were categories of exclusion from the Sacrament similar to Old Testament purification laws. For example, Jerome required married people to abstain from their marriage rights for several days before partaking of the Sacrament.[59]

The Lord's Supper continued to be the central act of Sunday worship, but its life-and-death importance, its joyful sense of a meeting with the crucified and risen Christ began to fade in the new state church. This fading was hurried along after the Council of Nicaea as the sacramental element (God's giving) increasingly receded into a hazy background while the sacrificial character (our doing) of the liturgy became increasingly prominent.[60]

This century also had profound impact on the church's calendar and lectionary (the Scripture readings appointed for the seasons and Sundays of the church year). Constantine had interest in the life of Christ and sites in the Holy Land and erected basilicas and shrines at the sites at which events recorded in the Gospels were reported to have occurred. This increased popular interest in and pilgrimages to Palestine encouraged a focus on special festival days.[61]

The Day of Pentecost as a feast day in its own right, Ascension Day on the fortieth day after Easter, and the individual days of Holy Week (especially Maundy Thursday and Good Friday) are among the celebrations that originated at this time in the church's history. There was much at work that called the church to know her history and her roots in the life of Christ. There was much at work to help the church order her liturgical time (her seasons) for the life of the world. But there was also much at work to tempt the church with a theology of glory. The coziness between the church and the state and the growing wealth and power of church leaders did not seem healthy to everyone. Some Christians fled to remote places to pursue the monastic life, especially to the deserts of Egypt. Some monks joined together to form monasteries and began to show leadership in theology, missions, and agriculture.

These monasteries would have both good and bad effects on the life of the church. Just as the church in society, monasteries would go through periods of decline and reform, but they were instrumental in keeping theological study, resources, and worship alive through some challenging periods. More than a thousand years later, one of those orders of monks, the Augustinians, was instrumental in training a young monk named Martin Luther. His connection to the recovery of weekly Communion both offered to the laity and received by the laity will be discussed in the fourth chapter.

The Fifth Century (AD 401–500)

For in Him dwells all the fullness of the Godhead bodily. (Colossians 2:9)

73

The political and military strength of the Roman Empire had been eroding for some time. In this century, Germanic invaders fought for and settled increasing portions of Roman territory. In AD 410, the Germanic takeover had become so complete that Rome was sacked by the Goths under Alaric. Rome's collapse was followed by another even more destructive sacking of the city in AD 455 by the Vandals.[62] For nearly a century, the Christians had been closely connected with the Roman government, so the effect upon them was considerable.

Centralized political stability gave way to feudalism with the lord or leader of one region warring against another. The results were devastating economically, socially, and, one might assume, spiritually. But as the invaders settled in and as the years and decades passed, the conquered often taught the faith to the occupiers. Through the witness of the weak and defeated people, many of the invaders received the Christian faith. From them came new generations of leaders for the church.[63] However, the invaders did have a destructive effect on the church of this time. For example, the rule of the Goths in North Africa was disastrous. They were Arians and persecuted those who confessed the Nicene faith. There was also great destruction of property and church books and resources throughout the Roman Empire.

In this chaotic century, the Church of the East and the Church of the West (Roman) went their separate ways. From this time on, the Roman orders of worship moved along somewhat different lines than orders of worship in the East. In the Eastern churches, the Lord's Supper was primarily a weekly celebration. In the Western churches, it became a daily occurrence.[64] It also became customary in the West to call observances of the Lord's Supper "Masses." While the origin and the meaning of the term remain uncertain, it is commonly traced to the word for dismissal: *missa*, that is, "mass."[65]

THE SACRAMENT IN THE EARLY CHURCH

From this century on, the number of adult candidates for Baptism diminished while the number of infant Baptisms increased.[66] It was common in the early church for Baptism, confirmation, and the giving of the Lord's Supper to form one single celebration. In the Eastern churches, this is still the case today, even for the Baptism of children.[67]

The practice in the early centuries was for both clergy and laity to stand for the reception of Holy Communion. The practice of kneeling to receive Communion began to appear in the early Middle Ages in the Latin West. In the East, clergy and laity to this day still stand to receive the Lord's Supper.[68] As will be noted in chapter 8, this posture may have some relationship to weekly Communion and the intersection of the length of the service and church architecture.

We have also noted that the Communion services were reserved only for those who were baptized and fully instructed. This practice continued, and there is witness also in this century that doorkeepers were in charge of guarding the entrances during the celebration of the Lord's Supper.[69] The loving work and witness of the church in the world consistently led the church to determine unity in confession of the faith and to know the life of those who came to the altar to receive Holy Communion.

Discussion Questions

1. In the first century, what instructions outside of the New Testament show how the early church worshiped? What two ways of worship does this instruction speak of? How early was this instruction written?

2. What does the *Didache* place at the center of worship? Does this mean there was no sermon? Discuss.

3. In the second century, why did Justin Martyr write his *First Apology*? In this document's description of worship, how does the Sunday service culminate?

4. The loving practice of closed Communion as expressed in Justin's *First Apology* took concern for both unity of _____ and a godly _____. Discuss.

5. In the third century, the *Apostolic Tradition* describes the Eucharist as the climax of Sunday worship. What dialogue still used in the liturgy today is recorded in the *Apostolic Tradition* as preceding the celebration of the Lord's Supper? Discuss its meaning.

6. Discuss the correlation between the cup of martyrdom and the cup of the Lord in Communion as it developed during the severe persecution of the third century.

7. What effect did the length of catechesis and the prevention from participation in the Supper until the end of such instruction have on the growth of the church in its early centuries? Discuss this in light of the relationship between worship and evangelism.

8. What relationship does the fish symbol have to the Lord's Supper? Discuss.

9. Until the third century, what was the meaning of the word *church*? Discuss.

10. Explain why it might be better to say that Sunday or weekly worship is a continuation of Easter rather than to describe it as a "little Easter."

11. Discuss how the mystery of Christ's real presence in the Lord's Supper goes hand in hand with the personal union of the divine and human natures in Christ.

12. After Constantine came to power, the external growth of the church was accompanied by symptoms of serious spiritual sickness, which included a decline in _____. How did the fight against the Arian heresy contribute to this decline? Discuss.

[Jesus] does not need daily, as those high priests, to offer up sacrifices, first for His own sins and then for the people's, for this He did once for all when He offered up Himself. (Hebrews 7:27)

CHAPTER THREE

The Sacrament during the Middle Ages

The Sixth, Seventh, Eighth and Ninth Centuries (AD 501–900)

As the Middle Ages began, two individuals had significant influence on the church and therefore also on the practice of the Lord's Supper. Early in the century (AD 530), the *Rule of St. Benedict* was written to correct monastic abuses and to guide monks in holiness of life. Because monasticism was central to the life of the church, Benedict's work had a profound effect for centuries to come. The second major influence came late in the century when Pope Gregory the Great (r. AD 590–604) used his outstanding administrative abilities to defend Rome militarily; help Spain accept Catholicism; reform the finances of the church; write scriptural commentaries; propose duties of bishops, highlighting the care of souls as the key activity for all pastors; regularize the celebrations of the Christian year; reform the liturgy; and promote plainsong music, which continues to influence sacred music today.[1]

Mark Noll states: "For over a millennium, in the centuries between the reign of Constantine and the Protestant Reformation, almost everything in the church that approached the highest, noblest, and truest ideals of the gospel was done either by those who had chosen the monastic way or by those who had been inspired in their Christian life by monks."[2] This included Bible translations, hymn compositions, theological studies, and Christian missions, as well as productive manual labor. Among other things, the monasteries provided a conscience to Christendom in stable, successful times and an anchor of stability in turbulent periods of severe social disorder.

The intellectual activity of the monks during the so-called Dark Ages is justly famous. When the light of learning barely flickered in Europe, monks preserved the precious texts of Scripture and other Christian writings. Monks kept alive an interest in languages. Monks and friars founded schools that eventually became the great universities of Europe. In short, monks preserved the life of the mind when almost no one else was giving it a thought. By God's grace, their efforts preserved the church.[3] Monks became adept at copying both the Bible and other books, thus they preserved these documents for later generations. Their houses also became teaching centers, particularly for the children who were placed under their care to be trained as monks.[4]

The *Rule of Saint Benedict* came to dominate and systematize the pattern of monastic life from the sixth through the thirteenth centuries. In addition to a daily quota of physical labor, Benedict required vows of obedience, chastity, poverty, and stability (the requirement that monks not move about at will). He formulated the practice of gathering eight times a day to pray and read Scripture. These became the traditional hours of prayer.[5]

Under Gregory the Great, the first monk to become pope, a significant change occurred in monastic life. For the purposes of missionary work, Gregory placed priests in the monasteries. The desire of these priest-monks to exercise the office for which they had been ordained led to the origin of private masses, first in the monasteries and later in a more widespread manner.[6]

Gregory's liturgical work directed the church throughout the Middle Ages with very few changes until the time of the Reformation. With his ordering and revision of the readings and the addition of sacred music, both beauty and continuity were enhanced. But in the process of his work, significant harmful errors also entered the life of the church. These errors included the development of the doctrine of purgatory, the concept of the Mass as sacrifice, and the acceptance of popular superstition as direct confirmation of Christian faith.[7]

Under Gregory, the central action of believing the teachings of Jesus and receiving the body and blood of Jesus in worship was displaced. Receiving the Word in the sermon was no longer an integral part of the Mass. The act of communicants receiving the body and blood of Christ was supplanted by the act of priests offering a sacrifice. According to A. L. Ramer, "Gregory's sacrificial theory of the Mass placed the chief importance upon the offering up unto God the Body of Christ. It was immaterial whether there were communicants present to partake of the Body thus offered."[8] Gregory also championed the doctrine of purgatory and attempted to adjust the teaching of the Lord's Supper to fit its properties. Ramer states that "Gregory had much to say of the miraculous power of the consecrated bread and even recounted cases where the dead appeared as phantoms begging that Mass might be said for the repose of their souls."[9]

In fact, according to the Lutheran Confessions, Gregory the Great is a turning point of bad theology.[10] Concerning private Masses, the Confessions state: "For nowhere do the ancient writers before Gregory mention the celebration of private Masses. For the present, we will forgo any discussion of their origins. It is clear that after the mendicant monks became dominant, private Masses spread—due to completely false beliefs and moneymaking."[11] Concerning Gregory's connection to Masses for the dead, we read: "[W]e do reject the transfer, *ex opera operato* [because of the doing of the deed], of the Lord's Supper to the dead. The ancients do not support our opponents' idea of the transfer . . . . And even though they have the support, especially of Gregory and of some of the more recent theologians, we set against them the clearest and surest passages of Scripture."[12]

In the process of Gregorian revisions, the cult of martyrs and saints was increasingly found in the liturgy. This focus upon the saints during the Mass tended to obscure the central saving work of Christ. During this period of church history, preaching also became infrequent.[13] At the end of the sixth century and under the leadership of Gregory the Great, the Mass was actually considered a repetition of the sacrifice on Golgotha.[14]

As one might expect, these false beliefs and practices had far-reaching negative effects on the frequency of lay Communion. The steadfast devotion to the apostles' doctrine and the Lord's Supper of the New Testament church was submerged in ways that would not be recovered until Martin Luther and the time of the Reformation.

For the most part in the two or three centuries after Gregory, the papacy struggled to overcome the final decay of the western Roman Empire, as well as a series of debilitating economic, political, and social reversals.[15] Feudalism led to a decline in trade and economic well-being. Many bishops became feudal lords and participated in the constant warfare. The church lost much of its moral and spiritual authority because some of its important leaders fell prey to the "conventional wisdom" of the culture as a means to survive in worldly terms and maintain hope of flourishing again.

It was a chaotic period in both the society and the church. As noted earlier, the active participation of the laity in weekly Communion began to decline during the rule of Constantine. For various reasons—including political and social turmoil, unsteady church leadership, and doctrinal confusion—this period of history did not foster a recovery of the understanding of the true nature of the Lord's Supper. One major barrier to its recovery was the growing presence of votive (special needs) Masses.

Since the time of Gregory, and perhaps even earlier, a Mass had been said for every kind of trouble. These votive Masses sometimes included the following requests:

> for getting rain, for preventing bad weather, for protec-tion against lightning, for safety when entering upon a journey, etc. Later on, masses were said to secure God's favor or help in other situations; to find a husband, secure happiness in marriage . . . make a business ven-ture prosper, give success to hunters, etc. Such masses resulted from the interpretation that the Lord's Supper is a work man performs to propitiate God or secure spe-cial favors.[16]

This, of course, is not the nature of the gift that Christ gave His church nor what the church celebrated and received in the first centuries after Pentecost. A tremendous decay in understanding and use had occurred regarding Christ's presence among His people to bring them forgiveness, life, and salvation in this gift. The Roman Catholic Church still believed rightly that the true body and true blood of Christ were present. But the decline in lay participation must be laid directly at the feet of the incorrect teaching and harmful practices that were at work. According to Theodore Tappert, "[o]ne effect of this was an individualistic concentration on one's own needs and a loss of the communal aspect of the primitive supper. Another effect was a tremendous multiplication of masses."[17]

Although the number of Masses was vastly increased—perhaps to fifty a week in an average parish church—reception of Communion by laypeople dropped from approximately three times a year at the beginning of the Middle Ages to only once a year after the thirteenth century. Monks who were deemed especially pious received Communion once a month or more often.[18] Votive Masses for special concerns or special needs became common. Ordained monks or priests were endowed by a wealthy donor to say Mass—often several times a day and with no one present except the celebrant himself.[19]

Missionary activity continued through the establishment of monasteries in pagan areas. This allowed the local population to see the application of Christianity to daily existence, as monks tilled the soil, welcomed visitors, and carried out the offices of study and daily prayer. So arose the saying that the monks civilized Europe with cross, book, and plow.[20]

In this period, another major barrier to recovering the understanding of weekly Communion received by the laity was the emergence of private Masses. The earliest monasteries were lay communities. As previously mentioned, Gregory's influence encouraged the monasteries to admit priests in great numbers. This meant that there were often more priests to celebrate Mass than monks to participate. These priest-monks naturally felt the need to exercise the office for which they had been ordained. Thus private Masses originated in the monasteries and became the general rule from the eighth to the tenth centuries.[21] Within many monasteries, a number of priests often celebrated a number of Masses on any given day, often without the presence of a worshiping community. The priest simply recited the text of the rite to himself.[22] Unfortunately, this practice, which had no foundation in the Word of God, did not remain isolated in the monasteries. In this century and the next, monastic worship practices flowed outward into the parish churches. These so-called private Masses became more common in all the churches of the West.[23]

From the daily private Masses evolved what came to be known as the Low Mass, which was a subdued and rather mechanical service said by a priest with his back to whomever might be present. There was no music and it was spoken in Latin, a language that most people no longer understood. In fact, the Canon of the Mass, formerly the Eucharistic Prayer or Prayer of Thanksgiving, was now said silently by the priest and was considered an act of priestly devotion and respect that made the presence of other people utterly superfluous.[24] In the High Mass, however, music, incense, and so on remained.

In many of the monasteries and larger churches, wealthy donors endowed a chapel, or chantry, in which priests were required daily to sing or say Mass for the souls of the donors. It was not uncommon for a large church or cathedral to have a dozen of these side chapels, each with its own altar, so many Masses were being said at the same time in the same church. The belief that merely saying Mass was in itself a work of righteousness was another factor that contributed to the creation of Masses. It thereby increased the fragmentation of the once unified Sunday Mass into a proliferation of daily Masses.[25]

The spread of this kind of private Mass was encouraged because of the penance system that assigned to a person pilgrimages or fast days or other actions in response to sins confessed. According to the rules of the system, it was possible to replace a required fast day with the celebration of a Mass. The spread of private Masses was also encouraged by the false belief that saying a Mass could help the souls of the dead. Sometimes one thousand

Masses would be said for a deceased person. It became necessary to forbid priests to celebrate more than thirty Masses in a day. Some priests resorted to a twofold or triple Mass in which they repeated the first part of the Mass up to the Preface two or three times before concluding with the Canon of the Mass or the Eucharistic Prayer. Thus the priest received two or three stipends.[26] This multiplication of Masses led to the establishment of secondary altars in churches that had lateral chapels along the nave and in small apses.[27]

Obviously, such abuses served to exclude the laypeople from active participation in the liturgy of the church and from receiving the gifts of Christ in the Lord's Supper. The intense weekly devotion to receiving Word and Sacrament that had flowed from the Holy Spirit's leading after Pentecost had been replaced with manmade prescriptions that lacked the promise of God concerning the presence of Christ. Instead of pressing their pastors to serve them Christ's gifts each week, the laity paid the priests to perform an act believed to have power over some need in life or some relative or friend in death.

The ninth century saw a dramatic shift in the political and geographic connections of the Western church. The crowning of Charlemagne's father by Boniface, the missionary bishop of Germany,[28] and the crowning of Charlemagne himself by Pope Leo III on Christmas Day in AD 800[29] signaled a transition from a Mediterranean, Eastern-oriented faith to an expressly European form of religion.[30] Constantinople and the emperor of the East could no longer secure Europe against the spread of Islam.[31] With former Christian centers such as Jerusalem, Antioch, and Alexandria all under Muslim control and the East under siege, the church of Rome looked elsewhere for military strength and protection.

For the next nine hundred years, the politics, learning, social organization, art, music, economy, and legal system of

Europe would be Christian in the sense of secular interest in and identification with churchly matters. That situation was not so much a result of the clear speaking of Law and Gospel in society but because the fate of the Western church, centered in Rome, had been so decisively linked with the new Roman emperor over the Alps.[32] At the time of his death, Charlemagne's empire included areas in modern France, Belgium, Holland, Switzerland, northern Spain, and much of Germany and Italy.[33]

Although the papacy received protection and status, Charlemagne also had more personal needs for which he sought answers in this state and church alliance. He had mistresses and concubines in addition to his five wives, and "[a]pparently the polygamous lifestyle troubled the emperor's conscience, as he had hundreds of monks praying for him. When he died in 814, he left all but a fraction of his enormous wealth to endow masses and the saying of prayers for his eternal salvation."[34] The effect of the church's erroneous teaching and practice concerning private Masses is seen in the death of Emperor Charlemagne himself. Christ redeemed him, as the Scriptures proclaim, not with gold or silver but with His holy precious blood and His innocent suffering and death. Charlemagne showed himself superstitious in leaving his immense wealth to pay for prayers and Masses to be said for him after death.

After the brief renaissance that had occurred under Charlemagne and his successors was past, the papacy entered a period of rapid decline.

A controversy in this period erupted over the miraculous bodily presence of Christ in the Sacrament versus merely a spiritual presence. Radbertus, abbot of Corbie, France, championed the first view in AD 844. Ratramnus, a brother in the same monastery, taught a spiritual presence. The teaching of Radbertus gained approval. Centuries later, at the Fourth Lateran Council in 1215, this teaching was officially accepted as the doctrine of transubstantiation.[35]

The Tenth, Eleventh, and Twelfth Centuries (AD 901–1200)

A bishop [pastor] then must be blameless, the husband of one wife, temperate, sober-minded, of good behavior, hospitable, able to teach. (1 Timothy 3:2)

Another major barrier to the church's recovery of steadfast devotion in receiving Christ's gifts in Word and Sacrament in these centuries was the leadership of the church itself. The Lutheran Confessions express well the Office of the Public Ministry that God ordained as the "the office of preaching, giving the gospel and the sacraments."[36] Church leadership in many of these decades, however, was focused on matters other than the support of Word and Sacrament ministry.

The moral decay of the papacy in the tenth century was deep and tragically ongoing. At times there were two and even three men claiming to be the pope at the same time. Throughout most of the century, papal tenures were brief and turnovers rapid. In AD 904, Pope Sergius III had his two rivals, Leo V and Christopher I, incarcerated and killed. Sergius had come to power with the support of one of the most powerful families of Italy. This family was headed by Theophylact and his wife, Theodora, whose daughter, Marozia, was Sergius's lover. Shortly after Sergius's death, Marozia and her husband, Guido of Tuscia, captured the Lateran palace and made John X their prisoner, subsequently suffocating him with a pillow.[37] This family continued to have interplay with the papal throne for decades with spiritually devastating results.

As had happened previously, a cycle of monastic renewal initiated a reversal and revival of this striking scene of degeneration. Although it took decades, some of the good effects of a monastery begun at Cluny, France, in AD 909 eventually reached the highest ranks of the Vatican.[38] There were, however, far-reaching negative effects that came from Cluny as well. The work of this monastery was free from secular control, and its serious and stable leaders exercised supervision over numerous other monasteries. While bishops and popes were often consumed with maintaining or advancing their positions as feudal lords and vassals, the monks of Cluny and its associates were devoted to the hours of prayer and Scripture reading.

The men who studied and trained in these monasteries would have some positive moral effect in the church for the next two hundred years. The social stability that surrounded this monastic system also offered protection to the populace from otherwise feuding noblemen. It encouraged and enabled economic and educational recovery. Unfortunately, it also encouraged practices that were contrary to the Word of God, such as the celibacy of priests. The long-range fruits of the Cluny monastic community were seen in Gregory VII, a Cluniac monk who became pope and then fixed the yoke of celibacy on the Roman clergy.[39]

Celibacy came to be seen as a form of personal purity essential for the men who handled the holy element of the body of Christ. Perhaps the saddest part of this erroneous teaching about celibacy and the handling of the Lord's Supper is that the Lord Himself is married. In fact, in the Divine Service He comes to give Himself to His bride, the church. He comes to unite with her in love that is both incarnate and intimate. The gifts she receives therein depend not upon the purity of the pastor, who is the earthly celebrant, but upon the Lord, who is the real celebrant. While the Scriptures are clear that Christ did not give the office of apostle or the office of pastor to women,[40] the Scriptures are also clear that celibacy is not a requirement of those men called to serve Christ's church as ministers of Word and Sacrament.

At the end of the eleventh century, the Crusades began. Economically and politically the Crusades were a vast outpouring of landless peasants and equally landless nobles, all hoping to carve a better future in the lands to be taken from the Muslims. Crusaders enjoyed a privileged status after assuming the cross. There was a moratorium on all their debts; they were promised the opportunity for new lands and property in the Holy Land; and they were granted a plenary indulgence that canceled the punishment for all previous sins.[41] Tragically, promoting the Crusades also became the major focus of twelfth-century preaching.[42] While the Crusades were being emphasized, the true place of recognizing and receiving the risen Lord continued to be ignored and abused. According to Frank Senn, "[e]ven though masses were being celebrated almost every hour of every day, the faithful were no longer receiving communion."[43] Sadly, the laity were reduced to being spectators, attempting to get a glimpse or view of the consecrated host.

Eucharistic cults (forms of honoring the elements) developed outside the Mass and took four principal forms: (1) devotional visits to the reserved host; (2) processions with the host carried about; (3) exposing the host to the eyes of the people; and (4) blessing the people with the eucharistic bread, often at the conclusion of a procession or a time of exposition.[44]

Concerning the third point, opportunities to view the Eucharist multiplied in this century with the introduction of the eucharistic elevation. Previously, the only point at which the people were invited to gaze at the Eucharist was just before Communion when the priest lifted the bread and the cup and said, in the words of the Western liturgy, "Behold, the Lamb of God." Now, with the introduction of the elevation of the host, people were also invited to look upon the Eucharist in conjunction with the consecration.[45] Seeing the elevation of the host came to be the high point of the Mass, and people were known to shout out instructions to the priest to hold it higher if they could not see and adore.[46] In larger cities people would run from church to church to see the elevated host as often as possible because looking at the host was considered by some to be salvific.[47] Priests were known to receive larger stipends for holding up the host longer at the elevation. Choir doors in monastic churches were opened at the consecration so the faithful could see the host when it was elevated. In some places, a dark curtain was hung behind the altar so the white host could be seen in clearer relief. In dark churches, a candle was held aloft so people could better see the host. From about the thirteenth century on (and apparently first practiced in Cologne, Germany), a bell was rung as a signal that the consecration was taking place.[48] James White writes:

> For the lay person attending the mass faithfully every Sunday and holy day, the trajectory of this whole period was that of mass becoming more and more remote. . . . The altar-table receded further and further until lodged against the East wall. . . . The bishop or priest who formerly had faced the people across the altar-table now turned his back on them. . . . Other instances of progressive remoteness include the disinclination to receive from the chalice which became common in the twelfth century for fear of spilling the blood of Christ.[49]

The steadfast devotion to the apostles' doctrine and the Lord's Supper recorded in Acts 2:42, which was present weekly in the church's earliest centuries, had been replaced by private Masses. Rather than gathering to hear the preached Word and to eat Christ's body and drink Christ's blood, the laity watched as the priest prayed silently.

The Thirteenth, Fourteenth, and Fifteenth Centuries (1201–1500)

For there is one God and one Mediator between God and men, the Man Christ Jesus, who gave Himself a ransom for all. (1 Timothy 2:5–6)

The height of papal power was reached under Pope Innocent III (1198–1216), who developed an international policy that made him the most powerful person in Europe. Innocent wielded organizational and political power in both the church and state. Despite his ruling that every Christian receive the Eucharist at least once a year, there was no recovery of the understanding of or right reception of this Gospel gift. Noncommuning attendance at Mass remained the norm for Roman Catholics until the reforms of Pius X, who in the early twentieth century encouraged Roman Catholic laity to commune frequently, even weekly.[50]

While at the beginning of the Middle Ages the reception of Communion by laypeople was about three times a year, it was reduced to once a year after the tenth century.[51] Many did not even partake once a year.[52] The normal public service had become so heavily influenced by the private Mass that the celebrant read the pericopes and chants to himself.[53] The medieval church had distorted worship to make man's work the chief thing, a sacrifice continually repeated and offered to God by the priest.

Meanwhile the people were encouraged to pray their own prayers and to adore Christ's presence in the Sacrament. Strong devotion to the person of Christ, continual reflection upon the suffering of Christ in His passion, and adoration of the blessed Sacrament became the core of late medieval piety. Genuflection, the rosary (prayer beads), and individual prayer books were created to keep the laity engaged in activity during the services. But these were activities that were personal, private, subjective, and individualized rather than the corporate activity of the worshiping community, activity that integrally related to the words and actions of the Mass itself. For the average faithful Christian, devotions outside of the Mass became the center of his or her piety. Within the Mass, the elevation of the host by the priest, accompanied by the ringing of a bell, became the main focus of popular devotion. Performing the Mass was viewed as the way to produce the real presence of Christ so Christ's people might *adore* Him rather than *commune with* Him.[54]

Another illustration of the subjective, privatized nature of the Christian life was the Movement of the Penitents, approved by the papacy in 1221. This was a group of laymen who lived a religious life and followed a program at home. According to one commentator, "[t]he penitents had to wear a robe made out of poor and undyed fabric . . . were required to fast more often and at greater length than other faithful and had to recite seven canonical hours daily. . . . In addition they were expected to make confession and take communion three times a year."[55] This and other movements indicate that religious life was viewed largely as a solitary search for reconciliation with God. Of such efforts the Lutheran Confessions state: "It is no minor scandal in the church to propose to the people a certain act of worship invented by human beings without a command of God and to teach that such worship justifies human beings."[56] Such solitary and humanly devised efforts flowed directly from uncertainty about Christ's promised gifts to His gathered people in His Word and Supper. The forgiveness He promised with His body and blood is not partial but carries with it life and salvation. With the weekly gathering around Word and Sacrament so sadly misunderstood and not received, all manner of spiritual inventions rose to fill the void. However, this spiritual void is not one that man can artificially fill. It also helps us understand the deep struggles of Martin Luther a few centuries later. He sought to find peace with God under this system of prayer and penance and precious little Gospel.

Added to the mix was a rising devotion to the memory of the saints and to Mary. Saints' days were added to the church's calendar at a rapid rate. Their popularity was perhaps spurred on to fill the void left by the increasing distance between the presence of Christ and the Christian. Remember that one of the original causes for the decline in lay Communion was the lack of proclamation of the gracious, mediating work of Jesus Christ. With the one mediator between God and man (1 Timothy 1:15) wrongly distanced and feared, other mediators were offered to fill the void.

This does not mean it is wrong to remember and praise God for the lives of the saints. Our hymnbooks have days and texts noted for doing so. In many ways the modern church is impoverished by not remembering and rejoicing in the cloud of witnesses that have gone before us. The Lutheran Confessions plainly say that we should give honor to the saints and remember how they experienced grace and were helped by faith. But we should not call upon them or seek help from them, for this cannot be shown from Scripture.[57]

In the thirteenth century, "[c]lergy were concerned more with the risk that the faithful, all of whom presumed to be sinners, would profane the sacrament of the altar, than with encouraging them to develop the habit of receiving the Eucharist more frequently than the annual communion mandated."[58] The issues that were at work in this century were exactly the type addressed by Luther in the Smalcald Articles. Indeed, the chief article spoken of is the merit of Christ and the righteousness of faith.

> That the Mass under the papacy has to be the greatest and most terrible abomination, as it directly and violently opposes this chief article. In spite of this, it has been the supreme and most precious of all the various

papal idolatries. For it is held that this sacrifice or work
of the Mass (even when performed by a rotten
scoundrel) delivers people from sin both here in this life
and beyond in purgatory, even though the Lamb of God
alone should and must do this.[59]

The Smalcald Articles also speak of the sacrifice of the
Mass and its trappings (not the Lord's Supper) as "a dangerous
thing, fabricated and invented without God's Word and will."[60]
They lament that it "is only used on behalf of the dead, although
Christ instituted the sacrament only for the living." They say that
purgatory "with all its pomp, requiem Masses, and transactions,
is to be regarded as an apparition of the devil." [61] They note that
"unspeakable abuses have arisen throughout the whole world
with the buying and selling of Masses."[62] And they give this invitation to those caught up in this human invention: "You can
receive the sacrament in a much better and more blessed way
(indeed, it is the only blessed way), when you receive it according to Christ's institution."[63] It is that institution and weekly
presence that Luther and his followers sought to recover in the
Reformation.

But before that recovery took place, another recovery would
dominate the fourteenth and fifteenth centuries. It was called the
Renaissance, which means "rebirth." This word describes a
humanistic recovery or rebirth of classical learning. The effects of
humanism and the Renaissance came on the scene at about the
same time. A renewed interest in the study of science, history, lit-
erature, art, and theology was undertaken. Classics in Latin and
then in Greek were studied and appreciated for their own sake.

At this time, the doctrine of purgatory, coupled with the
Black Death caused by the plague, which decimated much of
Europe's population, gave the Roman hierarchy one of its major
holds on the population. That hold was something to cling to in
the face of death, though it was something that did not have the

promise of God. The church offered indulgences to deal with the last enemy of death. Indulgences[64] "were granted from the pope reducing the amount of time that certain dead persons would have to spend in purgatory. The idea was that the pope possessed a treasury of the merits of the saints who had been better than they needed to be to get themselves out of purgatory and whose extra credit the pope could hand over to someone else in return for payment by living relatives."[65] With the introduction of uniform indulgence letters, the sale of indulgences became all the more popular and all the more businesslike. It was this errant and spiritually dangerous system that Luther addressed in writing the Ninety-five Theses. His fifth thesis states: "The pope neither desires nor is able to remit any penalties except those imposed by his own authority or that of the canons."[66] Thesis 21 states: "Thus those indulgence preachers are in error who say that a man is absolved from every penalty and saved by papal indulgences."[67] Thesis 32 states: "Those who believe that they can be certain of their salvation because they have indulgence letters will be eternally damned, together with their teachers."[68]

Tragically, there was no real change in the poverty of understanding and use of the Lord's Supper in the face of the plague and papal decline. The Mass was viewed as a sacrifice performed by the priest and the people were not communing. Frank Senn states: "In the fourteenth and fifteenth centuries the generally accepted theory was that the Mass had a limited value. A consequence of this theory was that a Mass that was offered for a single person benefited him more than a Mass celebrated for him and others together."[69] Thus in the face of illness and death, most people did not have the comfort of the Holy Sacrament.

Such erroneous thoughts were surely supported by the army of priests saying private Masses for special needs and intentions. To think of appeasing God in this mechanical way would offer a harmful perspective on one's standing before God. Instead of receiving God's sure and certain promises, the people were led to pray and pay for papal pronouncements. This system eventually led Luther and others to speak out against the works-righteousness of Rome. Under this system, the Lord's Supper was sometimes viewed as a charm and sometimes as a spiritual work of more elite Christians. Roland Bainton relates that "[a]ccording to one story, a woman kept a piece of bread in her mouth, took it home, and put it in the beehive in the hope of more honey, whereupon the bees built around it an entire cathedral in honeycomb."[70] Reports of raptures were also recorded in connection with receiving the Eucharist. There were reports of groups who received the Sacrament more frequently, such as the mystic women who received the Sacrament seven times a year, but such reception was detached from the liturgy of the church.[71]

The mystery of Christ's presence in the Lord's Supper for us Christians to eat and drink had been replaced with magical and mechanical perspectives of indulgences and the satisfaction of individual needs. And even where voices were raised against these abuses, they did not proclaim clearly the true treasure in the Sacrament. For example, while John Wycliffe taught rightly against many of the papal errors and made the first translation of the Bible into English, he also taught that Holy Communion was simply a celebration of the spiritual presence of the body and blood of Christ.[72] It would be more than a century before papal abuses were attacked and the scriptural treasure of the Lord's Supper was once again clearly proclaimed.

The martyrdom of two reformers bracketed the fifteenth century and signaled to many the need for the late medieval church to reform its doctrine and life. John Hus of Bohemia was burned at the stake early in the century. Savanarola, a Dominican of Florence, was hanged and then burned in 1498. His chief "crime" was seeking moral reform in the church and identifying the corruption of the papal state.

The "heresies" of John Hus, a professor at the University of Prague who embraced many, but not all, of Wycliffe's views, were more widely known. He preached against indulgences in the language of the people, challenged the primacy of the pope, and emphasized the supreme authority of Scripture. He also held that the persons communing should receive both the bread and the chalice.[73] Against the advice of many, Hus attended the Council of Constance while under the emperor's promise of safe conduct. The leaders of the council decided to ignore that promised protection, however, and ordered that Hus be burned at the stake on July 6, 1415. After the death of Hus, his followers in Bohemia were outraged and rebelled in a religious war that lasted more than two decades. The Roman hierarchy tried to crush these separatists with a series of crusades, but eventually they were forced to reach a settlement in 1436 and to make a number of concessions to the Hussites.[74] One of those concessions was to allow both the bread and the cup in Communion.[75]

The period of the Renaissance popes began in the mid-fifteenth century and was a period of extreme secularization of the papacy. E. G. Schwiebert writes:

> Rome was made into one of the most beautiful centers of Christendom . . . . A new Vatican was begun with hundreds of rooms covering acres of ground, and it was in some of these papal chambers that such great Renaissance artists as Raphael painted . . . . Nicolas V justified this magnificently ostentatious capitol with all its pomp and splendor by claiming that "only through the greatness of what they see can the weak be strengthened in the faith."[76]

The temptation to link God's presence and blessings with earthly splendor or soaring statistics or seeming success is always at hand. Such is not the witness of the Scriptures, however. The greatness of Christ in the flesh is hidden not in earthly splendor and pomp but in water and word and bread and wine. God's power is not perfected in earthly success but in weakness and suffering (2 Corinthians 12:9–10). While those who occupied the papal throne were occupied with matters of real estate and political power and building programs and book collecting and art promotion, the church continued to be impoverished in her preaching and in her sacramental life.

Even as Rome was infected with economic exploitation and corruption, the Byzantine Empire was under assault by military might. In this century, the Ottoman Turks continued their territorial conquest of Greece and Turkey, culminating in the fall of Constantinople. On May 29, 1453, the Turks captured the city and transformed the Church of Hagia Sophia into a mosque.[77] With the fall to Islam, many religious scholars fled to the West, taking important manuscripts with them. From this point on, the most important Eastern church would be the Russian Orthodox Church.[78]

This period of the history of the Sacrament ended where it had begun one thousand years earlier. At the opening of this period, as the church received approval and support from the state, the Lord's Supper became submerged and was subjected to additional erroneous teachings and practices throughout the centuries. The single service of Word and Sacrament by which the risen Christ came weekly to teach and feed His gathered church after Pentecost and in the early church had not been clearly proclaimed or widely received for more than a millennium. Such clear proclamation was soon to be heard again as God moved Martin Luther in the recovery of understanding the sum and substance of the Gospel.

Discussion Questions

1. Discuss the positive work and the errors introduced by Gregory the Great.

2. List some of the reasons for which special Masses were said. What part did the people play in these votive Masses?

3. Discuss the medieval church's teaching concerning private Masses. Why was it wrong?

4. How did the penance system encourage the spread of the private Mass?

5. Describe the perceived connection between the celibacy of priests and the Lord's Supper. Why did this introduce errors into the practice of the Lord's Supper?

6. Discuss the four principal forms of eucharistic cults that developed outside the Mass.

7. What was the average frequency of Communion reception by the layperson at the beginning of the Middle Ages? How often did laypeople receive the Sacrament after the tenth century? What were laypeople encouraged to do during the worship service?

8. What do the Smalcald Articles say about the Mass and purgatory? What do they say about the sale of indulgences?

9. In these centuries, what did the pope offer to the people to help them deal with death? How do Luther's Ninety-five Theses respond to indulgences?

10. Discuss the efforts of the Renaissance popes to link God's presence and blessings with earthly splendor and glory. If not in earthly success, then where does God promise to perfect His power?

Therefore we conclude that a man is justified by faith apart from the deeds of the law. (Romans 3:28)

Chapter Four

The Sacrament during the Reformation Era

The Sixteenth Century (1501–1600)

Pope Leo X (r. 1513–1521) continued the lavish building and spending activity of the Renaissance popes, saying, "God has given us the Papacy, let us enjoy it."[1] Leo's love of art, music, and theater made Rome the cultural center of Europe and also put the papacy deeply in debt. In 1514, he issued a bull, the most solemn and formal written command of the pope, calling for the sale of indulgences to pay for the construction of St. Peter's Basilica in Rome.

The First Battlefront

The sale of those indulgences impelled Martin Luther to post his Ninety-five Theses for theological debate. Indulgences were a major part of what Luther knew was wrong in the church. His great concern over the certainty of salvation also directed his attention to the certain promises of God in Word and Sacrament. Friedrich Kalb quotes Vilmos Vajta: "As soon as Luther speaks of God, he speaks also of the worship of God, which is inseparable from the God revealed in Christ. Worship of God is not so much the human reaction, the human reply to a relation established by God . . . rather, [worship is] where God deals with us."[2] The heart of God's dealings with us is where the risen Christ comes to teach us and to feed us. Therefore as the number and direction of his writings make clear, the Lord's Supper was at the center of Luther's concern for true worship of God.

From 1522 to 1530, from Worms to Augsburg, more essays flowed from the pen of Luther on the Lord's Supper than on any other single topic.[3] Next to justification, the Lord's Supper is the theme Luther wrote about most, for he understood orthodoxy as the right teaching and right worship of the triune God.[4] Frank Senn writes: "Luther's Reformation attacked the heart of the medieval church—the sacramental system. . . . His reforms aimed at liberating the evangelical sacraments that communicate Christ from their captivity to misuse."[5]

There was poverty, indeed, nearly a cessation, of preaching on the Scriptures read during the Mass. There was poverty, indeed, nearly a cessation, of laity receiving the body and blood of Christ. With little or no Gospel proclamation, the people were left as spectators, trying to glimpse the host as it was elevated. Luther's return to the Scripture's witness unveiled the mystery of the presence of Christ in the Sacrament to serve us. This affirmation attacked the Roman Mass in two ways. First, it made clear the Mass was not a work presenting our piety to God. Second, it made clear the Mass was not a sacrifice.[6]

Many consider the sacrifice of the Mass the primary cause of the Reformation. Luther said that "[i]t is the common belief that the mass is a sacrifice, which is offered to God. Even the words of the canon seem to imply this, when they speak of 'these gifts, these presents, these holy sacrifices,' and further on 'this offering.' "[7] When Luther published an order for worship, he removed those sections of the liturgy that emphasized sacrifice. The Lutheran Confessions describe as an abominable error "the teaching that our Lord Jesus Christ had made satisfaction by his death only for original sin and had instituted the Mass as a sacrifice for other sins. Thus, the Mass was made into a sacrifice for the living and the dead for the purpose of taking away sin and appeasing God. . . . Meanwhile, faith in Christ and true worship of God were forgotten."[8]

Luther's changes were not wholesale. The last thing he desired was for people to think he had started a new thing. As he said, "It is not now nor ever has been our intention to abolish the liturgical service of God completely, but rather to purify the one that is now in use from the wretched accretions which corrupt it and to point out an evangelical use."[9] Luther's changes clarified that the direction of the Sacrament was from God to us as a gift.

Such an understanding meant there absolutely had to be laity present, desiring to commune, when the Sacrament was celebrated. This may seem obvious or elemental, but for century upon century this basic truth had not been understood. Frank Senn points out that "[t]he most significant reform in the mass was the insistence that when it was celebrated, it was to be received by the faithful. If there were no communicants to receive the sacrament, the mass was not celebrated."[10] The word *mass* when used in the Lutheran context is not the Mass of the Roman sacrifice, but it is Holy Communion. (As Luther sometimes used the word *mass* to designate the rightly recovered Lord's Supper, some of the authors quoted will use it in that way also.)

There was a rediscovery of the purpose for which the risen Christ comes into the midst of His gathered people—to teach them and to feed them, to forgive them and give them life, to comfort them and give them rest, to strengthen them and give them peace, to love them and give them love for one another. This rediscovery was intimately linked with the heart of the Reformation's rediscovery of justification by grace alone for Christ's sake alone through faith alone. The two went hand in hand. In the Divine Service, Jesus is present primarily to serve us, not to be served by us. In other words, "[o]ne of the greatest achievements of the Reformation was the recognition that it is *Gottesdienst*! It is his, he is the one who runs it. And runs it in the way of such a God who delights in nothing more as giving out his gifts."[11] For Luther, *Gottesdienst* meant Divine Service, and the highest worship of the Gospel is to receive good things from God. This is not the only worship of God, for hearts that are receiving life and forgiveness from Christ also respond in love and service. But the foundational bedrock of weekly worship from which love and service proceed is the reception of the love and service Christ brings to His gathered people.

The Second Battlefront

Before we consider the frequency of the Lord's Supper as fostered by the Reformation, it is important to note the second battlefront that arose concerning Holy Communion. Influenced by Luther's writings, other theologians also opposed the errors of the Roman Church. Some of their opposition concerning the Lord's Supper, however, was carried beyond the abuses of the papacy and applied to the witness of Scripture concerning the Holy Meal. By 1526, Luther had to shift from the first battlefront of Roman additions to the Lord's Supper to the second battlefront of rationalistic subtractions from the Lord's Supper.

The Swiss reformer Ulrich Zwingli and others sought to govern biblical revelation with human reason. Should the revealed Word of God contradict reason, they thought Scripture's witness should be explained figuratively on the basis of reason. As applied to the Lord's Supper, this meant that if the body and blood of Christ were in heaven, then these elements could not also be present in the bread and wine. Zwingli, like Ratramnus, Wycliffe, and others before him, believed in a representative or figurative view of the Lord's Supper. In effect he taught that the word *is* in Jesus' words "This *is* My body" really meant "signifies." According to Luther biographer E. G. Schwiebert, Zwingli "held that in Communion the individual receives only bread and wine, but that by reflecting on the Lord's death the individual received a spiritual blessing from this symbolical eating and drinking."[12] Under Zwingli's teaching, "[t]he Lord's Supper is therefore not the Lord's act, but something Christians do. By remembering and giving thanks for Christ's death Christians make Christ present."[13]

Luther relied on the simple and straightforward Words of Institution: "This is My body." In the debate with Zwingli at Marburg in 1529, Luther wrote these words on the table before him and often pointed to them throughout the days of discussion. Scwiebert points out that "[t]he fact that the Lord who raised Lazarus from the dead, stilled the unruly sea, and Himself rose from the grave had said these words made them all-sufficient for Luther."[14] Christ, who comes into the midst of His gathered people, is not limited to time and space. He is both God and man in one person, and He can do what His Word says. For Luther, there should be no tampering with His words "This is My body."

These two opposing views concerning God's work in Christ and Christ's work among us have not disappeared. There are still those who view this gift figuratively and those who speak only of a spiritual eating. And it is still the Lutheran confession that Jesus' words should be taken at face value, with our reason taken captive to His words. In truth, it is no captivity at all, but it is the blessed freedom of trusting Jesus' own promise of what He comes to give us. Our reason or intellect should be used but always as a servant of the text of Scripture, not as lord over the text. In fact, our reason and intellect continually need the healing that the risen Christ brings to His gathered people for the life of the world.[15]

Lutheran Worship: A Return to Acts 2:42 and the Worship of the Early Church

Christ comes in the flesh to give us forgiveness and life in His Word and Sacrament. It is His presence *for us*, to serve us, that in large part guided the liturgical changes of Reformation worship. Luther said, "The service now in common use everywhere goes back to genuine Christian beginnings, as does the office of preaching."[16] Paul Kretzmann notes that Luther abolished "private masses, but not the daily Mass, gradually reducing their number, however, until Eucharist [was] celebrated only on Sundays or when communicants [were] present."[17] Luther did not experiment or try to come up with something of his own devising when he revised the liturgy. He primarily deleted those portions referring to sacrifice. He also emphasized the Verba (the Words of Institution) as a Gospel proclamation. In part for this reason he favored a free-standing altar so the Words of Institution could be clearly heard as the pastor faced the congregation.

The general structure of the inherited liturgy was for the most part preserved. However, instead of using it many times every day, as had been customary, it came to be used only once a week on Sunday morning and also on other festivals, such as Christmas, which might fall on a weekday. When there were no communicants, the Sacrament was omitted to avoid relapsing into "the idolatry of the sacrifice of the Mass."[18] It must be remembered that for more than a thousand years the laity of the Western church had communed only occasionally. In the centuries immediately preceding the Reformation, most laypeople communed only once a year at Easter under a papal requirement to do so. That was a tremendous history of false tradition to overcome. As James White observes: "To give up a weekly Eucharist would have been absurd to Luther. But getting the laity to commune weekly proved a major obstacle where most were accustomed to receiving communion only once a year."[19] White adds: "That Luther met with more success than is usually assumed is seen by the fact that as late as Bach's time, thousands of Lutherans in Leipzig and Dresden received communion each Sunday. If there were many communicants the service could last four hours."[20]

That Luther desired a weekly celebration of the Sacrament is seen in his 1528 letter to Lazarus Spengler in Nurnberg.

> First, that all masses without communicants should be completely abolished . . . . Second, that one or two masses should be celebrated on Sundays or on the days of the saints in the two parish churches . . . . Third, during the week mass could be celebrated on whatever day there is a need for it, that is, if there are some communicants present who ask for it and desire it. In this way no one would be forced to come to the sacrament, and yet everyone would be served [with the sacrament] in an orderly and sufficient way.[21]

Luther goes on to express the centrality of weekly administration of the Sacrament to the office of the pastor. After stating that the Lord's Supper should be celebrated once or twice on Sundays and during the week, if desired, he continues:

> If the ministers complain about this, however, alleging that they are thus forced [to celebrate the Lord's Supper], or lamenting that they are unworthy [to celebrate the Lord's Supper], I would tell them that no one compels them except God himself through his call. For since they have the office, they are already obliged and com-

pelled (on the basis of their calling and office) to administer the sacrament when it is requested of them; thus their excuses are void. This is the same as their obligation to preach, comfort, absolve, help the poor, and visit the sick, as often as these services are needed and demanded.[22]

Luther elsewhere wrote about the holy possessions or identifying marks of the church. He named seven of them: (1) the Word of God; (2) the Sacrament of Holy Baptism; (3) the Sacrament of the Altar; (4) the Office of the Keys (forgiving and retaining sins); (5) the pastoral office; (6) prayer, such as the Lord's Prayer, the Psalms, and so on; and (7) the holy cross of suffering and persecution.[23] Concerning the fifth identifying mark of the church, Luther makes clear that the Holy Spirit chooses only competent males to fill the pastoral office, not women. He also states that the pastoral office exists by the institution of Christ and that its purpose is to administer the first four holy possessions on behalf of the church.[24] The clarity of the work that God gives pastors to do is striking in these writings of Luther. Anchored in the Word of God and the Lutheran Confessions, the Rite of Ordination is also striking in its clarity of grounding the work of the Office of the Public Ministry in teaching God's holy Word and administering His Sacraments.[25]

Luther's counsel to the church at Nurnberg through Spengler made it clear that pastors were to administer the Lord's Supper when the church gathered on Sunday and perhaps once during the week, if communicants were present. While no one was to be forced to commune, neither was anyone to be forced not to commune when they came for regular weekly worship. Luther's counsel called for a radical decrease from the multiple Masses being said in the average parish before the Reformation. Gone from Lutheran congregations were Masses for the dead and Masses for special intentions. Gone were the private Masses of a multitude of priests. In reducing the number of Masses to Sunday and the weekdays, when desired, Luther and the reformers sought to undo the deformities that had arisen. (The word *mass* is used here to mean the serving of God's Word and Sacrament to God's gathered people—the Lord's Supper.) Luther and the reformers also sought to undo the deformity of noncommuning laity. While the errant votive and private Masses could quickly be adjusted to the weekly common service, it would take much longer for people to commune with frequency. In this regard, Luther and the reformers showed both patience and persistence. John Stephenson points out:

> While the reformer can enjoin weekly celebration of the Sacrament on the clergy, he noticeably refrains from ordering the laity to commune weekly. His reticence here perfectly parallels his softly-softly approach toward accustoming the laity to once again receive the Supper in both kinds. Age-old custom can be overcome only gradually, and just as it would take time for the laity to become used to receiving the chalice, so likewise gentle pastoral care and unremitting instruction would be needed to make inroads into the medieval habit of communing only once or twice a year. But Luther's refusal to dragoon the laity to the altar must not be so interpreted that we fail to mark his clear longing for frequent Communion to be the rule, not the exception, of congregational life.[26]

In other words, Luther taught that the Sacrament should be available when the people gathered to meet with the risen Christ each week to receive His gifts. Because of the tremendous weight of a millennium of wrong tradition, only a few may have initially desired it, but the minority would never be denied the gift because the majority declined it. Holy Communion was only to be omitted in weekly worship when absolutely no one desired to receive it.

A gift related to the Lord's Supper is the gift of confession and absolution. The Augsburg Confession states: "For the custom has been retained among us of not administering the sacrament to those who have not previously been examined and absolved. At the same time, the people are diligently instructed how comforting the word of absolution is and how highly and dearly absolution is to be esteemed."[27] Luther emphasized the Gospel gift of absolution. He repeatedly extolled its use and its value in the Christian life. In the above quote, the Augsburg Confession echoes that high esteem in the context of administering the Lord's Supper. But this did not mean that confession of sins was a requirement for Communion, as Rome had historically said. In fact, the Roman Church had solidified this legalistic link in 1215 when the Fourth Lateran Council decreed that annual penance was a prerequisite to receiving Communion.

Luther's own concern in relating confession and absolution and the Sacrament was a Gospel concern, not a concern of fulfilling the Law. He wrote: "Now concerning private confession before communion, I still think as I have held heretofore, namely, that it neither is necessary nor should be demanded. Nevertheless, it is useful and should not be despised."[28] Historically, this did not continue uniformly at the time of the Reformation or in North America. In the early decades of the LCMS, announcing the desire to commune the day before receiving the Sacrament was the prevalent practice. For pastors of multiple parishes separated by some distance, announcing the desire to commune the same day was also acceptable. This was at a time when the opportunity to receive the Lord's Supper was generally infrequent, perhaps only four to six times a year.

One explanation for the changes that occurred in moving toward our present practice was offered from the Cologne Church Order of 1543.

Those who had announced their intention to receive communion at the Sunday Service attended Vespers on Saturday evening. . . . This was followed by the examination of the communicants individually, with individual confession and absolution as well. . . . As the number of communicants became larger (a result of the pastors always exhorting the people to receive the sacrament more frequently), the examination and confession became more perfunctory and absolution was given to several penitents at once. From this it was but a short step to replacing private confession with a general confession.[29]

Church architecture offered one factor against an immediate and widespread increase in Communion attendance. As Lutherans took over the formerly Catholic buildings, they made only the most necessary changes: tearing out side altars and placing pews in the vacated space; removing tabernacles for the reserved host; and sometimes removing sanctuary lamps, which had become associated with transubstantiation.[30] The churches, however, had been built in the Middle Ages when the laity stood at a distance and watched the Mass. Thus the buildings were not constructed to accommodate all the people of the parish, sometimes thousands, at the altar. The adaptations to the nave and altar furniture did not address the physical limitations of space in the chancel, especially in view of the fact that the blood began to be distributed as well as the body. These space limitations sometimes slowed the encouragement and invitation for all in attendance to commune weekly. Whenever communicants were present, however, the Lord's Supper was celebrated every Lord's Day.

The change that came as God led Luther to clearly proclaim the Gospel and to lead the people to recover Word and Sacrament worship was overwhelming. A long period of controversy followed in both personal and political spheres. The recovery of

God's good gifts was neither uniform nor unopposed in the different regions of "Luther lands." For example:

> In Brandenburg . . . the attempt was at first made to retain daily observance of the sacrament in the cities and weekly observances in the country. In Strasbourg, on the other hand, where Lutheran influence was somewhat modified by that of the Reformed, the Lord's Supper was celebrated every fourth week in each of the parish churches in the city and at least every eighth week in the country. More common in the early years of the Reformation was the practice in Hanover, where the Lord's Supper was celebrated once every Sunday, "as often as there are communicants."[31]

The weekly opportunity to commune was central to the reforms Luther made as he sought to return to the worship practice of the Scriptures and the early church. Coupled with his proclamation of justification by grace for Christ's sake through faith was his weekly provision of the means by which the risen Christ brought the fruits of His cross to His people. The recovery of Communion received by the laity every Sunday was at the heart of Luther's efforts in the Reformation.

After Luther's Death

In the same year Luther died, both the pope and the emperor felt the time had come to deal Lutheranism its death blow. In 1546, the military threat posed by Turkish forces had lessened, freeing the military to consider armed struggle with the Lutherans. The pope realized that it was the time to enforce the Edict of Worms made a quarter of a century earlier in 1521. That edict had made Luther and his followers outlaws. Luther died on February 18, 1546, and within six months the pope and the emperor sprang into action. According to Charles Arand, "[a] pact was ratified between them on June 26, 1546, in which the pope granted

200,000 crowns and 12,000 infantry to the war effort."[32] The Lutheran forces were defeated by the combined forces of emperor and pope, and the practices of Roman Catholicism began to be reasserted.

Desiring to win over the populace and minimize opposition, the emperor was willing to make concessions even as the Roman system was reinstituted. To this end, he commissioned several theologians to compose the Augsburg Interim of 1548. This agreement allowed priests to marry and permitted communicants to receive the cup as well as the bread in the celebration of Holy Communion. Apart from these modest concessions, however, the Augsburg Interim reintroduced the teachings and liturgies of Roman Catholicism and required the German princes to ensure compliance.[33]

When the theologians of the University of Wittenberg summarily rejected this agreement, another agreement, the Leipzig Interim, was proposed, which reintroduced the sacraments of confirmation and extreme unction, approved of worship commemorating the dead, and forbade the eating of meat in Saxony on Friday and Saturday.[34] This agreement, approved by Melanchthon, basically agreed to regard many Roman rites and ceremonies of the Middle Ages as adiaphora or matters of indifference (things neither commanded nor forbidden in Scripture). This agreement met with stiff opposition by the Lutherans in Northern Germany, a group led by Matthias Flacius.

In these unstable post-Luther years, Flacius's publications and doctrinal teaching provided stability to the Lutheran confession.[35] Flacius and his followers said that Melanchthon was betraying the confession of Luther in the Smalcald Articles and giving in to papal heresies. Melanchthon contended that as long as justification by faith without works was allowed as a teaching, these other practices (seven sacraments, services commemorating the dead, etc.) didn't matter. Melanchthon felt that Roman ceremonies were a lesser evil than imperial persecution. His Lutheran opponents maintained that one should confess the truth and suffer whatever consequence might follow.[36]

Those who opposed Melanchthon were called Gnesio-Lutherans, meaning "authentic" Lutherans. They contended that "[l]iturgy and doctrine are correlative. Whatever rites and ceremonies a church observes will reflect the doctrine of that church."[37] The subsequent writing of the Formula of Concord would echo these same concerns and confess that not only our words but also our rites and ceremonies may sometimes deny the Word of God. In other words, the public witness of actions can compromise the verbal proclamation of the truth. This is especially true in times of persecution or when there is public pressure to give the appearance of agreement in doctrine, even where there is none.

Even as it confesses this truth, however, the Formula also makes it clear that having fewer or more ceremonies is not a reason to condemn each other when there is agreement in teaching and in all the articles of the faith, as well as in the proper use of the sacraments.[38] This means that a minimal verbal agreement, such as, "Yes, we believe that Jesus died on the cross to forgive our sins," is not sufficient for joint spiritual life and worship. The agreement in doctrine set forth here includes teaching all the articles of the faith, and it includes worship that faithfully confesses what Christ is present to bestow in the Lord's Supper.

The years immediately following Luther's death were filled with turmoil and testing. In 1552, however, the political struggle turned in the Lutherans' favor, and Emperor Charles retreated across the Alps. The Peace of Augsburg in 1555 granted religious toleration to Lutherans, depending upon the beliefs of local leaders. The phrase that was used to describe this settlement was *cuius regio, eieus religio*, which literally means "whose rule, his religion." As Robert Clouse explains, the religion of the prince or ruler of a region was to be the religion of the people of that region. Sometimes this provided freedom and support for Lutheran teaching and worship and sometimes just the opposite. Territorial rulers often controlled pastors not only in legal matters but also in doctrinal areas. Sometimes they were even described as "Protestant popes."[39]

The most serious threats against the Lutheran confession did not come from emperor or pope or prince but from within the church, primarily from the Lutheran pastors and laity themselves. C. F. W. Walther, the first president of the LCMS, studied this era of history to better deal with issues of Lutheran unity in the United States as the Synod was beginning. As Charles Arand notes, "[t]ime and again, Walther pointed out that the chief cause for the disintegration of the Lutheran Church in the 16th century was the failure on the part of its people and leaders to cling to the pure doctrine as proclaimed by Luther."[40]

There was pressure to compromise the true confession, and that compromise occurred first with the Roman demands and later with Protestant leanings regarding the Lord's Supper. Walther believed that during Luther's lifetime and immediately after his death, Melanchthon and his colleagues did not openly teach false doctrine. They did, however, show "less and less earnestness and enthusiasm to fight against it, and thus opened themselves to suspicion of false doctrine, especially with regard to Holy Communion."[41] The laxity and unsteadiness of Melanchthon and his Wittenberg colleagues encouraged younger theologians to go further than their teachers. Melanchthon's students not only accepted his teachings but also expanded and elaborated on them.[42]

Those teaching falsely concerning the Lord's Supper were referred to as Crypto-Calvinists, though "[t]he Formula of Concord itself uses the term 'subtle sacramentarians' for this party. . . . [T]hey were trying to develop Melanchthon's theology faithfully and at the same time held 'secret' their spiritualizing interpretation of the Lord's Supper."[43] The Crypto-Calvinists were students of Melanchthon who desired to modify the teaching of Luther and the Lutheran Confessions concerning the Lord's Supper while concealing their intention to do so. They desired to unite with other Christians and were willing to minimize doctrinal disagreements about the Sacrament that had arisen between the Lutheran confession and that of the Reformed Protestants who followed John Calvin. According to Arand, "Walther blamed these students for the controversies which brought the Lutheran Church to the brink of destruction."[44]

Calvin became the spiritual leader of the Swiss in 1549, and his influence spread to Germany, France, and England. The theological document he signed, called *Consensus Tigurinis*, "had declared that the body of the ascended Christ is finite and contained in heaven far distant from the earth where the mind seeks it through faith. To confess Christ under and united to the elements of the Lord's Supper is an absurd, perverse, impious, superstition."[45] Calvin himself said, "I teach that Christ, though absent according to his body, is nevertheless not only present with us according to his divine power, but also makes his flesh vivifying for us."[46] Calvin's desire to speak of Jesus' divine presence nonetheless denied the straightforward meaning of Jesus' words "This is My body."

In time, the efforts to secretly change the confession and practice of the Lutheran Church from the inside were recognized and confronted. In 1580 the Formula of Concord ended the confessional chaos. As one commentator notes, "Article 7 rejected a spiritual presence of the divine nature of Jesus Christ in the Lord's Supper which also confined his human nature to heaven far away from earth."[47] The Confessions clearly taught that in the Lord's Supper the true body and the true blood of Jesus are received orally by both worthy and unworthy communicants.

This teaching gives God's heavenly comfort to poor sinners who come to receive the Holy Supper of our Lord. The promises of Jesus are sure and certain. His Word gives what it says. Walther identified three benefits of the Formula of Concord that are still valid today. The Formula (1) identified and united all true Lutherans; (2) exposed those who sought to cling to non-Lutheran doctrines and the name of Lutheran at the same time; and (3) provided a true understanding of the other Confessions in the Book of Concord and a catalog of accepted confessions.[48]

As we have said, there has never been a golden age in which the presence of Christ in Word and Sacrament was perfectly understood and uniformly received. The decades following Luther's life and death were no different. Parish visitation protocols spoke of frightening ingratitude toward God and a flagrant contempt for the servants of God's Word.[49] There were accounts of people entering church when the service was half over and at once going to sleep, of barking dogs running about in church, of the congregation leaving once the minister began to preach, and of pastors waiting in empty churches while people relaxed under the trees or in the tavern. In Pfalz-Neuburg of the Palatinate in 1576 a posse of council members and men-at-arms made rounds during church hours to require attendance.[50]

When there were no communicants to receive the Sacrament, the Lord's Supper was not offered. In some parishes, this led to a decrease from the weekly schedule of offering the Sacrament to a more occasional practice. In other words, the opportunity to receive was adjusted downward to reflect the lack of communicants to receive.

After centuries of papal rule devoid of lay Communion but filled with frequent sacrifices of the Mass by the priests, with widespread ignorance of the Scriptures and the Small Catechism, with some pastors who were not Lutheran in confession, with wars and attempts to force a return to the papal system, with the unsettled economic and social conditions of the sixteenth century, with threats of doctrinal compromise from within Lutheranism, and with administrative action by the state that caused uncertainty, these decades were filled with struggle for the Lutheran Church and the Lutheran laity. That struggle clearly complicated Luther's desire to return to the form of worship seen in the Scriptures and the early church. That struggle clearly complicated Luther's leading toward the recovery of weekly Communion widely received by the laity.

The Seventeenth Century (1601–1700)

> And you will hear of wars and rumors of wars. See that you are not troubled; for all these things must come to pass, but the end is not yet. For nation will rise against nation, and kingdom against kingdom. And there will be famines, pestilences, and earthquakes in various places. (Matthew 24:6–7)

The conditions of struggle that ended the sixteenth century did not disappear in the seventeenth century. It was an age some call Baroque, which means brilliant and ornate. It was an age in which the old and new did battle in science, politics, music, architecture, and religion. It was an age in which Germany was dominated by the Thirty Years' War.

In 1618, the population of the federated regions in what is now Germany was approximately eighteen million and growing. Both Protestants and Catholics felt threatened by questions of security, population, and economics.[51] In addition, there was ongoing religious antagonism between the Lutherans and Calvinists and Catholics. Because the political leader of a region determined the religion, religious questions had definite political consequences. Thus Ronald Asch points out that "[i]t is not surprising that it was the confrontations between the three great confessional groups which brought the struggle over the future of the empire to a head."[52]

In 1618, Protestant Bohemians rebelled, and Catholic troops violently suppressed the rebellion not only in Bohemia but also in other lands in which the rebels had allies. In the early years, Catholic armies had their way, and the Counter-Reformation reached the height of its power in 1629. In that year, the Edict of Restitution was issued that demanded the return of all Protestant property to the Catholic Church and threatened the existence of Protestantism.[53] But the conflict had widened in scope. The Danes had intervened in defense of the Protestants and fought several battles. The Swedes also invaded Germany under the command of King Gustavus Adolphus and won several victories for the Protestant side before the king was killed in battle.[54]

Frank Senn notes that "Germany became a battleground in which Spaniards, Frenchmen, Austrians, Bohemians, Germans, Danes, and Swedes contended in a chaotic, protracted struggle. While the leading figures were looking out for their own interests, this was sometimes merged with religious devotion and even fanaticism."[55] From the late 1630s onward, starved and half-starved soldiers were a common sight, and desperate conditions led to atrocities. The spread of infectious diseases and the shortage of food caused as much or more suffering than the military conflicts and violent carnage.[56] Social organization broke down. Money became worthless, and it was necessary to barter for daily necessities. Self-preservation became the only law with meaning.[57]

Ultimately, Germany become a wasteland as the movement of armies and the military sieges of cities devastated the population and the countryside.[58] Some estimates were that Germany's population of eighteen million when the war began decreased to only twelve million when the war ended. Senn states: "This had as

deleterious an effect on church life as on civic life. Church buildings and books were destroyed, there was a shortage of pastors,
and congregations were demoralized."[59] The war's destruction,
therefore, had a disruptive effect not only on family and community life but also on parish life and weekly worship.

One result of the war that negatively affected the weekly
opportunity to receive Communion was the unsympathetic attitude it engendered toward confessing the faith. For three decades
a war had occurred in which armies and destruction were often
linked to the names Catholic, Protestant, or Lutheran. This was
caused in large part by the unscriptural link between religion and
political rule. Nonetheless, part of the reaction against Lutheran
confession and worship after the war came from that connection.

The response in Lutheran lands after the war did not always
help.

> In face of ignorance, lawlessness, and competition from
> Calvinism, church leaders sought to bring order into
> chaos by legally enforcing catechesis, attendance at wor-
> ship and doctrinal preaching. Fines were imposed for
> noncompliance and nonattendance. Relations between
> church and state were such that civil offenders were sen-
> tenced by the courts *to go to confession and receive the
> sacrament.*[60]

In other words, there were attempts at external compliance with
sound worship and teaching, but the motive was sometimes the
Law (even civil law), not the Gospel. While this secular law
approach to Gospel gifts was not uniform, it was a factor in how
Lutheranism was perceived in this period following the devasta-
tion of the Thirty Years' War.

"Enough of this conflict!" people exclaimed. Enough of the
confession of faith linked with the conflict! Enough of pastors
who were treated as state employees! Enough of the bleak spiritual circumstances of some regions! Enough of the view that the

Christian faith could be treated as mere intellectual assent to religious propositions! The Peace of Westphalia in 1648 officially ended the war, after which a religious movement became prominent that called for personal piety (godliness) and spiritual discipline. These are not bad emphases. Indeed, godliness and discipline are enjoined and praised throughout the Scriptures (e.g., 1 Timothy 4:7–8; 6:11). However, the rules and regulations of the three recognized state religions—Catholicism, Lutheranism, and Calvinism—during and after the war did not always seem to be pursuing godliness and exercising personal spiritual discipline. There is spiritual harm when politics and legalism are at work in the church.

The new emphasis of Pietism was not indifference. Its adherents generally cared deeply for the Christian faith and the abuses they saw in the church of their day. They emphasized cross bearing and moral reform. Nor was this new emphasis fanaticism, that is, a movement that recklessly abandoned Scripture. Rather, the Pietists emphasized reading and discussing the Bible. The spiritual danger of this movement, however, was that the pursuit of piety was given predominance over the pursuit of revealed truth.[61] While the movement took on different forms, some of its universal characteristics were a personally meaningful relationship of the individual to God (related to medieval mystics and stressing the assurance of salvation), religious idealism (a pressure toward perfection and emphasizing a devotional life), and a biblical emphasis (including trusting the religious opinions of theologically untrained laypeople).[62]

Whenever any pursuit, even one God has given—such as piety or missions or family or country or outward harmony—is regarded more highly than the truth, then spiritual harm will result. The "truth" does not mean a body of laws to be learned. Instead, it is the Word made flesh and the words by which Christ brings us life and salvation, even those words that run contrary to reason and contrary to human feelings. This would include the apostles' doctrine. This would include the truth that no one comes to the Father but by the Son, Jesus Christ. This would include words about the true presence of the living Christ as He comes among us to forgive us in Word and Sacrament. This would include His promise that with the bread and wine we receive His body and blood.

There were failings in the life of the Lutheran Church in this period, as there are in all periods. There were abuses in general practice that Pietism correctly identified, such as the needed connection between faith and conduct. This is teaching and exhortation that is always needed in the church. But Pietism's ultimate response to those failings was not a return to the anchored-in-Scripture faith of Luther. It was also, therefore, not a return to the Holy Spirit's leading after Pentecost, which is centered in Word and Sacrament, the practice that was seen in the early church.

While there is no confessional book for Pietism and while there were differences in its expression, Pietism largely located the certainty of salvation within, not on God's promised gifts from without. It was the sincerity of one's faith that was considered the true test, and this was largely determined by one's feelings about that sincerity. Emotion ruled. Ronald Feuerhahn states: "While the Pietists gave great emphasis to Bible reading, nevertheless the Scriptures were viewed differently than had been in the Church of the Lutheran Reformation . . . the norm was now inner experience or feeling."[63]

The preaching of the Gospel was understood not so much as a proclamation of the forgiveness of sins for the sake of Christ but as the fact that Christ is the source of the newness of life and the enabler of God-pleasing works.[64] Sermons were practical, focusing more on the ethical than the theological and were sometimes legalistic. Indeed, "that legalism quickly became and always remained the greatest temptation of Pietists should be acknowledged."[65]

Public worship ceased to be primarily a celebration of redemption and became chiefly an act of edification, of learning and instruction. Pietism succeeded in introducing a new theology of worship grounded not in the delivery of the fruits of Christ's redeeming work but in the edification of the saint.[66] In other words, worship became more like a classroom or lecture hall to reform and improve life and less like a hospital for dying sinners to receive Christ's gift of life.

Practical behavior was stressed. This behavior flowed from the most characteristic experience and central point in the life of a Pietist—regeneration. Pietism, of course, was not of one variety, but a common emphasis in Pietism's many expressions was the need for the emotional as opposed to the intellectual. A major point of attack of the Pietists was directed against the orthodox stress on doctrine.[67]

This emphasis coincided with and was in part a reaction to strong Lutheran orthodoxy, which arose after the publication in 1580 of *The Book of Concord*. This Lutheran orthodoxy was not dead orthodoxy. It flowed from committed confession of God's truths, including evangelical concerns for worship and the Sacrament of the Altar. Confessors such as Johann Gerhard and Abraham Calov preached and wrote on God's good gifts in Word and Sacrament. The orthodox Lutherans were in agreement that confessional unity was central to communing together. They were also in agreement that the Words of Institution be repeated articulately and distinctly whenever the Sacrament was administered. Concerning the presence of Christ in the Divine Service, the following quote from Gerhard is representative of orthodox teaching.

> Christ our Savior instituted and distributed to His disciples this holy Sacrament not only on the night that He

was betrayed. Rather, it is He who also today is present when [believers] come together to celebrate this His holy Lord's Supper, and it is He Himself who distributes His true body and blood in this worthy Sacrament. . . . Yet, Christ no longer performs the administration or handles this Sacrament of the holy Supper without intermediary persons, as it happened once at the original institution. Rather, He employs for this the servants of the office of the preaching ministry, i.e., pastors.[68]

There was liturgical deterioration as the influence of Pietism increased. Coarse Pietists saw God's means of grace as only ceremonies and signs. Subtle Pietists regarded the means of grace as mere natural things when piety was not present.[69] The Lord's Supper was celebrated less frequently and was given less emphasis in preaching. The hymns and preaching directed the hearers inward to find in themselves the genuine marks of a true conversion to God.[70]

This does not mean that the Lord's Supper was uniformly emphasized in preaching before the influence of Pietism became widespread. Nor, as we have seen, does it mean that Communion attendance was frequent even when the Lord's Supper was celebrated weekly. Nor does it mean that some Pietists did not highly value the Lord's Supper. It does mean that the general focus of Pietism that favored a subjective or internal test of religious truth did not direct the focus to the objective, external gifts of God delivered in such humble means *for us.* The promised presence of Christ among His gathered people in Word and Sacrament became secondary to a pursuit of piety that felt personally meaningful. Although not initially so intended, the small-group gatherings, called conventicles, increasingly became the focus of spiritual life for some groups in Pietism.

Adding to the speed and the swell of the deterioration in Word and Sacrament worship in this century was the rise of

Rationalism, which was also known as the Enlightenment in Germany. Here reason became a tyrant. Here the church became a lecture hall. Here revealed truth was put in subjection to the truth of human perception. Here was indifference to the church's past. Here religion was reduced to a system of ethics and common sense.

Rationalism did not become full blown until the next century, but already in this century revelation was seen as necessarily harmonizing with reason (rational supernaturalism).[71] Therefore the early presence of Rationalism is noted here because human reason soon gained the upper hand over revelation. This directly affected the worship of the church in Europe immediately before the immigration to North America. It thereby greatly impoverished the worship of the earliest Lutherans in the New World.

The North American continent was settled by Europeans during this period of marked liturgical deterioration. The hymnbooks and prayer books that were brought to this continent and translated in this and the next centuries closely connected the forms of worship of the period of Pietism, Rationalism, and Deism in Europe.[72] In other words, a clear and widespread understanding of the liturgy that confessed Christ's bodily presence in Word and Sacrament in weekly worship did not emigrate from Europe with the Lutherans.

After 1600, settlers began to fill up the New World and brought with them different forms of religion. In December 1619, there was the first known Lutheran service on the continent. A Danish expedition, attempting to find a northwest passage to Asia, wintered at Churchill, Manitoba. They were accompanied by a Lutheran minister, Rasmus Jensen, who led the group in a service of Word and Sacrament: "The Holy Christmas Day was celebrated in customary fashion. We had a sermon and Communion and our offerings to the minister after the sermon were in accordance with our means."[73] Two months later the minister died of scurvy.

The first permanent Lutheran settlement in North America began in 1623 when New Netherlands was colonized. Because of religious intolerance by the Dutch West India Company, only Reformed ministers were permitted to serve the colonists. Appeals for a Lutheran pastor and the right to worship according to the Augsburg Confession were ignored and rejected in 1649 and 1653. Lutherans who protested were arrested and fined. In 1657, an ordained Lutheran pastor, John Ernst Gutwasser, came, yet local Reformed pastors forbade his preaching or holding services. He departed within two years.[74] In 1664, the English took over New Netherlands and renamed it New York. In 1669 a Lutheran pastor, John Fabritius, began services in New York City.[75] Meanwhile, Delaware was settled by Swedish Lutherans, and a Lutheran minister first conducted services there in 1639.

The first English colony was begun in 1607 in Jamestown, Virginia. According to Mark Noll, "Virginia's earliest legal code made attendance at Sunday services compulsory and contained harsh laws prohibiting violations of the Sabbath."[76] Captain John Smith, the leader of the colonists, described the first services this way: "[W]e built a homely thing like a barn, set upon cratchets . . . yet we had daily Common Prayer, morning and evening; every Sunday two sermons; and every three months the Holy Communion."[77]

While the Thirty Years' War was raging in Europe, the Separatists, or Puritans, were seeking to reestablish the holiness of early Christianity and witness to those who remained in England as "a city on a hill" in the colonies around 1620. The Puritans intended to finish the Reformation. They came from England in part to escape persecution. Their faith was based largely on Calvin's teaching and emphasized the sovereignty of God and evinced a strong belief that God works through covenants, or solemn agreements, with local congregations and with nations. The Puritans hoped for a total reform of life through faithfulness to the covenant of grace and the national covenant in this new land. As children and grandchildren failed to fulfill the requirements of the covenant, a halfway covenant was proposed and implemented in the 1660s. This allowed those who did not step forth to testify of special grace to have their children baptized. However, "[p]articipation in the Lord's Supper remained a privilege for those who could testify to a specific work of God's grace in their lives."[78]

What seemed so new and promising as North America was first settled was not the promised land. The same sin that infected the Old World infected the New World. There was disappointment and disaster, disease and death here as well as there. What Pastor Jensen and that Danish expedition received on Christmas Day 1619 is our life in this dying world. The Savior whose birth they celebrated was born to die and so defeat death for us. The Savior who was wrapped in the humble dress of swaddling clothes and laid in a manger at Bethlehem came to those early explorers wrapped in the humble means of Word and bread and wine.

Discussion Questions

1. Next to justification, what theme did Martin Luther write about most in the Reformation? Discuss the intimate connection between these two themes.

2. Was it Luther's intention to abolish the liturgical service or to purify it? How did Luther's efforts affect the private Mass said by the priest with no one to receive it?

3. What is the highest worship of the Gospel? Discuss. Does this agree with Luther's hymn stanza on the Third Commandment recorded on p. 22?

4. Luther did not experiment when he revised the liturgy. He deleted portions referring to _____. His most significant reform was that when the Mass was celebrated, _____ had to be present. Luther also emphasized the Words of Institution as _____ proclamation. This contributed to his preference for a free-standing _____ so the Words of Institution could be clearly heard as the pastor faced the congregation. Discuss.

5. What was the second battlefront that Luther confronted regarding the Lord's Supper? Under this teaching, the Lord's Supper is not the Lord's act but something _____ do. Discuss.

6. What advice did Luther give to pastors in Nurnberg who might object to celebrating the Lord's Supper once or twice on Sundays and during the week if desired? Discuss.

7. Was Luther's concern in relating private confession and absolution one of the Law or of the Gospel? How does this compare to the decree of the Fourth Lateran Council in 1215?

8. According to C. F. W. Walther, what was the chief cause for the disintegration of the Lutheran Church in the sixteenth century? Was the chief problem a desire to teach false doctrine or simply less emphasis and commitment in fighting against it? Discuss Walther's analysis as it pertains to the temptation to minimize doctrinal truth in our day.

9. What were some of the negative effects of the Thirty Years' War on confessing the Lutheran faith and on weekly worship?

10. What was the spiritual danger of Pietists?

11. When reading the Bible, what did Pietists regard as the norm for viewing or understanding the Scriptures? What became and still remains the greatest temptation of Pietists? How did Pietism contribute to liturgical deterioration?

12. How did Rationalism join Pietism in impoverishing worship? Discuss.

13. How did the religious movements of England and Europe affect the worship life of the earliest colonists in North America? Discuss.
14. When and under what circumstances did the first recorded Lutheran service in North America occur? Was it a service of Word and Sacrament?

Trust in the LORD with all your heart, And lean not on your own understanding; In all your ways acknowledge Him, And He shall direct your paths. (Proverbs 3:5–6)

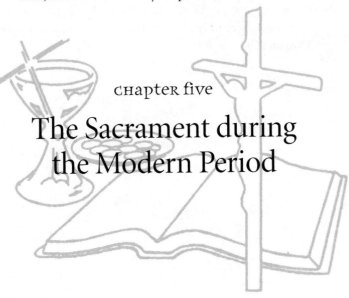

CHAPTER five

The Sacrament during the Modern Period

The Eighteenth Century (1701–1800)

The Pietist and Rationalist movements that began in the 1600s blossomed in the eighteenth century. The two movements had little in common except the effect they had on decreasing the value placed on doctrine and the Lord's Supper. Pietism was an attempt to be truly spiritual, to have a religion that seemed to matter more in daily life. This led to a decreasing emphasis on the Lord's Supper. According to Byron Northwick, "[a]s a religious movement, Pietism opposed what it saw as a rigid formalization in the church's theology and, importantly, in its worship."[1] The presence of Christ's body and blood in the Sacrament was de-emphasized in favor of internal or subjective religion. Rationalism, on the other hand, was a philosophical and academic movement that made reason the judge in questions of religion. Human reason judged the sacraments to be superstitious relics from the past and emphasized a common-sense religion. Concern for doctrine and worship was replaced with concern for reason and education.

Again, the intention of each of these movements was entirely different. Pietism sought to rescue religion and restore true worship. Rationalism sought to elevate human reason over religion and relegated worship to its own purposes. Yet each in its own way had negative effects upon God-given Word and Sacrament worship. Each in it its own way had negative effects upon the opportunity to receive the Lord's Supper in weekly worship and the desire to receive it.

Pietism rightly stressed Luther's arguments for the inner spiritual life of faith in a period when worship could sometimes be legalistically rigid. But its popular expression often neglected the sacramental basis of worship. Despite retaining the "external forms," Pietism emptied them from the inside and thus theologically destroyed the forms of worship.[2] Rationalism, on the other hand, was an assault on the supernatural. Miracles were considered beyond proof and superstitious. God's gifts in water and word, in bread and wine—things Lutherans confessed as great New Testament miracles—were considered irrational and therefore irrelevant. Thus Rationalism attacked from the outside the sacramental presence of Christ in the flesh.

The combined result of Pietism's effect from the inside and Rationalism's attack from the outside was a shocking deterioration in Word and Sacrament worship. Hermann Sasse described this eighteenth-century deterioration in Europe as the "Supper crisis" or "the dying of the Sacrament." He supported his general conclusion with specific parish statistics that showed the decline of attendance at the Lord's Supper. For example, in one parish in Breslau, Sasse cited a drop in Communion attendance from

35,930 people per year in 1701 to 9,500 people per year in 1800. He noted that this is a drop from 700 communicants per Sunday to 180 per Sunday (nearly a 75 percent decrease). Sasse also noted that the devastating effects of this single century were felt throughout German Protestantism.[3]

The one place of noticeable exception to this decay for most of the century was the church in Leipzig where Johann Sebastian Bach wrote some of his greatest music. According to Günther Stiller, "[t]hroughout the eighteenth century . . . the regular main service in Leipzig, in agreement with the old Lutheran order of service with its two high points, the Sermon and the celebration of Holy Communion, was incontestably the center of worship life on all Sundays and festival days, and this fact applies not only to the two main churches of the city but also to New Church."[4] It should also be noted that not only was weekly Communion present as an opportunity, but also that some of the worshipers were partaking of it every Sunday.[5] It was not until 1785 and following that the destructive effects of Rationalism became more strongly present in Leipzig.

In its early stages, Pietism showed respect for the structures of worship and tried to make conscious the spiritual significance of Baptism and Communion. But in stressing the avoidance of doctrinal controversy and favoring an experiential knowledge of religion over revealed knowledge, strange things began to creep in.

For the various kinds of Pietists, Luther's separation between Law and Gospel became a concept applied to different groups of people.[6] Only the reborn—and here *reborn* did not mean those baptized and instructed and confessing the faith but those conscious of some special grace—were thought worthy to eat and drink. The importance of the action of preparation for Communion and the penance involved became overemphasized. As Vilmos Vajta states: "The sacramental gift of the body and blood of Christ are devalued by the spiritual eating and drinking:

the meal has become the love feast of the small group of believers (the truly converted)."[7] The word *worthy* for some meant "make myself worthy," as Theodore Tappert notes: "Occasionally Pietists showed reluctance to receive Communion either because they felt that they themselves were unworthy or because they were unwilling to receive it with unworthy people at the hand of unworthy ministers."[8] People of the upper strata of society insisted on reception of Holy Communion separate from the common people. At the very least, they desired the use of a separate cup.[9]

Rationalism, on the other hand, had no compunctions about worthiness to commune. Everybody was welcome at the Lord's Table no matter what they believed it to be. According to the value system of Rationalism, Holy Communion was beneath moderate, balanced, clear reason. Thus sacraments lost their meaning. Sermons degenerated into educational lectures on morality or civic duty or science. According to Frank Senn,

> Lutheran liturgy was most subject to changes influenced by Rationalism, either because local pastors were given the freedom to experiment with liturgical orders and texts or because new worship books reflected the spirit of the times. . . . Official liturgies, when revised, tended to become simpler and sentimental expressions found their way into prayer texts as well as hymns. . . . With the elevation of the sermon above the rest of the liturgy, pulpits were typically placed on a longitudinal wall or above the altar-table, with seating arranged around it on the ground floor as well as in several tiers of balconies.[10]

Everything had to be reasonable and educational under Rationalism. There was no room for the mystery of the supernatural. Therefore there was a total disregard of what occurs as the risen Christ comes in the flesh into the midst of His gathered people to teach them and to feed them. The essence of religion under Rationalism was seen as the pursuit of virtue. God was viewed as retired. God's past work in Jesus Christ was to be remembered but not experienced afresh. The human became not so much the recipient of the sacraments but their performer.[11] There was a tendency to reduce the Lord's Supper to a memorial service to celebrate Christ's struggle to death for truth and to encourage his disciples to lead lives of virtue and stimulate fellowship. Tappert explains: "Characteristic of the tendency, even if extreme, was this form for distribution: Enjoy this bread. The spirit of devotion rest upon you with its full blessing. Enjoy a little wine. Virtue does not lie in this wine but in you, in the teaching about God, in God."[12]

This is the seedbed from which formative thoughts about Lutheran worship and practice were transported to North America. In large measure, the Lutheran immigrants to this continent were not arriving with the understanding of worship shared by Luther and the early church. Rather, they were arriving with worship practices that had been greatly impoverished by Pietism and Rationalism in this century of the "death of the Sacrament." One commentator states: "Historians have noted that the effect of the Enlightenment (Rationalism) in Europe in the eighteenth century was to reduce church attendance by 90 percent—a falling away from which the church has never recovered."[13]

In North America

The general religious scene in North America continued to be diverse. The Deism of England's upper classes was held by Americans such as Thomas Jefferson and Benjamin Franklin. In Deism, miracles were inadmissible because everything beyond proof and reason was considered mere superstition. Jefferson pasted together his own Bible with no virgin birth, no vicarious atonement, no resurrection, and so on. Liturgy and the sacraments were dismissed by Deists as irrelevant. George Washington was on the vestry of his Anglican parish, but his views were largely socially oriented. Mark Noll notes of our first president that "[h]e was a Christian as a Virginia planter understood the term. He seems never to have taken communion; he stood to pray, instead of kneeling; and he did not invariably go to church on Sundays."[14] As in Europe, these beliefs tended to suppress the Lord's Supper.

For the most part, the Christian expression in North America tended toward a democratic and popular style. In the first half of the eighteenth century, there was a time of revival called the Great Awakening. George Whitefield, an English preacher, conducted preaching tours in the colonies and became a sensation. He popularized revival preaching in open-air gatherings or in large buildings—but not necessarily in churches. One church in which he did preach was in Northampton, Massachusetts. It happened to be the parish of the American Congregationalist preacher and writer Jonathan Edwards, who was influential in this period in raising the consciousness of many to man's sin and the need for God's grace. The preaching of Whitefield and the writing of Edwards found their doctrinal basis in the teaching of Reformed Calvinism. Noll notes that "[t]he revivals that Whitefield and Edwards encouraged led, at least for a time, to a rapid increase in the number of people making personal profession of their faith and joining a church."[15] But statistics also show that these numbers soon declined to levels present before the revivals and to extremely low levels by the time of the Revolutionary War.

The Great Awakening played a part in altering the shape of religion in the colonies. In contrast to the reserved covenant approach of the Puritans and the formal ceremonial worship of the Calvinists, there emerged a new, more emotional, individualized expression that had more in common with the Baptists. This was to have significant influence on the shape of American religion in the decades to come. The doctrines of Calvinism would be supplemented with increasing emphasis on the individual and his or her liberty and need to make a decision and choose God.

Before the 1740s were over, Edwards lost favor with his own congregation when he altered the long-standing Northampton practice of allowing all members of the community to participate in the Lord's Supper, even if they had not yet joined the church by a profession of faith. Edward's new proposal that only the "professedly regenerate" be allowed to take Communion upset many of the town's leading citizens, who had come to look upon church membership as an important glue that preserved the traditional order of the community. After bitter debate, Edwards was dismissed from his pulpit.[16]

As the Scriptures and church history make clear, a pastor and congregation should have concern for the faith and life of those who commune. Concerns about "community glue" in Edwards's day or "the appearance of friendliness" in our day should not displace the loving God-given concerns for the faith confessed. Congregations should encourage their pastors in the loving and scriptural practice of closed Communion, not attempting to treat them as Northampton treated Pastor Edwards. Closed Communion is not fencing the altar in an elitist manner; rather, it is faithfulness to Christ's altar in an evangelical manner.

In 1742, there were only nine active regular Lutheran ministers in the thirteen colonies. These men were serving about twenty-one organized congregations and an undetermined number of preaching points.[17] As noted previously, eighteenth-century American Lutherans had largely been members of the state churches of Europe. This brought them to North America with an initial orientation heavily anchored in Pietism and Rationalism. Doctrinal concern was subservient to personal experience. A deep understanding of the true presence of the living Christ to teach and feed His gathered people in the Divine Service would be challenged by other more reasonable views. The rationalistic, individualistic, and revivalistic nature of popular American Christianity would greatly impact Lutheran worship as well.

Earlier we noted how Pietism could decrease Communion attendance by turning thoughts inward as the basis of certainty, then producing feelings of unworthiness to receive the Lord's Supper. In its questions for those communicants preparing to come to the Lord's Supper, *The Lutheran Church Agenda* of 1748 demonstrates this type of Pietistic influence:

> I now ask you in the presence of omniscient God, and upon testimony of your own conscience: I ask you: Whether you are fully resolved, with the help of God, to yield yourselves entirely to the gracious direction of the Holy Spirit, by His Word; in order that by His power, the help, the grace of the same, sin may be subdued in you, the old man with all his evil deeds and corrupt affects be weakened and overcome by daily sorrow and repentance, and that you may win a complete victory over the world and its allurements? If this be your serious purpose, confess it and answer, Yes.[18]

This is a much different emphasis than we find in Luther's teaching in the Small Catechism. The communicant who answers *yes* to the questions above will have his confidence directed inward to his own resolve. By comparison, the section entitled "Christian Questions with Their Answers" found in the Small Catechism directs the communicant's inward thoughts to one's sin and great need, not the strength of his or her resolve. These questions in the Small Catechism also direct an outward focus toward the satisfaction for sins that only Christ has made, toward Christ's love for the Father and us, and toward the presence of Christ's true body and true blood in the Sacrament.[19] The resolve spoken of is not our strength as the basis of worthiness to commune. Rather, the resolve spoken of is that which we ask God to strengthen in us in

Holy Communion: "Finally, why do you wish to go to the Sacrament? That I may learn to believe that Christ, out of great love, died for my sin, and also learn from Him to love God and my neighbor."[20]

The 1748 *Lutheran Church Agenda* was used by Henry Melchior Muhlenberg, the pastor who in that year organized the Ministerium of Pennsylvania, the first Lutheran Synod in North America. While Muhlenberg gave confessional moorings to his congregations, Lutherans "moved steadily toward a more generic Protestantism, which had become equated with an 'American' civil religion."[21] The influence of Pietism, as glimpsed in the *Agenda*, was a major reason for this. Rationalism and the intellectual changes at work in North America pulled Lutheranism in this direction as well. According to Reginald Dietz, "[a]mong Lutherans, confessional subscription disappeared. The new constitutions of the Pennsylvania (1792), New York (1796) and North Carolina (1803) synods contained no confessional text."[22] Likewise, Charles Arand points out that, "[i]n fact, no rite of ordination during this period contained a confessional reference."[23] That meant pastors were not pledged to preach and teach the scriptural faith as confessed in the Lutheran Confessions.

Preparations for Communion in the colonies were complicated, but the actual celebration of Communion was extremely rare. As Dietz observes:

> Confessional examination, usually private, was held in advance of administration. Members were expected to announce their intention to commune. Their names were recorded and carefully reviewed by pastor and deacons. . . . In congregations without a resident pastor, Communion was administered only as frequently as an ordained minister happened to pass by. In settled parishes, the sacrament was apparently administered regularly from two to four times a year: Christmas,

Easter, Pentecost, and August-September. Muhlenberg mentions twice a year as his own practice.[24]

The decay of confessional subscription, the sparse and occasional use of the Sacrament, the pietistic focus on self, and the rationalistic drift toward a generic religion did not bode well for retaining or recovering an understanding of the mystery of Christ's true bodily presence in the Lord's Supper. Nor did it bode well for worship and liturgy that flowed from and faithfully confessed Christ's life-giving presence.

This deteriorating drift was clearly seen when the synod of Pennsylvania published its first printed liturgy in 1786. In it there was no announcement to stand for the reading of the Gospel. The confession of the Creed was omitted. The collect was replaced with a voluntary prayer. The Words of Institution began with "Jesus said."[25] In both the reading of the Gospel and in the distribution of Communion, the liturgy's normal leading in recognizing the true presence of the risen Christ as the one giving His gifts had been deleted. Additionally, the words "Jesus said" used with the distribution were specifically avoided by the Lutheran confessors because they allow the interpretation that while Jesus said it back then, one wasn't really sure whether it is His body and blood now.[26]

The Nineteenth Century (1801–1900)

And truly if they had called to mind that country from which they came out, they would have had opportunity to return. But now they desire a better, that is, a heavenly country. Therefore God is not ashamed to be called their God, for He has prepared a city for them. (Hebrews 11:15–16)

Politically, the military campaigns of Napoleon dominated the early years of the nineteenth century for most of Europe.

Theologically, the Prussian Union dominated the early decades of this century for most Lutherans in Germany. The struggle against Napoleon had increased the desire for German nationalism. Because the church was linked so closely with the state in Europe, many in Germany were agitating for religious unionism before the king actually made his declaration. Frederick Wilhelm III was Calvinist, that is, Reformed. Most of his subjects were Lutheran, as was his wife. Because of the effects of Pietism and Rationalism, doctrinal indifference was quite common. There was a steady surrender of the religion of revelation for the religion of reason and practicality and feeling. Practically and politically speaking, it seemed reasonable and expedient to subject the church to the needs of the state.

In 1817, the king declared a voluntary union of the Reformed and Lutheran churches of Potsdam. He encouraged the people to put away their Lutheran and Reformed liturgies and use a new one. He wanted pulpit and altar fellowship, the sharing of preachers and communion altars between the Reformed and Lutherans. Other churches were urged to follow this example, but widespread opposition followed. Therefore the voluntary portion of this proposed union was replaced with mandates. The first of the compulsory measures came in 1821 when all candidates for the ministry were required to pledge loyalty to the union at their examination. In 1822, the king added great controversy to the struggle by publishing a service book, or agenda, that he himself had compiled. The Words of Institution in his book incorporated the words "Our Lord Jesus Christ says: 'Take and eat, this is My body.'" The addition of the phrase "Our Lord Jesus Christ says" allowed each communicant to make his own interpretation of Christ's presence in the Sacrament.[27] The king's agenda also insisted on the fraction, or the breaking of the bread. Because that is what Jesus did and because this was viewed as a memorial meal to Him, the king thought the priests should break the bread too.

After 1830, the three hundredth anniversary of the Augsburg Confession, all thoughts vanished that only voluntary compliance with the union was necessary. Confessional Lutherans who continued to use Lutheran orders of worship saw their pastors suspended and imprisoned and their property seized. Troops were used to force compliance with the king's wishes. Unionism was considered loyalty to the king and an expression of German patriotism.[28] Conversely, this meant that faithfulness to the Scriptures and the witness of the Lutheran Confessions was viewed as unpatriotic and as a rebellion against the crown. Yet even in the face of persecution, many continued to use the Lutheran liturgy and its confession of Christ's true bodily presence in the Lord's Supper.

Was it really that important? According to David Gustafson, "[m]any pastors were imprisoned for refusing to conduct services according to the union Agenda. Laity who refused to cooperate with the union had their homes confiscated and sold by the government."[29] Would pastors today be willing to face prison for the same reason? Would laity today be willing to lose their homes for the same reason? To keep the peace and hold on to property and personal freedom, why not change a few words here and break the bread there? But pastors and laypeople wouldn't change for the same reason that Luther, at Marburg, clung to Jesus' promise that "This is My body." They wouldn't compromise their worship practice for the same reason St. Paul wrote to the Corinthians: "Whoever eats this bread or drinks this cup of the Lord in an unworthy manner will be guilty of the body and blood of the Lord" (1 Corinthians 11:27). Ultimately, it was for the same reason the Holy Spirit led the church after Pentecost to be steadfastly devoted to the apostles' doctrine and the breaking of the bread. As Luther said of this gift, it is the sum and substance of the

Gospel. Those who suffered for confessing it during the Prussian Union were not being intolerant but deeply loving in their actions. And their concern for this loving confession did not stand alone.

A few decades into the nineteenth century, a recovery of the historic Lutheran Confessions began in some areas. Perhaps in part a response to the state-forced union, perhaps in part a response to the rationalistic denial of scriptural teaching, the Scriptures and the Lutheran Confessions became objects of renewed study. This movement was called Old Lutheranism or new confessionalism. It called people back to the realities of human sin and divine grace and gave special attention to the Lord's Supper.[30] There was the desire to worship God in continuity with Christians of past centuries. Worship was seen as the Gospel in action.[31]

One proponent of this confessional recovery was Pastor Claus Harms of Kiel, who wrote his own ninety-five theses contradicting the Prussian Union and Rationalism. Thesis 43 spoke against Rationalism: "When reason lays its hands on religion, it throws the pearls out and plays with the shells, empty words."[32] Thesis 73 speaks against the Prussian Union: "If the body and blood of Christ were present in the bread and wine at the Marburg Colloquy in 1529, this is still true in 1817."[33]

Another example of the confessional recovery in Germany was Wilhelm Loehe, a Lutheran pastor in Bavaria. He worked toward more frequent celebration of Holy Communion in the context of what is today called closed Communion. Through his sending of mission pastors and his support of Lutheran pastors in North America, Loehe had considerable influence on the doctrine and practice of the LCMS in its early years. Loehe and those who supported his mission efforts founded a seminary in Fort Wayne, Indiana, in 1846; started a mission to Chippewa Indians in 1844; created the concept of the church extension fund; and trained men for work in North America.[34]

The church was the center of Loehe's thought, and for him the Sacrament of the Altar was the center of the church. He taught that the sermon leads to the Lord's Supper "as to the innermost mysterious connection of Christians to their Christ."[35] He believed that the Lord's Supper of the New Testament was the Lord's Supper of the Lutheran Church. Therefore Loehe encouraged the weekly offering of Communion, and that good influence was felt in some of the Franconian congregations in Michigan that participated in the formation of the LCMS. Loehe spoke of a change in his own perspective that is helpful to a contemporary approach to this gift. That perspective is to approach the Lord's Supper not primarily as a doctrine but to focus on the sacramental life.

The confessional influence of Loehe, though from across an ocean, was sorely needed. So was the confessional influence of C. F. W. Walther as the LCMS was founded in mid-century. The direction of American Lutheranism in the eighteenth century and in the first third of the nineteenth century was not toward the Scriptures and Lutheran Confessions but away from them. One commentator states:

> While in some measure cherishing their distinctive Lutheran heritage, these leaders reflected, also, the free-wheeling liberty with which Americans, having little national history, treated the various traditions out of which they came. They shared the adolescent assurance, the historical rootlessness, and the confident rationalism of much of American Protestantism. They did not hesitate to propose revisions in their tradition or to subject their heritage to modifications dictated by the "wisdom" of the American experience. The Bible alone should be the church's authority. In any case, if the church makes creeds it could surely change them. These liberal and flexible concepts were applied quite frankly by some

Lutherans to the doctrine of the Lord's Supper. Leaders of "American Lutheranism" said—and repeated with increasing insistence as their position was challenged—that the Augsburg Confession, though substantially correct, had failed at several points to disregard the superstitious vestiges of Roman Catholicism.[36]

Holy Communion, Holy Absolution, and Holy Baptism were considered to be the front line of those superstitious vestiges. Samuel Simon Schmucker was the leading theologian of American Lutheranism at this time. He proposed *An American Recension of the Augsburg Confession* (1855) in which he denied the real presence of the body and blood of Christ in the Lord's Supper and denied what the Augsburg Confession taught concerning the ceremonies of the Communion service. The other three changes he desired to make to the Lutheran Confessions to make them more American included the denial of baptismal regeneration, the denial of private confession and absolution, and the addition of the divine obligation of the Lord's Day. The doctrines he wished to remove he described as Romanizing elements.

In this frontal attack on God's means of grace, Schmucker focused his attention not on the church's agreed upon collective confession but upon the individual's rights. According to Charles Arand, "Schmucker emphasized the individual rights to believe and teach as he wished over the rights of the church to monitor the teaching and preaching of its ministers. At this point an unmistakably 'American' tone and emphasis appears in the writing and speech of Schmucker."[37] His attitude stands in marked contrast to that of Walther, the first president of the LCMS. It was Walther's belief that confessional binding does not compromise the freedom of the Christian, but it frees one to be a teacher of the truth instead of a slave of human opinion.[38]

While the confessional recovery in Europe would soon have a major impact by way of immigration, American Lutheranism was not without its own clear witnesses to the treasures of Scripture that are discarded when the Lutheran Confessions are disregarded. The Henkel family, objecting to the doctrinal laxity of the Lutherans in the early decades of this century, formed the Tennessee Synod, the first confessional synod, in 1820. They were maligned by the majority of American Lutherans, but their loyalty to confessional Lutheranism remained steady. They published Lutheran catechisms and hymnbooks and even the first English translation of *The Book of Concord* in 1851.[39]

In the nineteenth century, hundreds of thousands of immigrants from Europe came to the United States. Uncertainties of life included the industrial revolution, which displaced farmers and craftspeople; the Napoleonic Wars (1799–1815); the redrawing of boundaries because of armed conflict; religious turmoil; and the forced merger of the Lutherans and Reformed in the Prussian Union.[40] This emigration included German and Scandinavian Lutherans and largely took place between 1830 and 1880.

In 1838, F. C. D. Wyneken arrived in Fort Wayne, Indiana, and was received as a missionary of the Pennsylvania Ministerium.[41] He wrote to Germany about the lack of Word and Sacrament ministry to the German Lutherans in the United States, describing the deplorable frontier conditions and desperate need for pastors. In 1841, he returned to Germany to raise mission support and to receive medical treatment. Wilhelm Loehe responded to Wyneken's plea by sending both funds and volunteers to the United States.

Wyneken returned to the United States in 1843 as a more mature and confessional pastor. Seeing the persecution brought on by the Prussian Union, he took a more decided stand against unionism. Previously he had had pietistic leanings and held Methodist-style prayer meetings. He also had allowed ministers of other confessions to occupy his pulpit and had permitted intercommunion with the Reformed.[42] When Wyneken returned, he was more concerned with the doctrine and practice of his congregation, which led the Reformed element of his parishoners to form a separate congregation. It also led many Lutheran members to question his "Lutheranism." They dubbed themselves American Lutherans, and many referred to Pastor Wyneken as "a Jesuit in disguise."[43]

Wyneken took a unique approach in answering the Romanizing charges leveled against him. He invited the Synod of the West to convene at his congregation, St. Paul's in Fort Wayne, in October 1844. He also permitted his congregation to accuse him before this synod so he would have opportunity to explain his actions on the basis of God's Word and the Lutheran Confessions. As a result, the synod acknowledged Wyneken as a loyal Lutheran pastor, as did his congregation.[44] Wyneken joined the LCMS in 1848, the year after its founding. The LCMS did not find his confessional Lutheranism, his use of the liturgy, and his practice of closed Communion to be Romanizing in any way. Wyneken served as the second president of the Synod from 1850 to 1864.

C. F. W. Walther, the first president of the LCMS, had also developed his confessional convictions in Germany. He arrived in the United States as part of the 1839 Saxon immigration, the year after Wyneken's arrival. This immigration had been sparked by a desire to escape the pressures of Rationalism and the Prussian Union; however, "Walther and the Saxons found themselves confronting the very things they had hoped to escape. Upon landing in Missouri, they encountered criticism and opposition from Germans who accepted enlightenment thought."[45] Walther expressed the depth of his concern:

> Reason has taken the place of the pope. (Human) virtue
> with its secret societies (lodges) has taken the place of
> monasticism. Works of humanism and philanthropy
> temperance and abstinence, have taken the place of self-

chosen works of fasting, penances, indulgences, pilgrimages, the mass, etc. Unbelief, the mocking of religion, rationalism, atheism, and materialism have taken the place of superstition. The swindle of liberation, self-deification, and the deification of the human mind have taken the place of human authority and the deification of the saints.[46]

Two different immigrant groups with conservative confessional Lutheran perspectives formed the LCMS in 1847. They were the Saxons in Missouri and the Franconians in Michigan. A point of great interest for this study is that the frequency of offering the Lord's Supper was high in some congregations of both groups compared to subsequent decades in LCMS history.

Ludwig Fuerbringer, a pastor who studied at Concordia Seminary in St. Louis near the end of Walther's life, had contact with worship in both camps. His home congregation in Frankenmuth, Michigan, celebrated the Lord's Supper every Sunday in the 1880s. As a seminary student in St. Louis, he found that the four churches that the students could attend celebrated the Lord's Supper every second week.[47] Walther had founded these four churches, and at the time they were considered one congregation or a *Gesamtgemeinde*. Statistics also indicate that some members of the LCMS communed far more frequently in 1850 than in 1930. Parish records from Trinity Lutheran Church in St. Louis indicate roughly six receptions of Communion per communicant per year in 1850. In 1930, the first year these were indicated in a statistical yearbook, the synodical average was 2.1 receptions of Communion per year.[48]

There is both a surprising and a sad aspect to these statistics. Surprising is the witness of a rich sacramental presence at the start of the LCMS. Indeed, the presence of the Lord's Supper in weekly worship was apparent in Fuerbringer's Michigan congregation and in the St. Louis congregations every other week. It is important to note that this would not have been true in the majority of situations in the LCMS because of pastoral shortages, multiple parishes over considerable distances in frontier conditions, the complicated Reformation and post-Reformation history previously considered, and, most significant, the pietistic and rationalistic attitudes inherited from Europe. Yet after centuries of challenges from outside and inside the church, there is clear witness to frequent Communion in some LCMS congregations from the start.

Sadly, statistics indicate that the early practice of weekly Communion was not passed on to the hundreds and thousands of congregations that joined the LCMS in the coming decades. The witness of Scripture was there. The witness of the Lutheran Confessions was there. The witness of church history was there. But there also were wars and Pietism and Rationalism and the pressures of life in a new country. In addition, anti-Roman Catholic sentiment sometimes downplayed Christ's presence in the Sacrament even as it condemned the pope. Finally, the desire to fit into the largely Protestant United States and its new, more unstructured forms of worship seems to have had a suppressing effect on liturgy and Sacrament.[49]

The Twentieth Century (1901–2000)

Therefore since we are receiving a kingdom which cannot be shaken, let us have grace, by which we may serve God acceptably with reverence and godly fear. For our God is a consuming fire. (Hebrews 12:29)

The twentieth century, though bloody and turbulent, saw an increase in the frequency of Communion attendance by members of the LCMS. This was a time of great upheaval in the church and in the world, and perhaps the instability and rapid change of modern life contributed to a return to the Lord's Table.

Early in the twentieth century, higher criticism began to take over in the seminaries of the major Lutheran denominations. World War I brought with it a widespread anti-German hysteria, and overnight most Lutherans were forced to drop their mother tongue.[50] Meanwhile, Pope Pius X (r. 1903–1914) had encouraged more frequent Communion by Catholics, an emphasis viewed with suspicion by Lutherans. But the liturgical renewal of the twentieth century affected all churches, Catholic and Lutheran alike, with its emphasis on worship and the sacraments.

The first year for which communing statistics appear for the LCMS is 1930; however, this information was not printed until the 1950 *Statistical Yearbook*.[51]

Year	Av. Times per Communicant	Year	Av. Times per Communicant	Year	Av. Times per Communicant
1930	2.10	1937	2.26	1944	2.70
1931	2.11	1938	2.32	1945	2.72
1932	2.07	1939	2.43	1946	2.83
1933	2.09	1940	2.45	1947	2.91
1934	2.16	1941	2.58	1948	2.91
1935	2.18	1941	2.59	1949	3.09
1936	2.21	1942	2.63	1950	3.22

In 1930, most congregations offered Communion four to six times a year. The Lutheran congregations in the United States had mirrored the American Protestant model. There was some background to this infrequent timetable already in Europe, where the Lutheran schedule of offering the Sacrament had been decreased when no one would come to receive it. Amid the occasional offering of the Lord's Supper in the United States in these decades, teaching about this gift largely emphasized correct doctrine to combat errors. Generally it did not emphasize the abounding treasures of this gift or the witness of Scripture and the Confessions and church history to the weekly offering of Communion. What was taught was correct. That which impoverished the congregations in the area of worship and Communion frequency is what was not taught and therefore not practiced.

When the quarterly offering of the Lord's Supper was discussed by LCMS members, Luther's statement in the preface to the Small Catechism about four Communions a year was sometimes noted. His teaching there, however, cannot be applied to the quarterly offering of Holy Communion in LCMS history. Attempting to use his statement to justify the quarterly offering of the Lord's Supper is incorrect for the following reasons.

First, Luther spoke of abolishing the tyranny of the pope and how people subsequently treated the Sacrament with contempt. He told pastors they should not fix or compel a law or time for the people to commune. Luther then gave this instruction to pastors:

> Instead, we should preach in such a way that the people make themselves come without our law and just plain compel us pastors to administer the sacrament to them. This can be done by telling them: You have to worry that whoever does not desire or receive the sacrament at the very least around four times a year despises the sacrament and is no Christian, just as anyone who does not listen to or believe the gospel is no Christian.[52]

Clearly, Luther was not encouraging only a quarterly offering of Holy Communion. Remember the clear proclamation of the Confessions that Lutherans celebrate the Lord's Supper every Lord's Day. Remember also the centuries of tradition of laity communing only once a year under the false teaching and papal requirements of Rome. Remember also, in view of the renewed proclamation of the Gospel, that the sinful nature's desire is to despise this Gospel freedom.

Luther was not saying to pastors, "Let's give Christ's church the opportunity for Christ to teach and feed them four times a year." He was, in effect, instructing pastors to say to their hearers, "If you cut yourself off from the risen Christ who comes to His gathered people each week to teach and to feed you, how can you be Christian?" Luther clearly gave a warning of the Law here that said, "Wake up, and don't separate yourself from the grace of God where He has promised to give it to you." Luther clearly did not give a prescription of the Gospel here, saying, "You can get by on this."

Concern over the infrequent reception of Communion eventually began to appear in *The Lutheran Witness*, the official communication vehicle of the LCMS. From 1928 to 1938, there were no less than a dozen articles dealing with poor church attendance and reception of Holy Communion. Five articles were entitled "Contempt for the Sacrament."[53] While there was concern for infrequent reception, the concern for infrequent celebration was rarely expressed until after World War II.[54] One 1929 article was entitled "The Altar Is Neglected" and addressed the Lord's Supper. It expressed how the Reformed discarded the altar and Luther kept it; however, poor Communion attendance was showing contempt for the Sacrament of the Altar. "Oh the pity and shame of it," the article exclaimed, adding the following exhortation:

> Right now before the year 1929 has advanced still farther, let us determine to show such neglect of the altar no more. Let us read Luther's introduction to His small catechism.

> How can you expect God to bless you and your children if you do not appreciate His greatest spiritual blessings as they are offered in Holy Communion? Are you seeking first the kingdom of God and His righteousness

when you are neglecting the very means through which
God bestows those blessings upon you?[55]

Only two brief articles in one issue of *The Lutheran Witness*
in the entire year of 1930 addressed the Lord's Supper.[56] The first
article stated that not communing was a symptom that points to
a serious malady of the soul. Loss of appetite with the soul, as
with the body, is an alarming symptom. Some pastors would mail
out special announcements when Communion was celebrated,
but the article contended that it would also help if some instruction was given concerning frequent attendance at Holy Communion. The second article asked if the main cause of infrequent
communing was indifference, modernism, or the Lodge. This
article also spoke of sending out notices of the celebration of the
Lord's Supper to tardy members.

As we have seen from the scriptural witness, from the early
church, and from the church of the Reformation era, the discussion of whether to send out notices identified a foundational part
of the problem. The Sacrament had become an appendage or an
occasional extra. Weekly worship was not largely understood as
meeting with the risen Christ to be taught by Him and fed by
Him. The opportunity to receive the body and blood of Christ
was offered so infrequently that pastors agonized over how best
to alert and inform members that something unusual was taking
place, that is, that Holy Communion would be available on a
given Sunday.

There were also many members for whom the infrequent
presence of the Sacrament was the high point of the church calendar. No reminder card would have been necessary for them
because the Lord's Supper was anticipated and prepared for with
diligence and reverence. Preparations for this mountaintop meeting with Christ to receive His body and blood for the forgiveness
of sins included prayer and announcement to the pastor of the
intent to commune. They ensured physical cleanliness and

appropriate clothing for the occasion. These members had not determined that Communion should be so infrequently given nor did they see it as infrequent. It is what they were taught and what they experienced throughout life. In repentance and love, they went to receive the love of their Savior in this gift when it was given.

As the century moved on through World War I, the Great Depression, World War II, military conflicts in Korea and Vietnam, and the struggle to advance civil rights on U.S. soil, there was a slow increase in the opportunity to receive the Lord's Supper and in the frequency of its reception in congregations. The LCMS statistical yearbooks indicate the following change in average number of Communion receptions per communicant member through these decades: 3.22 in 1950; 4.62 in 1960; 5.91 in 1970; 7.45 in 1980; and 8.445 in 1990.

As in all previous centuries and in the twentieth century, the central gifts of Christ to His church were not without opposition and attack. The fruits of the historical-critical method of Scripture interpretation influenced nearly all the mainline denominations in the United States. This method of biblical study approaches the Bible as the words of man, a document that contains errors and contradictions. Therefore historical-critical commentators often approach the fellowship of the Lord's Supper without concern for careful instruction in the faith and without concern for unity of confession by those who commune.

The denial of the Bible's truthfulness and authority yields a foundation wherein Scripture is approached as uncertain. Therefore man's reason and intellect must choose that which is true and that which is false. Upon this foundation, the pressures of society will direct what is said and done. Thus fellowship concerns for the Lord's Supper have little place and outward union can be declared without agreement as to the nature of Christ's presence in Communion or in the faith confessed by those who receive the Sacrament.

The fact that the LCMS has fought against higher criticism does not mean that the Synod has no creed but the Bible. This was the slogan confessed by many early American Protestants. It is enlightening to see, however, the explosion of denominations that took place in the United States under the banner "No creed but the Bible." By separating themselves from the history of the church, these denominations have often drifted in a multitude of unscriptural and antisacramental directions.

Trust in God's written Word does not deny that the Holy Spirit has also been at work in the church's history in confessing the truth and rejecting heresy. Lutherans confess the historic creeds along with the historic church. Nor does trust in God's written Word mean that the Bible is treated as a code book to predict the future or as a set of rules or facts to be learned to earn good standing with God in preparation for Christ's return. The Scriptures bear witness to the Word made flesh. They are written that we might believe in Christ. But they are breathed out by the Holy Spirit through human authors in truthful testimony, not in errors or falsehood.

Those advocating liturgical worship and more frequent Communion during the twentieth century were sometimes viewed as advocating a liberal view of Scripture and open Communion. Because of concern for conserving the truthfulness of the Scripture's witness in the 1960s and 1970s, many thought *conservative* meant no changes in the frequency of offering the Lord's Supper. As the biblical, confessional, and historic witness is recounted here, however, it is clear that the opportunity for weekly closed Communion is not a liberal setting aside of the truth—just the opposite. In the deepest way, it is conservative of the faith once handed over to the saints at Pentecost. It is conservative of the biblical faith and worship practiced by the early church. It is conservative of the faith and worship confessed by Luther and the Lutheran Confessions in the Reformation.

Discussion Questions

1. The intentions of Pietism and Rationalism were quite different, yet each in its own way had negative effects on God-given Word and Sacrament worship. Discuss the combined result of Pietism's effect from the inside and Rationalism's attack from the outside.

2. Discuss Hermann Sasse's description of eighteenth-century European worship as "the dying of the Sacrament."

3. Pietism's efforts to avoid doctrinal controversy and its propensity to favor experience over revelation led to some strange results. Discuss some of these results as applied to the Lord's Supper.

4. What effect did the Enlightenment (Rationalism) have on worship in Europe? What shape did sermons take under the influence of Rationalism? Describe the Lord's Supper under Rationalism.

5. Discuss this falling away in relation to the current scene in European Christianity.

6. Read Luther's "Christian Questions with their Answers" (see pp. 39–42 in *Luther's Small Catechism*). Discuss the difference between the focus of these questions and the questions for communicants in the 1748 *Lutheran Agenda* (see pp. 135–36).

7. Discuss the reason many German Lutheran pastors were suspended and imprisoned under Friedrich Wilhelm III after 1830. What were some of the actions taken against Lutheran laity? Were the actions of these persecuted pastors and laity narrow-minded and unloving? Discuss.

8. In an attempt to make the Lutheran Confessions more American and less Roman, what doctrines did Samuel Simon Schmucker propose removing? Discuss.

9. When C. F. W. Walther arrived in this country, he said, "_____ has taken the place of the pope." What did he say had taken the place of monasticism, of self-chosen works and indulgences, and of superstition? Discuss.

10. Why was F. C. D. Wyneken referred to as a "Jesuit in disguise"? How did the LCMS view Wyneken's use of the liturgy and his practice of closed Communion? Discuss.

11. In 1930, most LCMS congregations offered Holy Communion four to six times a year. Does Luther's statement in the preface to the Small Catechism support this quarterly practice? Discuss.

12. The battle for the Bible in the LCMS in the 1960s and 1970s helped identify the error in a liberal view of Scripture and in advocating open Communion. Discuss why the same concern for liberal error does not apply to advocating liturgical worship and weekly Communion.

Now Jesus called His disciples to Himself and said, "I have compassion on the multitude, because they have now continued with Me three days and have nothing to eat. And I do not want to send them away hungry, lest they faint on the way." (Matthew 15:32)

сhapter six

The Lord's Supper in the LCMS Today

During the 1999 Easter season, I conducted a survey of all LCMS pastors. Its intent was to measure the frequency of the opportunity to commune in the worship of LCMS congregations. I also wanted to determine if there was any change in understanding of the scriptural, historical, and confessional witness to weekly Communion. Finally, I wanted to identify the major barriers to recovering the opportunity for weekly Communion in the LCMS. Following are the survey questions:

1. How frequently is the Lord's Supper available in the congregation you serve?

2. If your congregation offers the Lord's Supper in each Lord's Day service (and weekly alternative), for how many years has this been the case?

3. If such is not the practice, are you at this time attempting to teach and lead your congregation in the recovery of the Lord's Supper in each weekly Divine Service?

4. If such instructional effort is not taking place presently, is such your desire for the future?

5. If such is not a focus of attention now nor your desire for the future, would you briefly express your thoughts concerning its importance or lack thereof?

6. What percentage (to the nearest 10 percent) of your sermons would you estimate proclaim God's grace in the Sacrament of the Altar?

7. Within your congregation, which concerns would you anticipate in recovering the Lord's Supper on the Lord's Day?

8. Does your congregation offer a routine time for individual confession and absolution?[1]

A total of 2,494 responses were tabulated from pastors serving in parish settings. This was more than 48 percent of the total parish pastors at the time (5,187) the surveys were received. The percentage returned from each of the nine geographic regions of the LCMS provided an acceptable representation of the congregations in those areas. Thus the rate of response and the geographic representation comprised a helpful statistical sample. The general information of active pastors concerning the frequency of Communion in their parishes was as follows:

Each Sunday service and weekly alternative	495	(19.8 percent)
Each Sunday in rotating services	403	(16.2 percent)
Twice monthly	428	(17.2 percent)
Twice monthly and fifth Sundays	153	(6.1 percent)
Twice monthly and major feasts	564	(22.6 percent)
Monthly	57	(2.3 percent)
Other variations and combinations	369	(14.8 percent)
Not indicating	25	(1.0 percent)

Of eleven possible concerns listed on the survey that pastors would anticipate in recovering the opportunity for weekly Communion, four were noted by more than 40 percent of the respondents:

1. The concern of members that the opportunity to receive the Lord's Supper weekly would make it too common (1,363 or 55 percent)
2. Length of service concerns (1,315 or 53 percent)
3. The lack of understanding of the scriptural, confessional, and historical witness to every Sunday Communion at this time (1,235 or 50 percent)
4. The tradition of the last two and a half centuries of occasional Communion that is now understood to be the Lutheran tradition (1,003 or 40 percent).

Before discussing the pastoral practices and perspectives reflected in the survey, let's examine the four chief concerns anticipated by pastors as barriers to recovering weekly Communion. The first concern, noted by 55 percent of the pastors responding, has also been the foremost concern expressed to me during eighteen years of conversations concerning weekly Communion.

The Major Concerns

The Sacrament Will Become Too Common

In one sense the primary concern listed here is understandable because it holds true for many things in life. Whether it is leftover turkey in the days after Thanksgiving or our favorite dessert served daily for a month, too much of a good thing quickly becomes wearisome. It is the way of our sinful human nature to become satiated and desire change, even from good things. It is in our sinful human nature to take good gifts for granted: our spouse, our family, our work, our country, freedom.

But the Lord's Supper is no ordinary "good thing." It is the body and blood of Him who alone is good—God (Luke 18:19). It is heavenly food that is every bit as holy and healing as God's holy Word. As noted earlier, Luther described it as the sum and substance of the Gospel. Therefore the frequency of its use should not be compared to other good things of this life. The frequency of its use should only be reasoned out the same way we would reason out the use of God's holy Word. What would you think if someone argued that we should not have a sermon each week because it would become too common? Indeed, this is the real temptation that Luther confronts in his explanation of the Third Commandment: "We should fear and love God so that we do not despise preaching and His Word, but hold it sacred and gladly hear and learn it."[2] Satan does tempt us to be inattentive to the preached Word, to treat it in a common way. But this does not change the sermon's proper place when Jesus comes into the midst of His gathered church to serve her. The potential misuse of God's forgiving and life-giving Word should not lessen the opportunity to hear it.

In the same way, Satan's tempted misuse of Christ's forgiving and life-giving Meal should not lessen the opportunity to receive it. There is no question that Satan tempts us to treat the visible Word, the Lord's Supper, in a common way, just as He tempts us to treat the preached Word in a common way. But this does not change the Sacrament's proper place when Jesus comes into the midst of His gathered church to serve her.

Potential misuse should not lead to disuse of the apostles' doctrine, for in the Divine Service Christ is present to teach us and strengthen our faith, which comes by hearing. Potential misuse should not lead to disuse of the breaking of the bread. In the Divine Service, Christ is present to feed us, and His food brings forgiveness of sins, life, and salvation. As Luther explains: "What is the benefit of this eating and drinking? These words, 'Given and shed for you for the forgiveness of sins,' show us that in the Sacrament forgiveness of sins, life and salvation are given us through these words. For where there is forgiveness of sins, there is also life and salvation."[3] In other words, the problem with abuse or treating the Lord's Supper in a common way lies in our sinful hearts, not in the availability of the gift. Baptism indicates that we are given grace to drown those sinful desires that tempt us to treat the Sacrament in a common way, just as we are given grace to drown those sinful desires that tempt us to treat the sermon in a common manner. The battle is real. It will go on until the day we die. Along our earthly journey, the heavenly food of our Lord's body and blood is not the problem; rather, it is the nourishment we need to help deal with the problems of sin, death, and the devil.

The Sacrament Will Take Too Much Time

The second major concern—that the Lord's Supper would make the service too long—is one that is best handled by each pastor and parish in planning service times. This concern was expressed by 53 percent of the pastors responding. Timing and scheduling can become a problem when there are numerous services on a Sunday morning, when there are parking considerations, when there are Bible classes and Sunday School classes to juggle, when there is a dual parish being served by one pastor, or when there are any number of factors that squeeze the clock. Time is like money in our day—valuable and in short supply.

Thorough planning and preparation are called for in all these areas. Congregations might also want to look at Communion distribution practice. Such planning and preparation also would extend to the liturgy and the sermon so maximum attention is given to the central treasure of making available Christ's Word and Sacrament. There are extra and unnecessary things—announcements, stage directions, summarizing speeches, awards, and so on—that sometimes squeeze their way into the service. What is central to weekly worship is the true presence of the risen Christ to teach and feed His people.

Because the presence of the Lord's Supper is already scheduled on some Sundays in each parish, it would seem that such consideration has already been given to starting times, service length, and so on. Christ's presence in Word and Sacrament each Sunday is exceedingly worthy of whatever other adjustments are necessary. Someone has said that in our hurried, overcommitted, hyperactive age, time is the new currency. Indeed, time is a precious gift from God. In examining our own Christian piety and use of time, the question must be asked, "Is a Divine Service that runs 65 to 75 minutes really the noble sacrifice our flesh tells us it is?" In view of the time we spend at our children's sports or music events, the time we spend reading the paper, the time we spend watching a movie or television, and the time we spend for ourselves and others, is the real problem an additional fifteen minutes on Sunday morning?

The liturgy should be well planned and flow smoothly. The King of kings is in our midst. His people have come to hear Him. They are dying people in a dying world. Their greatest need is His Word and Meal of life. Of all the voices in the world, only His can renew their hearts. Of all the food in the world, only His can refresh their souls and prepare their bodies for the resurrection of all flesh. The eternal purpose of what He is present to do will govern the reverent and joyful focus of receiving His gifts and the responding prayer and praise.

Church architecture can occasionally aggravate the concern of service length. It can also be a barrier to frequent Communion. If the membership is large and the altar area at which to kneel is small, Communion may take much longer. It may be necessary to restructure the altar area or adjust the logistics of distribution.

What better reason than to give God's flock more opportunity to eat from the Table that the Good Shepherd prepares for them?

In the early church, until well into the fourth century, communicants stood to receive the Lord's Supper. A more efficient Communion distribution that does not involve kneeling need not be irreverent. A congregation could have continuous distribution without harming people's faith. This may not be the first choice, but would the posture of the first four centuries of the church not be preferable if the only other alternative was denying God's people the opportunity to commune when they come for weekly worship?

People Do Not Understand the Witness to Every Sunday Communion

The third greatest concern, expressed by 50 percent of the pastors, was the lack of understanding of the scriptural, confessional, and historical witness for every Sunday Communion. For this, the best remedy is for pastors to patiently teach. Perhaps a study of the history of the Sacrament through the centuries and its recovery at the time of the Reformation would be helpful. The LCMS Commission on Worship also has excellent resources on the Divine Service. The questions at the end of the chapters in this book may prove helpful. Sensitivity and patience is needed but so is serious purpose and persistence. Recovering the weekly opportunity to commune is not a program or a policy of an organization but the presence of the Lord of the Sabbath to teach and feed His people.

Occasional Communion Is Considered the Lutheran Tradition

The fourth concern, expressed by 40 percent of the pastors responding to the survey, is closely related to the concern just noted—understanding the scriptural, historical, and confessional witness to weekly Communion. When the young man asked me the question noted at the beginning of this book, I, too, thought that occasional Communion was the Lutheran tradition. I was confident it would only take a little research to answer in defense of that perspective.

A careful look at the Lutheran Confessions, along with the teachings and writings of Luther outside the Confessions, will help alleviate this concern. As this is done, it is important not to disparage the teaching and ministry of former pastors who served God's people in former decades. For example, my grandfather was a pastor on the South Dakota prairie from the late 1800s until the 1940s. To hear of his struggles with horses and blizzards and traveling between parishes and ministering to the dying in sod huts and losing three teenagers to typhus and the transition from German to English and receiving hardly any pay through-out the Depression and having no Concordia Retirement Plan helps me more fully appreciate the lack of those particular hardships in pastoral service today. Grandpa also served in decades of high anti-Roman Catholic sentiment in the nation and also in the Lutheran Church.[4] Communion was offered in the churches he served about four times a year. For me to find fault with his service in the ministry and say he should have taught and recovered weekly Communion would show pride and ignorance. Let us not find fault with what has occurred in LCMS history or any pastor's service in the ministry as they fought the battles of their time. We honor those who went before while we foster the recovery in our present time of what was at work after Pentecost and in the early church and at the time of the Reformation.

The pastor that served before me in my present congregation came in 1970. Because of the doctrinal threats so prevalent in the LCMS at the time, the congregation wanted to be assured that he believed the Bible was the written Word of God, that he believed that God created the world, that he believed Jonah was swallowed by a great fish, and that he believed Christ rose bodily from the grave. For me to find fault with the battles he fought in his generation and say he should have done this or that would show pride and ignorance. I am thankful that he and others did confess the truthfulness of the Scriptures against threats that have harmed so many denominations. Let us not find fault with the service of others but foster recovery of Word and Sacrament in regular weekly worship today.

Other Concerns

The only other concerns expressed by more than 20 percent of the pastors were increased preparation and cleaning for the altar guild, concern over more frequent pressures of closed Communion coming with the weekly Eucharist, and the lack of understanding of sin as our greatest problem and of understanding the desire to receive forgiveness as the highest worship in the Gospel.

The concerns of the altar guild may perhaps be addressed in a study regarding the opportunity for every Sunday Communion. Some members who may be led to see its importance may also be inclined to assist with the preparations that the altar guild oversees. It may well be that the altar guild grows through such study. The preparation of individual cups and reverent care of them after Holy Communion certainly multiplies the work of the altar guild. A discussion of the common chalice may help alleviate this concern.[5] The kindness shown to altar guild workers in using the common chalice could also be part of the discussion.

The concerns about more intense pressures on the faithful practice of closed Communion will not lessen in our age. Understanding the loving nature of this practice is perhaps the best help to explain it and practice it with joy and thankfulness. As has been noted, it is the historic practice of the church through the centuries.[6]

The concern regarding the understanding of sin as our greatest problem and of understanding the highest worship in the Gospel as the desire to receive forgiveness of sins is a concern that will be with each of us throughout life. The first treasure of the Lord's Supper that is discussed in chapter 7 is the forgiveness of sins and has application to this matter.

Is Recovering Weekly Communion Legalistic?

A few survey responses suggested that recovering weekly Communion was being legalistic and forcing people to do something they may not want to do. Those responses helped me see how varied the perspectives can be on the place of this treasure.

If recovering weekly Communion were done in a heavy-handed manner within a few weeks and without adequate teaching, perhaps the perception of legalism would be applicable to the method of recovery. Our hearts are quite capable of trying to turn God's beautiful Gospel into the Law. But surely the word *legalistic* cannot be rightly applied to the actual recovery of weekly Communion. What we are speaking about, in Luther's words, is the sum and the substance of the Gospel. The Lord's Supper is Gospel. As St. Augustine put it, it is the visible Word. What we are speaking about in its recovery is the opportunity for Christ's sheep to receive the food of the Good Shepherd. The recovery of this treasure would in no way coerce them to receive it weekly. Perhaps not everyone will desire it or receive it in every Divine Service. There is no legalistic requirement for them to do so. But if it is not present, then is it not true that absolutely everyone is automatically denied the opportunity to receive the body and blood of their Savior, even if they deeply hunger and thirst for this gift? Surely allowing no one the opportunity to receive Communion must be more aptly considered "legalism" than giving people the opportunity to commune.

In the Large Catechism, Luther wrote: "We must never regard the sacrament as a harmful thing from which we should flee, but as a pure, wholesome, soothing medicine that aids you and gives life in both soul and body."[7] When the Great Physician comes into the midst of His gathered sin-sick congregation, is it really fitting for someone to tell another, "You don't need the medicine of His body and blood today"? That would certainly not be anyone's intent. But if providing the opportunity is viewed as a matter of the Law, then Luther's thought here may be a helpful corrective.

In addition, there is a richness to this gift and the treasures it bestows that goes beyond the individual forgiveness of sins. Forgiveness is the heart of this gift, but where there is forgiveness of sins there is also life and salvation. These treasures come from the flesh of Christ. Where He is present to serve His people, the treasures abound.[8]

The Opportunity to Commune in the LCMS in 1999

As indicated above, 495 of the 2,494 parish pastors responding (19.8 percent) indicated that the Lord's Supper was made available in each weekly Divine Service. That is, whenever members came for regularly scheduled weekly worship (e.g., Saturday evening, Sunday morning, Thursday evening, etc.), both Word and Sacrament were available to them. Another 403 pastors (16.2 percent) indicated that the Lord's Supper was available each week in the parish they serve but at alternating services.

The largest number of pastors, 1,145 (46 percent), indicated a celebration of the Lord's Supper that was some combination of twice monthly. More than half of these pastors also celebrated the Lord's Supper on major feasts such as Christmas and Easter in addition to the twice monthly schedule. About 13 percent of these pastors included every fifth Sunday in the Communion schedule. This would mean that the members they served would not need to go more than one week without the opportunity to receive the Lord's Supper. Only 57 of the 2,494 pastors (2.3 percent) responded that Holy Communion was offered just once a month.

Most encouraging was the survey's deeper indication that a recovery of opportunities for members to commune when they come for regular weekly worship is underway. Of the 495 pastors whose congregations had the Sacrament at each Sunday service and weekly alternative, 241 indicated that this opportunity had been recovered in the previous five years. This indicates nearly a doubling in the number of pastors leading their parishes in recovering weekly Communion from 1994 to 1999. The survey also indicated that an additional 512 pastors (20 percent) were studying the Sacrament with their congregations with the hope of leading them to recover weekly Communion. Because of the synodical history of occasionally offering Holy Communion, such study needs to be both patient and persistent. But these 512 pastors expressed an understanding of the scriptural, historic, and confessional place of the Lord's Supper in the weekly service and desired its recovery.

Also encouraging was the answer of another 481 pastors (19 percent) who did not offer the Lord's Supper every Sunday and were not currently involved in a study to recover it but desired such an instructional effort in the future. This would indicate some positive thoughts for the continued recovery of the availability of the Sacrament in LCMS parishes.

In his preface to the Small Catechism, Luther told pastors that "we should preach in such a way that the people make themselves come without our law and just plain compel us pastors to administer the sacrament to them."[9] The results of this survey give some indication that many pastors have a strong desire for their members to compel them to serve the Sacrament and recover the opportunity for this weekly treasure.

Anti-Roman Catholic Sentiment Has an Effect

Growing up in a Midwestern LCMS congregation in the 1950s and 1960s, I was aware of some anti-Roman Catholic sentiment. Sometimes this sentiment was helpfully directed at false teaching and practice such as Luther identified in the Reformation. At other times, however, it seemed to broaden harmfully to such a helpful and beautiful sign as the crucifix or to such a practice as making the sign of the cross, which Luther taught in the Small Catechism and which Lutheran hymnals have acknowledged postively.

I believe such sentiment caused me to perceive negatively as Roman Catholic some things that are more accurately perceived as historically Christian and positive for the life of the church. This would include the weekly opportunity to commune. Since her earliest days, the United States has viewed Roman Catholicism with some degree of concern and even fear because of papal claims to authority in the earthly realm. However, the political maneuvering of the papacy—best seen in the Crusades, the Inquisition, the execution of heretics, military participation in the Thirty Years' War, etc.—is not part of the work of the true catholic (universal) church. Rome has flexed worldly muscles that God has not given to His church on earth. That immigrants to North America should have some fear of the papal abuse of civil power is only natural. The Puritans of Massachusetts and the Anglicans of Virginia feared and hated Rome because their fathers had witnessed wars with Catholic France and despaired for their faith at the ascension to the throne of the Catholic Queen Mary. In addition, there were consistent threats from the Jesuits.[10]

The early colonists feared that the papacy would abuse earthly power in North America as it had in Europe. Their fear was deep and rooted in historical experience. So general was this anti-Catholic fear that by 1700 only Rhode Island gave Catholics full civil and religious rights. In 1696, all inhabitants of New Hampshire were required to take an oath against the pope. In 1755, a measure was passed in Maryland forcing all Catholics to pay double the land tax that Protestants were assessed. During the colonial period, service in public office was denied to those professing the "Popish religion." The game "Break the Pope's Neck" was popular in New England, and textbooks such as the *New England Primer* were sometimes illustrated with grotesque pictures of the pope.[11]

A popular early colonial holiday was celebrated on November 5 and related to England's Guy Fawkes Day, which celebrates the failure of a 1605 plot to blow up King James I and Parliament. The plot was led by Roman Catholic activists, among them Guy Fawkes, who was subsequently hanged. Thus in the American colonies November 5 came to be called Pope Day. It was observed with parades and the burning of effigies of the pope. In 1775, this became a political problem in the context of the Revolutionary War. Congress was attempting to obtain the aid of Catholic Canada against England. Given those political sensitivities, George Washington found it necessary to issue an order to the Continental Army forbidding the troops to observe the November 5 "holiday."[12] After the war, seven state constitutions banned Catholics from state office in the 1770s. In the 1780s, 1790s, and 1800s the limitations gradually dropped as fears of Rome decreased.[13]

Anti-Roman sentiment was heightened again in the 1820s with the Papal Jubilee of 1827 and with increased immigration following the Napoleonic Wars. By 1827, there were thirty Protestant newspapers that attacked popery.[14] Hostile attitudes toward Catholics were raised even more in the 1840s with the arrival of poor Irish immigrants. The American Protestant Association was formed in 1842 to oppose the principles of popery. In 1844, there were riots in Philadelphia in which thirteen Catholic parishioners were killed and two Catholic churches were burned. This was the peak of the Nativist movement, which took public and private action against foreigners and Catholics.[15] From 1854 until the Civil War, the American Party, also known as the Know-Nothing Party, fostered the dislike of Catholicism and the foreign born. As Abraham Lincoln campaigned, he said, "I am not a Know-Nothing, that is certain. . . . When the Know-Nothings get control, it will read 'all men are created equal except negroes and foreigners and Catholics.' "[16]

To make matters worse, Pope Pius IX published a syllabus of errors in 1864. In it the pope included the condemnation of "errors" such as religious freedom and the separation of church and state. Then, in 1870, the First Vatican Council proclaimed the infallibility of the pope.[17] People remembered how the papacy in times past had gained its desires through violence, so these actions naturally intensified Protestant suspicions concerning Catholic involvement in U.S. politics and business. Few things could have heightened fears more than the pope's condemnation of religious freedom and the separation of church and state.[18]

At this time anti-Roman thoughts began to fester, particularly in the Midwest. In 1887, the American Protective Association formed in Clinton, Iowa, and grew to approximately one million members in the mid-1890s. Among other things, the secret oath of this association promised "that I will not employ a Roman Catholic in any capacity if I can procure the services of a Protestant . . . that I will not vote for, or counsel others to vote for any Roman Catholic, but will vote only for a Protestant, so far as may lie in my power."[19]

This anti-Roman Catholic sentiment also affected the LCMS. The founder of what became known as Lutheranism was excommunicated by a pope and put under the sentence of death.

As soon as Luther died, the pope supplied money and twelve thousand troops to the emperor to help stamp out Lutheranism. Lutherans, as well as other Protestants, had been battered and bloodied by Catholic military might in the Thirty Years' War. The false teaching of the pope regarding his earthly powers had caused real destruction for the ancestors of American Lutherans. The false teaching of the pope regarding salvation centers on the chief article of the Christian faith, justification by grace for Christ's sake through faith. It is not surprising, therefore, that there should be some anti-Roman sentiment and fear in the LCMS.

What is enlightening to note concerning the focus of this book, however, is the strength of the anti-Roman message as compared to the positive proclamation of God's gifts in the Lord's Supper. One gauge of this relationship is the occurrence of anti-Roman articles and articles on the Lord's Supper in *Der Lutheraner*, an official German publication of the LCMS from 1847 to 1974, and *The Lutheran Witness*, an official publication of the LCMS since 1911. To gain perspective on this, I took a random sampling of index titles or articles in these two publications from the 1870s to the 1930s. In *Der Lutheraner*, the index was compared using German titles indicating the papacy, Rome, or Jesuits and titles indicating Communion or the Lord's Supper. The results were as follows:

	Papacy/Rome/ Jesuits	Communion/ Lord's Supper
Oct. 1872–Dec. 1873	29	2
1882	19	1
1883	24	2
1892	25	0
1893	17	0
1902	6	0
1903	19	1

In *The Lutheran Witness*, the results were as follows:

	Papacy/Rome/ Jesuits	Communion/ Lord's Supper
1912	14	2
1913	37	0
1922	14	4
1923	7	0
1932	11	2
1933	10	1

This random sample from the 1870s to the 1930s is quite representative of the other years in these six decades. The anti-Catholic word was strongly predominant over the pro-Communion word. Many of the 230 or more anti-Roman Catholic articles were brief and dealt with such matters as Catholic statistics, actions of cardinals or popes, church and state issues, the work of Jesuits, false teaching, and the like. Many of the fifteen Communion articles were also brief and spoke of such matters as announcing for Communion, the hygiene of the common cup, errors in teaching, synodical statistics, and so on.

Important warnings were sounded against papal errors, including errors concerning the Mass and worship. While this was done, however, the true treasures of the Sacrament were not extolled with anywhere near equal frequency or vigor. The anti-Roman sentiment in this period was complicated even more because in the early decades of the 1900s, the Roman Catholic Church began to encourage more frequent, even weekly, communing by its membership.[20] This was not an errant emphasis. It is in keeping with the scriptural witness, with the history of the early church, and with Luther's rediscovery of the blessings of the Lord's Supper in the Reformation. In my upbringing, however, and in that of many I have served, anti-Roman sentiment wrongly lumped together Rome's encouragement of frequent Communion celebration and reception with its errors.

Here we can learn from Martin Luther, who addressed the error of the Anabaptists and enthusiasts of his day who said, "Whatever is of the pope is wrong" or "Whatever is in the papacy we must have and do differently." Luther wrote:

> In fact they remind us of what one brother in the forest of Thuringia did to the other. They were going through the woods with each other when they were set upon by a bear who threw one of them beneath him. The other brother sought to help and struck at the bear, but missed him and grievously wounded the brother under the bear. So these enthusiasts. They ought to come to the aid of Christendom which Antichrist has in his grip and tortures. They take a severe stand against the pope, but they miss the mark and murder the more terribly the Christendom under the pope. For if they would permit baptism and the sacrament of the altar to stand as they are, Christians under the pope might yet escape with their souls and be saved, as has been the case hitherto. But now when the sacraments are taken from them, they will most likely be lost, since even Christ is thereby taken away.[21]

Whenever a threat or a fear becomes a greater focus than the proclamation of the treasures of God's grace, errant results seem inescapable. In these decades, friendly fire appeared to be a contributing factor in the decline of opportunities to commune in some of the founding congregations of the LCMS. This same sentiment would seem hard to escape by the hundreds of congregations started in those years. As the decades passed, weekly Communion was often seen as Roman Catholic while occasional Communion was seen as the conservative, Lutheran practice. Take, for example, an article in *The Lutheran Witness* in this period that helps highlight the link between the anti-Catholic sentiment described above, the pro-Protestant sentiment expressed below, and the resultant omission of strong and steady extolling of the treasures of the Lord's Supper.

In the August 2, 1932, issue of *The Lutheran Witness*, there is an article on a eucharistic conference in Dublin, Ireland. It describes the fanfare, the procession, the glorification of the Mass. The Catholics' love of pomp and display is noted, which, the article states, "Protestants view as glittering robes covering a poverty of true religion." The article continues: "In the sight of God the humblest gathering of true believers worshipping in a rental store or country school house . . . is more glorious than all thirty one Eucharistic congresses." In this article, there is no positive teaching on the true glory of the Lord's Supper, that is, the very presence of the living Christ to give us His body to eat and His blood to drink for the remission of sins, life, and salvation. Nor is there mention of the centrality of the Lord's Supper in weekly worship in the early church and in the church of the Reformation and the reverence with which it was received. The Lutheran readers are simply lumped together with Protestants over against Catholics. This linkage would likely leave the impression that Protestant worship without the Sacrament is the humble yet glorious gathering spoken of in this article. We note that in 1932, the communicant members of the LCMS communed on average only 2.07 times.[22]

Pro-Protestant Sentiment Has an Effect

The pro-Protestant sentiment expressed in this article relates to the predominant religion in North America when the LCMS was founded. Protestants have traditionally been broadly defined as those who split from the Roman Catholic Church in the Reformation and formed church bodies such as the Reformed, Lutheran, Anglican, Presbyterian, Methodist, and so on. A narrow definition will identify Protestants as those German princes who protested the Edict of the Diet of Speyer in 1529. By that edict, the Catholic majority of princes had sought to crush the reform movement by taking away from other princes the right to determine the religion in their regions. The evangelical princes protested and sought a unified political front against the Roman Catholic princes.

In the political sense, Lutheran princes were among those first Protestants. In the religious sense, however, Luther and his followers soon distinguished their confession from Zwingli, Calvin, and others chiefly over the Lord's Supper. During the Reformation, Luther fought a theological battle on two fronts. The first was against superstitious Roman Catholic additions to the historic Christian faith; the second was against rationalistic Protestant subtractions from the faith, chiefly in the area of the sacraments.

Thus while dictionaries lump together all who sought to address the abuses of Rome as "Protestant," it is important to distinguish the political realities from the theological realities. If *Protestant* means all those denominations that teach a figurative or spiritual or symbolic view of the real presence, Lutherans are not Protestants. This important theological distinction is the basis for discussing the effect of pro-Protestant sentiment on the Sacrament in the LCMS.

Luther was immovable over this difference concerning whether the true body and true blood of Christ are present in Holy Communion. Here he maintained that Roman Catholics were confessing more clearly the truth of the Scripture than were the Protestants. In 1528 he wrote: "I do not argue whether the wine remains wine or not. It is enough for me that Christ's blood is present; let it be with the wine as God wills. Sooner than have mere wine with the fanatics, I would agree with the pope that there is only blood."[23] Luther is overstating the case to make his point because he taught that the error of the enthusiasts on this doctrine was worse than that of the pope.

Luther identified those who taught only a spiritual presence of Christ's body and blood in the Sacrament as enthusiasts. Far from receiving Communion from a pastor who taught accordingly, Luther taught that people should be "ready to die on this account and suffer everything before that."[24] If there was uncertainty about whether a pastor believed that the true body and true blood of Christ are truly present in the Sacrament and received bodily with the mouth, Luther says: "[B]e free to inquire of him, and have him say quite plainly what it is he gives out to you with his hands and what you receive with your mouth. . . . One should put to him the straight question: 'What is held here in hand and mouth!' "[25] If the pastor did not acknowledge that the promised body and blood of Christ were present in the Sacrament, he should be abandoned.

Luther's deep concern for the external gifts of God was, however, not reflected on the North American religious scene. Already in the eighteenth century at the time of Jonathan Edwards and the First Great Awakening, a more subjective, individualistic emphasis was being fashioned in Protestant North America. Increasingly the focus moved away from God's dealing with the church and was placed on the direct act of God in converting the individual sinner. As Philip Lee says, "[T]he American preoccupation was dramatically shifted from the mighty acts of God to the religious experience of the Christian person."[26] This is a preoccupation that Screwtape described quite positively to Wormwood as he expressed Satan's temptations. Screwtape encouraged his nephew to keep human minds turned inward because such a focus would keep people looking for something inside themselves as the means for conversion.[27]

The Second Great Awakening in America (1800–1860) was based primarily upon revivalism and Methodism. What mattered most was subjective emotion. The individual was the center of reality, and his or her feelings were exalted as the true test of what was right and good. While this is widely recognized as the predominant expression of Christianity on the frontier, what is not so widely noted is "that by the period of the western expansion the founding colonial churches were no longer offering a theological alternative. The moment of truth, the inner feeling and assurance of conversion has become the distinguishing feature of the Christian person."[28]

Three major worship traditions were added in this period of U.S. history: the Methodist, the Frontier, and the Pentecostal.[29] In these traditions, the Lord's Supper was seen largely as a memorial that was kept merely because Christ commanded men to keep it. In essence, the Eucharist was moralized: "If Jesus could die for you, why can't you live righteously?" or, in a shortened version, "Jesus died. Be good."[30]

In American Protestantism in general, the sacraments were put on the sidetrack. What really mattered was Jesus in your heart or, rather, Jesus in your heart as determined by your own will and feelings. Man's response became elevated over God's action. Philip Lee notes: "The more conversion as a technique grew in importance, the less significant became the mighty acts of God."[31] This included the mighty act at the center of the church's life in which the risen Christ comes to teach and feed His gathered people in Word and Sacrament.

American Lutheranism, the Lutheranism led by Samuel Schmucker and in place before the LCMS began, "was characterized by revivalistic theology, the right of individual judgment in biblical interpretation, indifference toward doctrine, and the hope of rapprochement with an amalgamated American Protestantism."[32] In other words, American Lutherans were pulled toward the subjective ways of worship in American Protestantism and away from worship that centered on the presence of the living Christ to teach us and to feed us with His body and blood. There was a desire to fit in with the predominant religious emphases of the new country. The effects of Pietism and Rationalism on Lutherans in the decades before emigrating to the

United States added their effect to this pull away from Christ's promised gifts in the Lord's Supper. This effect can be glimpsed in *Hymns Selected and Original*, a hymnbook used by American Lutherans in 1828. John Pless notes that "[n]o sacramental hymns of Lutheranism are included. Not a single hymn of fourteen on the Lord's Supper confess the Lord's Supper as the place where Christ's body and blood are bestowed for the forgiveness of sins."[33]

There was a strong common-sense aspect to the various new expressions of Christianity in the United States in the nineteenth century. Inherited from the Scottish Enlightenment, this philosophy taught that we could find spiritual and moral resources within ourselves. Faith in reason was aligned with faith in God. Mark Noll states: "In a word, the basic principle of the Scottish philosophy—that people could reason naturally from the evidence of their own consciousness to the existence of God and the validity of traditional morality—had become very widespread by the early nineteenth century."[34]

This was the religious climate encountered in the United States as the LCMS began. In the first two decades before and after the Synod's founding, preacher Charles Finney was the most important theologian setting the direction of religious life in the United States. He emphasized getting in touch with God directly. He became known as the father of modern revivalism and made use of the "anxious bench" and "protracted meetings" for the purpose of soliciting decisions for Jesus. The revivals and the individualistic tenor of religion that he popularized largely set the tone for American Protestantism. Here was religion that was individualistic and immediate and the result of the person's own present choice.

The Baptists and the Methodists, whose theology fit the method of these revivals, mushroomed in numbers. The Lutherans, insofar as they used liturgy and vestments and kept the

Lord's Supper central, were viewed as clinging to outdated relics. They were also viewed with suspicion by American Protestants as being too closely connected in ritual to the errors of the papacy and Roman Catholicism. As we have seen, the effect of the anti-Roman Catholic sentiment was strong. An article in Walther's *Der Lutheraner* shows that the first president of the LCMS clearly felt the pressure of this Protestant sentiment and its accusations of Romanizing tendencies.

> Wherever the Divine Service once again follows the old Evangelical Lutheran agendas or church books it seems that many raise a great cry that it is "Roman Catholic" when the pastor sings "The Lord be with you" and the congregation responds by singing "And with thy spirit;" or if the pastor sings the collect and the blessing and the people respond with a sung "Amen." Even the simplest Christian can respond to this outcry, "Prove to me that this chanting is contrary to the Word of God, then I too will call it 'Roman Catholic' and have nothing more to do with it. However, you cannot prove this to me. If you insist upon calling every element in the Divine Service 'Roman' that has been used by the Roman Catholic Church, it must follow that the reading of the Epistle and Gospel is also 'Romish'; indeed it is mischief to sing or preach in church, for the Roman church has also done this." . . . Those who cry out should remember that the Roman Catholic Church possesses every beautiful song of the old orthodox church; the chants and antiphons and responses were brought into the church long before the false teaching of Rome crept in. . . . For more than 1700 years orthodox Christians have joyfully participated in the Divine Service; should we today carry on that such joyful participation is "Roman Catholic"? God prevent it.

> Therefore we continue to hold and restore our wonder-ful Divine Services in places where they have been for-

THE LORD'S SUPPER IN THE LCMS TODAY

gotten, let us boldly confess that our worship forms do
not unite us with the modern sects or the church of
Rome, rather they join us to the one, holy Christian
Church that is as old as the world and is built on the
foundation of the apostles and prophets.[35]

Walther, like Luther, desired that the worship of his day be
in harmony with the worship of the early church. Worship in the
early church included the presence of the risen Christ in Word
and Sacrament to serve His people. Notice Walther's statement
"let us boldly confess that our worship forms do not unite us
with the modern sects." By "modern sects," Walther meant the
new Protestant groups that had sprung up in the United States
that modeled worship after revivals and focused on the individual's emotions rather than the gifts of God to His gathered people. The modern sects also denied the true bodily presence of
Jesus Christ in Holy Communion. For all these reasons, Walther
clearly distinguished between the meetings of the modern sects
and orthodox Christian worship built on the foundation of the
apostles and prophets.

Protestant Americans were suspicious of the churchly and
the sacramental. Jesus was spiritualized in ways that were in the
control of one's own thoughts and emotions. As Mark Noll says:
"American Evangelicals never doubted that Christianity was the
truth. They never doubted that Christian principles should illu-
minate every part of life. What they did do . . . was make most
questions of truth into questions of practicality. What message
would be most effective? What do people most want to hear?"[36]

Most Protestant congregations celebrated Communion no
more than four times a year, a practice that had become so common it was considered normal.[37] In the final decades of nineteenth century and the opening decades of the twentieth century,
many LCMS congregations adopted the practice of quarterly
Communion. Frontier conditions were sometimes a factor. The

pietistic and rationalistic influences at work in Europe and the United States were a factor. But another influence that discouraged the recovery of weekly Communion was the emphasis of American Protestantism and its strong anti-Roman Catholic sentiment.

The pastors and congregations of the LCMS largely continued to confess the scriptural truth concerning the real presence in the Lord's Supper as taught in the Small Catechism and the Lutheran Confessions. There was, however, no movement to recover its weekly celebration, a practice also taught in the Lutheran Confessions. The movement, even among some of the earliest LCMS congregations that practiced frequent Communion, was to offer the Sacrament less often.

Pro-Protestant sentiment still has its effect today. There is the temptation to experiment with worship by borrowing from traditions that believe Jesus is absent. But the omission of understanding the true presence of the living Christ *for us* in the Divine Service is the most impoverishing of omissions. There are many alternatives that blur Walther's clear distinction of biblical and historic worship from other activities. But the way one worships will have an effect on what one believes, which is why it is encouraging to see a greater awareness of the scriptural, confessional, and historical presence of every Sunday Communion.

There are indications of a growing understanding of the promise and presence of the Lord's Supper in the Divine Service. As that understanding is founded on the very presence of the risen Christ to teach us and feed us in His serving of Word and Sacrament just as He did after Pentecost, the worship of our congregations will be enriched. As Christ's presence *for us* is treasured so dearly that worship is kept at the center of life each week, that witness will be conveyed to others. Here is life, for here is Christ serving us. It is God's desire for none to perish but for all to receive the life Christ brings into our dying world. Here is reason to guide the family and invite the neighbor and give our first fruits. Here is God in action—loving, saving, forgiving action for the life of the world.

Discussion Questions

1. What are the four major concerns in recovering the weekly opportunity to commune in the LCMS? Discuss the first concern in relation to removing the sermon from the weekly service.

2. Discuss concerns related to how much time weekly Communion might require.

3. Why did early American colonists fear Roman Catholicism? Discuss anti-Roman Catholic practices and observances in colonial and early U.S. history. How did the syllabus of errors (1864) and the proclamation of papal infallibility (1870) heighten anti-Roman Catholic sentiment?

4. From the 1870s to the 1930s, what is true about the anti-Roman Catholic articles in *Der Lutheraner* and *The Lutheran Witness* as compared to pro-Communion articles? How does Luther's story of the brothers in the Thuringian forest (p. 172) help explain some possible effects of these emphases?

5. Discuss the difference in being Protestant in the political sense and being Protestant in the theological sense.

6. What did Luther teach concerning pastors who taught only a spiritual presence of Christ's body and blood in the Sacrament?

7. What was the American Protestant view of the sacraments? Questions of truth often became _____. How often did most Protestant congregations celebrate Communion? In the late nineteenth and early twentieth centuries, how often did many LCMS congregations offer Communion?

What shall I render to the LORD For all His benefits toward me? I will take up the cup of salvation, And call upon the name of the LORD. (Psalm 116:12–13)

chapter seven

The Treasures Abound

Central to the recovery of the opportunity for weekly Communion and to the desire to receive this mystery is the awareness of how deep and rich this treasure is. In this chapter I have sought to review and reinforce some of what we readily speak about in relation to Holy Communion, such as the forgiveness of sins. I have also sought to touch on some aspects that are less familiar, such as the rich meaning of "Do this in remembrance of Me" (Luke 22:19 ESV) or how we receive holiness from the Holy of Holies. Each benefit or topic offered in this discussion includes a hymn stanza as a focal point.

After the forgiveness of sins, this chapter will discuss four benefits of the Sacrament that flow from one another. They are Christ in the flesh—heaven on earth; union with Christ; a blessed exchange; holiness from the Holy of Holies; and the communion of saints. There are also three key topics that flow from the words and phrases of Scripture concerning the Lord's Supper: thanksgiving (*eucharist*); "This do in remembrance of Me"; and proclaiming Christ's death until He comes. A fifth benefit is that the Lord's Supper is food for both soul and body, a truth commonly overlooked in our spiritualized age. The final topic flows from the Post-Communion Collect: encompassing the love of Christ and love for the neighbor.

First, the Lord's Supper is not a doctrine but a gift, a gift of the risen Christ in the flesh. Luther extols the richness of this gift in the Large Catechism:

> But those who feel their weakness, who are anxious to be rid of it and desire help, should regard and use the sacrament as a precious antidote against the poison in their systems. For here in the sacrament you are to receive from Christ's lips the forgiveness of sins, which contains and brings with it God's grace and Spirit with all his gifts, protection, defense, and power against death, the devil, and every trouble.[1]

This Sacrament is the sum and substance of the Gospel. It is a holy mystery. Unlike a secret, a mystery remains a mystery even after it is revealed. God's mystery is that which He longs to reveal yet that which is never fully understood by us in this life. God's mysteries contain the depth of His undeserved love, the eternity of His provision, the promise of His presence, and so on. No discussion of benefits that flow from the Lord's Supper, including this brief chapter, will exhaust the mystery of what Christ is present to bestow. Nor is this discussion of other benefits intended to lessen our thoughts and thankfulness for the nucleus from which all other benefits derive. That nucleus is the very presence of our risen Lord in the flesh to feed us with His true body and true blood for the forgiveness of sins, life, and salvation.

The Forgiveness of Sins

For this is My blood of the new covenant, which is shed
for many for the remission of sins. (Matthew 26:28)

Luther frequently and forcefully stressed that Holy Communion bestows the forgiveness of sins. The church had forgotten this, and the Roman hierarchy did not properly proclaim it. Indulgences, a system of penance, works-righteousness, the sacrifice of the Mass, and Communion taught primarily as something to be feared had choked out Jesus' inviting words "for the forgiveness of sins."

The forgiveness of sins must never become the grand "of course" in the Christian life. *Of course* we have forgiveness of sins, so now let's get on with more important matters. The very name of God in the flesh, "Jesus," was given because He would save His people from their sins. God was, in Christ, reconciling the world to Himself, not counting men's sins against them (2 Corinthians 5:21). It is no accident that Jesus taught us to pray daily for the forgiveness of sins in the Fifth Petition of the Lord's Prayer. Without the forgiveness of sins, we could never stand before God (Psalm 130:3–4). The highest way to worship Christ is to seek the forgiveness of sins from Him.[2] Therefore there is no higher worship than to receive our Savior's body and blood in faith. This gift is not a mere reminder that God is forgiving nor is it a mere reminder that Jesus shed His blood on the cross for our forgiveness. By His own promise, Jesus bids us to drink His blood for the remission of sins. As Luther taught:

What is the benefit of this eating and drinking?

These words, "Given and shed for you for the forgiveness of sins," show us that in the Sacrament forgiveness of sins, life and salvation are given us through these words. For where there is forgiveness of sins, there is also life and salvation.[3]

The Lord's Supper, then, is not a general idea about the chance of forgiveness nor is it a message offering vague assurance that God is a merciful God. Rather, it is the concrete gift of forgiveness from the risen Christ, who stands in the midst of His gathered people to feed them with His very body and very blood. In the eating and drinking of this heavenly food, He has promised the remission of sins.

We need Christ's gift of forgiveness because sin is a daily business, as Luther reiterates in his explanation of the Fifth Petition of the Lord's Prayer. We need Christ's gift of forgiveness because sin is a deceitful business (Psalm 19:12; 90:8). We need Christ's gift of forgiveness because sin is a dirty business (Isaiah 64:6). We need Christ's gift of forgiveness because sin is a devilish business (1 John 3:8). We need Christ's gift of forgiveness because sin is a deadly business (Genesis 3:19; Romans 6:23). More than anything else, even more than healing from paralyzing physical illness (Mark 2:1–12), we need the forgiveness of sins that Christ bestows.

Sin is as great as the God offended by it. Therefore Luther had much to say about the hereditary sin that infects us and the many sins this causes in our life. Luther said that the Bible was a closed book without the knowledge of sin; that as Adam wanted to be God, so do we and that all other sins come from this sin; that Scripture looks especially into the heart and at the root and source of all sin, which is unbelief at the bottom of the heart; that we should dwell on sin and its terrible effects, for if we do not know the magnitude of the disease, we shall neither know nor desire the remedy; that we should have an exaggerated fear of sinning; that God does not save pretended sinners; and that sin will be removed completely at death.[4]

When Luther wrote the Small Catechism, he changed the order of earlier catechisms and placed the Ten Commandments first. In so doing, he placed first the Law, which shows us our sin.

The confession of the Gospel in the Apostles' Creed then follows. That is what we pray for in the Lord's Prayer. In using the Small Catechism as a prayer book or a handbook for daily life, that order is part of what instructs our life before God.

In examining ourselves in preparation for receiving Holy Communion, Luther directs us to the Ten Commandments. Such examination is essential both in knowing what sins to confess in receiving the gift of absolution and as we perceive our need to receive the Lord's Supper. The questions below[5] provide an invaluable resource for those who wish to understand and teach the faith.

First Commandment

- Do I look to God, my heavenly Father, for all love, good, and joy? Is everything measured for me by what pleases me?
- Do I love the things God gives more than I love Him? And do I cling to what God takes away, even though He gives me Himself?

Second Commandment

- Do I pray with fervor in times of trouble? Am I bored and indifferent in prayer?
- Is it so that I cannot speak about God truly because I am bored with God's Word and neglect the study of the catechism and doctrine?

Third Commandment

- Do I use the Word of God and prayer to make my time, work, study, and life holy day by day? Am I lazy and bored with the Word of God? Have I any fear of God over this neglect?
- Do I love my fellow Christians by being present with them in the Divine Service to sustain them? Am I quick to make excuses for neglecting the divine liturgy because of what

someone else has said or done or to do other things that I like more?

Fourth Commandment

- Has the fear and love of God shaped my honor and obedience to parents and others in authority over me?
- Have I helped those who carry responsibilities of governing? Do I pray for parents, leaders of the nations, schools, and the church? Do I grumble about work given me to do?

Fifth Commandment

- Have I injured my neighbor with violent actions, hitting and beating my neighbor, spoken debasing and insulting words, using foul or dirty words to describe my neighbor, or murdered him with thoughts of anger, contempt, and hatred?
- Do I abuse my body with neglect of health care, excess of food, drink, tobacco, or drugs?

Sixth Commandment

- Have I dishonored marriage by ridicule, divorce, or neglecting to encourage others to be faithful to their spouses in the fear of God?
- Have I neglected to pray for my spouse, to attend the Divine Service together, and to live in the fear and love of God in times of sexual temptation?

Seventh Commandment

- Have I been lazy at work, doing poor work in school or at my job, or working hard only when the teacher or the boss is around?
- Have I been stingy in paying my workers?
- Have I been stingy when it comes to giving to the Lord a generous portion as thankoffering for all that He has given me?

Eighth Commandment

- Have I gossiped, delighting to tell others about the faults or mistakes of another, excusing myself especially by saying that I spoke only the truth?
- Have I slanted stories to my benefit or deceived others by withholding some elements of their story?

Ninth Commandment

- Have I longed for the honor, wealth, happy life, or what seemed the ease of the lives of others? Has my life been full of craving for these things?
- Have I tried by claims of various rights to make the property of others my own, saying they don't really deserve it and I do?

Tenth Commandment

- Have I urged friends and spouses and workers to go back to their calling, holding their marriages, friendships, families, and work together?
- Have I fostered discontent with the congregation, its pastor, or leaders, and failed to urge members to stay and do their duty in the divine liturgy, praying, giving, and serving?

Our sin is always death deep (Romans 6:23). Our missing the mark of God's holy Law is always a total miss (James 2:10). Our righteousness compared with God's is nothing but unrighteousness. Johann Gerhard wrote: "A lamp that gleams in the darkness is obscured in the light of the sun."[6] Whether we feel the sad state of our sinfulness or not does not change our true condition.

There is nothing in the whole world that can deal with our sin except the grace of God in Jesus Christ, our Lord. He is the one to whom we sing in the Communion liturgy: "O Lamb of God, who takes away the sin of the world, have mercy on us" (see John 1:29). That's why He comes into our midst, to serve us with forgiveness, life, and salvation. The forgiveness of sins He brings is not received in a magical way, simply by going through the motions. It is received in faith that recognizes the mercy Christ is present to bestow. According to the Formula of Concord:

> The true and worthy guests, for whom this precious sacrament above all was instituted and established, are the Christians who are weak in faith, fragile and troubled, who are terrified in their hearts by the immensity and number of their sins and think that they are not worthy of this precious treasure and of the benefits of Christ because of their great impurity, who feel the weakness of their faith and deplore it, and who desire with all their heart to serve God with a stronger, more resolute faith and purer obedience. As Christ says, "Come to me, all you that are weary and are carrying heavy burdens, and I will give you rest" [Matt. 11:28], and, "Those who are well have no need of a physician, but those who are sick" [Matt. 9:12].[7]

The rest that Jesus gives for our souls is rest from the futile, everlasting effort of trying to mop up the sloppy stains of our sins. In His cry of victory from the cross, "It is finished," Jesus proclaimed a redemption that was and is full and free and finished. Baptized into His death, that finished redemption is now His gift to you.

Without the shedding of blood, there is no forgiveness (Hebrews 9:22), but Christ has poured out His blood in the once-for-all sacrifice on the cross. In His shed blood there is cleansing from sin (1 John 1:7), redemption (Ephesians 1:7; 1 Peter 1:19), peace with God (Colossians 1:20), and freedom from our sins (Revelation 1:5). It is Jesus' shed blood that He bids us to drink for the remission of sins in the Lord's Supper. God does not forgive pretend sinners but real sinners. In the Lord's Supper, Jesus does not serve us with pretend blood but with His true blood.

> Weary am I and heavy laden,
> With sin my soul is sore opprest;

Receive me graciously and gladden
My heart, for I am now Thy guest.
Lord, may Thy body and Thy blood
Be for my soul the highest good![8]

What follows are four benefits that flow from one another. They fit well under Luther's expression above that along with the forgiveness of sins we receive God's grace and Spirit with all His gifts, protection, defense, and power against death, the devil, and every trouble.

Heaven on Earth, Christ in the Flesh

Whom have I in heaven but You? And there is none upon earth that I desire besides You. (Psalm 73:25)

The Divine Service is not an escape from the world. It is the crucified and risen Christ's entry into our world through His church. In faith, it makes us partakers of the world to come because He who controls that world comes into our midst. One Communion prayer of our forefathers expressed it this way: "Thy Supper be my heaven on earth, till I enter heaven."

Hermann Sasse identifies this thread of understanding the Sacrament as "heaven on earth" weaving throughout the history of the church, from its earliest times to the time of the Reformation and into the present.[9] The early church's prayer "Come, Lord Jesus" has a twofold meaning: a prayer for Christ's second coming and a prayer for His presence in the Sacrament. Sasse explains: "This coming of the Lord in the Real Presence makes the Lord's Day a day of unspeakable joy, a day of praise and thanksgiving. It makes the Eucharist not only an anticipation of the blessed future, but also a participation in the eternal worship in heaven, which St. John saw in the great vision he had at Patmos just at the time when the churches of Asia assembled for their divine service (Rev. 1:10; 4:1ff)."[10]

There are members of the congregation and visitors who come and go quickly on Sunday morning, not realizing what only the eyes of faith can see. Other things preoccupy their minds and hearts. Their priority is to get out of church quickly and back to the "real" world. According to Richard Eyer, "there are those who realize that the experience of the Divine Service is the real world at a glimpse, a door to heaven opened to us each week so we do not lose heart and are sustained for this life until we walk through that doorway at our Lord's invitation for more than a glimpse."[11]

At the altar the Lord stands before us. He is our peace. He is our righteousness. He is our life. He is love itself. He comes to give us His peace. He comes to robe us in His righteousness. He comes to nourish the life He breathed into us at Baptism. He comes to love us. At this Meal, He does it by feeding us the very body and very blood He once offered on the cross for our redemption. John Kleinig writes: "In the Lord's Supper we enter heaven itself together with our great High Priest (Heb 10:19–22). There we eat Christ's flesh, the bread from heaven."[12] He also explains that "[t]he sacred meal was only a small part of the sacrificial ritual at the tabernacle, but by Christ's institution, the new Meal is the heart of the Divine Service in the NT church. In the Lord's Supper, the triune God reveals his glory to the assembled congregation and blesses his people with every spiritual blessing in the heavenly realms (Eph 1:3–14)."[13] Gustaf Wingren expressed it in this manner: "Christ is just as much present in the Lord's Supper now as he will be in the heavenly Supper, but his real presence now is in accordance with this phase of the history of redemption in which we stand—the phase between Easter and the Parousia (Christ's Second Coming), faith's phase, not sight's."[14] And Gene Edward Veith states: "It has been said that this contact with Christ is more direct and closer and more intimate than what His disciples enjoyed. Again, Christ comes to us.

It is not something we do, but something Christ does, which we have only to receive."[15]

In the miracle of the ages, God became man and dwelt among us. In the miracle of the Lord's Supper, the God-man comes to serve us heavenly food. Speaking of His true bodily presence as heaven on earth is not meant to say that the eternal pleasures of God's right hand are fully seen and felt. For now we live by faith, not by sight (Hebrews 11). But it is meant to say that He who opened heaven to us comes into our midst to feed and strengthen us here below. Or, as Luther expressed it, "in this sacrament he offers us all the treasures he brought from heaven for us, to which he most graciously invites us in other places, as when he says in Matthew 11[:28]: 'Come to me, all you that are weary and are carrying heavy burdens, and I will give you rest.'"[16]

> Soul, adorn yourself with gladness,
> Leave the gloomy haunts of sadness,
> Come into the daylight's splendor,
> There with joy your praises render.
> Bless the one whose grace unbounded
> This amazing banquet founded;
> He, though heav'nly, high, and holy,
> Deigns to dwell with you most lowly.[17]

Jesus' offering of all the treasures He brought from heaven for us is wonderful encouragement to recover the opportunity for God's people to commune in weekly worship. And that's not all—Christ's true bodily presence also brings with it union with Christ.

Union with Christ: Blessed Exchange and Transforming Power

But we all, with unveiled face, beholding as in a mirror the glory of the Lord, are being transformed into the

192

same image from glory to glory, just as by the Spirit of the Lord. (2 Corinthians 3:18)

The image of God in which we were created was shattered by our rebellion and fall into sin. In Adam, death reigned over us. In Adam, we were without strength. In Adam, we were ungodly and stood condemned. "Therefore, as through one man's offense judgment came to all men, resulting in condemnation, even so through one Man's righteous act the free gift came to all men, resulting in justification of life" (Romans 5:18).

God doesn't give this free gift of justification and life from a distance. God comes so close to man that He becomes man. The free gift that transforms and gives life is Christ Himself, the Word made flesh. In Baptism He gives us Himself (Galatians 3:27), unites us with Himself. Through the preaching of Christ, He enters the lives of His people today. In Holy Communion, He nourishes us with His body and blood, continuing to unite Himself with us. In this union, Jesus takes what is ours and gives us what is His. It is a blessed exchange, a joyous exchange. Not that man is deified. Rather, Christ comes to restore man in the image of God, in union with Christ, the God-man.[18] As Veith says:

> Not only is Christ present at the altar, He gives Himself to us. As we eat the bread, we are receiving, in an intimate and personal way, His body that was broken on the cross. When we sip the wine, we are receiving His blood that sealed the covenant, assuring the forgiveness of sin. We are literally united with Christ—Christ crucified, resurrected, ascended—bridging the gap between here and Golgotha, now and eternity.[19]

Discussing Jesus' gift of Himself in the Lord's Supper, Luther wrote: "For Christ and I are being baked into each other in such a way that my sins and death become His and His righteousness and life become my own. In short, a most blessed exchange is taking place here."[20] This exchange is not halfway or piecemeal. At the Lord's Supper your self-centeredness becomes Christ's. His self-sacrifice becomes yours. Your untamed tongue becomes His. His peace-bestowing tongue becomes yours. Your rebellion becomes His. His obedience becomes yours. Your lusting becomes His. His chastity becomes yours. Your envy and coveting become His. His charity and compassion become yours. Your hate becomes His. His love becomes yours. Your worry becomes His. His perfect trust becomes yours. Your self-promotion and self-pity become His. His self-giving becomes yours. Your willingness to compromise the truth becomes His. His perfect speaking of the truth in love becomes yours. Your mind, set on earthly things, becomes His. His mind, set on heavenly things, becomes yours. Or as Luther strikingly pictured it:

> To give a simple illustration of what takes place in this eating: it is as if a wolf devoured a sheep and the sheep were so powerful a food that it transformed the wolf and turned him into a sheep. So, when we eat Christ's flesh physically and spiritually, the food is so powerful that it transforms us into itself and out of fleshly, sinful, mortal men makes spiritual, holy, living men. This we are already, though in a hidden manner in faith and hope; the fact is not yet manifest, but we shall experience it on the Last Day.[21]

As Harold Senkbeil aptly summarizes: "On his cross Jesus pulled off the greatest swap in history. He took our sin and gave us his own righteousness."[22] Do we deserve such a royal, life-giving exchange? In no way! Does God desire to give us such a bold and beautiful exchange? In every way! He desires us to put off the old man and put on the new (Ephesians 4:22–24). That is why He continues to feed us with the heavenly food of His very body and very blood.

The centurion whose servant was ill told Jesus, "I am not worthy that You should enter under my roof" (Luke 7:6). That statement has been used since ancient times in connection with all that we receive in the Lord's Supper: "Lord, I am not worthy to have You come under the roof of my mouth." This is true for all of us, yet Jesus comes to give us what we cannot give ourselves.

> By faith your Word has made us bold
> To seize the gift of love retold;
> All that you are we here receive,
> And all we are to you we give.[23]

> Break forth, my soul, in joy and say:
> What wealth has come to me today,
> What health of body, mind, and soul!
> Christ dwells within in me, makes me whole.[24]

The risen Christ's union with us and the blessed exchange He bestows is wonderful encouragement to recover the opportunity for God's people to receive this gift when they come for weekly worship. It is also the basis for the next benefit.

Holiness from the Holy of Holies

> Therefore, brethren, having boldness to enter the Holiest by the blood of Jesus, By a new and living way which He consecrated for us, through the veil, that is, His flesh, and having a High Priest over the house of God, let us draw near with a true heart in full assurance of faith, having our hearts sprinkled from an evil conscience and our bodies washed with pure water. (Hebrews 10:19–22)

In the Old Testament, God located Himself in the Holy of Holies, the Most Holy Place, or as stated in the translation above, "the Holiest." The curtain separated the Holy of Holies from the holy place in the sanctuary and showed the exclusion of sinful mankind from the presence of God. Only the high priest could enter the Holy of Holies and then only once a year on the Day of Atonement. When he did so, sacrificial blood was in abundance.

When he did so, a rope was tied to him in case he died while inside. His body could then be pulled out, for no one else was allowed entrance into the presence of God.

But in the fullness of time, the Holy One came in the flesh. On Friday of Holy Week, Jesus offered a sacrifice so complete that the curtain in the temple was torn in two from top to bottom (Mark 15:38). It is a sacrifice that is once for all (Hebrews 7:27). God has acted to open the way into His holy presence through the body and blood of Jesus Christ offered up on the cross.

Baptized into Christ's death (Romans 6:3), we can draw near to God with a true heart in full assurance of faith. And as Hebrews 10 also makes clear, this drawing near to God, this entering the Most Holy Place by the blood of Jesus, is joined to our gathering together in worship. Richard Eyer states that "in the Divine Service we are led up to the door of heaven weekly and given a taste of the holiness that awaits us in heaven. Here and now, in the celebration of the Lord's Supper, the Lord opens the door of heaven and comes down Himself to feed us the bread of life."[25] This is Jesus' promised presence *for us.* The holiness received is not our own doing, it is the gift of Christ who is our holiness, our sanctification (1 Corinthians 1:30). It is a borrowed holiness. What we cannot manufacture, the Holy One bestows upon us as a gift, namely, His perfect holiness.

This is in perfect keeping with how God has always bestowed His holiness on sinful man. Since the fall into sin, no one is holy by nature. However, God acted to share His holiness with His people in an ongoing process. John Kleinig explains:

> *God communicated his holiness physically with his people through the holy things. . . .* By meeting with them in the daily service he made and kept them holy (Ex 29:43). Their holiness therefore depended on him and their association with him at the sanctuary. . . . His holiness never was their own possession apart from him. It was

always received anew from him, like nourishment for the body from food, through their involvement in the divine service.[26]

No sin can enter God's holy presence, and our attempts at inventing ways to approach Him and worship Him are just that—our inventions. The church of our day needs to be reminded that offering God a strange fire, attempting to approach Him with our own devices, has serious spiritual consequences. When Nadab and Abihu, the sons of Levi, experimented with worshiping God, the strange fire they offered was met with God's consuming fire (Leviticus 10:1–3). Seeking life on their own terms, they received death. But receiving Jesus' Word and Sacrament, feasting on His body and blood for the forgiveness of sins, is not strange worship. These are the very gifts Jesus gave on the night of His betrayal. These are the very gifts the Holy Spirit led Christ's church to be devoted to after Pentecost. This is not offering to God a strange fire but receiving the fire of His love.

Where the risen Christ is present *for us*, to give us Himself, there we also receive His holiness and the power for holy living. Sin will never stop clinging to us in this life (1 John 1:8–10; Romans 7), but that does not change the holiness that is Christ's gift to us. By a strange paradox, we are saint and sinner at the same time. If we make our peace with sin, if we willfully, unrepentantly continue in sin, we drive the Holy Spirit out. But as God continues to bestow His peace on us in Christ Jesus, as He absolves us, the Holy Spirit strengthens us to drive sin out. It is a battle that will continue until the day God calls us from this life.

> The energy of the Christian life and the focus of holy living does not consist in trying harder to be good. It is humbling to have to admit to oneself that spiritual self-improvement is an impossibility. It may be pride, as much as conscientious desire for self-improvement, that causes us to refuse to believe our holiness is a gift of God

in Christ, enjoyed and lived by faith, not by our own efforts. Faith requires us to entrust our lives to God, relying on the Holy Spirit to transform us. As our faith takes charge, we leave behind the narcissistic preoccupation with self-evaluation and put our spiritual energies into serving the needs of others.[27]

The Lord came no closer to His people in the Old Testament than He did in the Holy of Holies. By His design, on the Day of Atonement, through the mediation of the high priest, God provided forgiveness for the nation. The Lord comes no closer to His people in the New Testament than He does in the holy body and holy blood of Christ. By His design, God bestows this gift in bread and wine for us Christians to eat and drink. Jesus is the embodiment of holiness and purity: "As the 'Holy One of God,' whatever Jesus touches and proclaims clean and holy—no matter how unclean and unholy it might be . . . is holy because it has been transformed by the Creator who has broken into His creation to make all things new."[28] Kleinig states:

> Since Christ's body has been offered up as a sin offering and a reparation offering to God the Father, it is now most holy. It is therefore eaten as a part of the Divine Service in a holy place, the assembly of saints in the heavenly sanctuary (Heb 10:19–22). This is typified for us by our reception of the Lord's Supper in the sanctuaries of our churches. Contact with that most holy flesh makes and keeps God's people holy (Heb 10:10). In this way we come to share more and more in God's life-giving holiness.[29]

> > The holy Lamb undaunted came
> > To God's own altar lit with flame;
> > While weeping angels hid their eyes,
> > This Priest became a sacrifice.
> >
> > But death would not the victor be

Of Him who hung upon the tree.
He leads us to the Holy Place
Within the veil before God's face.

God's unveiled presence now we see,
As at the rail on bended knee
Our hungry mouths from Him receive
The bread of immortality.[30]

The benefits of union with Christ and the reception of His holiness are surely encouragement for the weekly opportunity to receive this gift. Union with Christ brings with it another benefit as well— union with the holy Christian church.

The Communion of Saints

But you have come to Mount Zion and to the city of the living God, the heavenly Jerusalem, to an innumerable company of angels, to the general assembly and church of the firstborn who are registered in heaven, to God the Judge of all, to the spirits of just men made perfect, to Jesus the Mediator of the new covenant, and to the blood of sprinkling that speaks better things than that of Abel. (Hebrews 12:22–24)

Luther's first point in recovering a scriptural understanding of the Lord's Supper is the fellowship that God gives us therein with Himself and with one another. This is clearly seen in Luther's 1519 sermon on the Sacrament. The church had lost sight of this fact as it offered private Masses said by a priest with no communicants. The Reformation addressed this by mandating that there be absolutely no Communion service unless there were communicants to receive the Sacrament. The Lord's Supper was not a solo performance by the priest for the people. Rather, it is the Supper Christ came to serve to His *gathered* people.

As the risen Lord gives union with Himself in this meal, He also gives union with one another as His body. This fellowship has meaning for the faith that is mutually confessed, the love that is mutually given, the burdens that are mutually borne. Luther explains: "This fellowship consists in this, that all the spiritual possessions of Christ and his saints are shared with and become the common property of him who receives this sacrament."[31]

This truth is confessed in the Third Article of the Apostles' Creed in the phrase "communion of saints." According to Hermann Sasse, "[t]he Latin text . . . can mean either 'communion of holy things (sancta)' or 'communion of holy persons (sancti). Both interpretations occur in the early centuries of the formula."[32] Along with St. Paul (1 Corinthians 10:16–17), we confess that the bread in Holy Communion is the body of Christ, a holy thing, and that those who eat it are the body of Christ, a holy people—the Church.[33] This communion or fellowship is an unearthly reality that connects Christians with the Holy Trinity and extends from this world into the world to come.[34]

Christ and His saints are one spiritual body, a vital union even as the human body is joined with the head. This spiritual body includes the saints who have already departed this life in the faith. Christ is eternal, and His body cannot be divided by our limits of time. As the hymn says: "The saints on earth and those above But one communion make."[35] We are divided only by the narrow stream of death. We do not eat in isolation but as part of the church across space and time. The apostles, prophets, and martyrs are in the presence of Christ who comes into our presence. Our worship is one with the train of the faithful called home through the sweep of the centuries.

When the Lord, the head of the church, comes into our midst, He does not do so in isolation from His body. Those who have died in Christ are always with Him, even when He comes to serve us. Their bodies may be temporarily present in the cemetery, but their living souls are with Christ, who comes to teach and feed us. It is no accident that the liturgy leads us to say: "Therefore with angels and archangels and all the company of heaven we laud and magnify Your glorious name." In Holy Communion, the seen and the unseen, the temporary and the eternal meet. Heaven is more than a dream, and the King of heaven comes to teach you and to feed you. As the head of the church does so, His body is with Him.

The Sacrament of the Altar is the closest meeting point between us and our Lord. How can He come closer to us than to come under the very roof of our mouths with His holy body and holy blood? This means that the altar, the Lord's Supper, is also the closest meeting point between us and the body of the Lord— His church, His saints. This includes our loved ones who have died in the faith. They are with Him who comes bodily to feed us.

In the Divine Service, I sometimes thank God for our daughter Bethany, who died at 6 weeks of age. She was baptized in Christ and clothed in Him (Galatians 3:27). We rejoice in the eternal pleasure at God's right hand that Bethany receives from Him (Psalm 26:11). As together with all the company of heaven we laud and magnify God's name, is it not proper for me to think about Bethany and other loved ones, including the many individuals I have served as pastor through their dying time? Is it not proper for you to think with thanksgiving about those dear to you who have departed this life in the faith? Jesus, with all the authority of God's right hand, comes into our midst to give us a foretaste of the eternal pleasure they now enjoy in His presence. Their focus is not upon us, but upon the glorified Christ. The center of our thoughts is also upon Christ, but as He enters our midst to serve us, it is not wrong that we rejoice also in the company of heaven. Gaylin Schmeling points out that Norwegian churches often feature an altar rail in a half circle. This symbolic design reminds communicants that the circle at the altar is completed by those feasting in heaven. This is a powerful reminder that we still have a close relationship with those who have died in the faith and that we will dine with them forever in heaven.[36]

Richard Eyer, noting the church of the firstborn whose names are written in heaven (Hebrews 12:23), expressed the fellowship of the saints on earth and those in heaven in this way:

> Here, we stand with those who have died in faith and who were once lost to us. I have heard people say that they cannot attend public worship because they become too emotionally upset following the recent loss of a loved one, but there is nothing wrong with quiet tears in worship. Even greater than the tears of grief and loss expressed in public worship are the tears of joy that come in rediscovering loved ones at worship with us among the host of heaven.[37]

Describing the singing of the Sanctus—"Holy, holy, holy Lord, God of power and might"—during the Communion liturgy, Eyer beautifully summarizes this blessing that Christ brings in Holy Communion:

> At this point in the Divine Service the curtain separating this life from the next is drawn back and we sing with those who have gone before us the glory of Christ's victory over sin and death. Here, in the Divine Service, as nowhere else on earth, we are together as one, saints above and saints on earth. Here, more than anywhere else in this life, we are near to those who have died in Christ. No memories or private devotions can rival the reality that all the community of heaven worships with us when we worship together in the Divine Service on a Sunday morning. What better place to find healing and reunion with loved ones than in the gathering of God's people before the altar?[38]

Death is up ahead just a bit for us. We don't know the time or the manner of our death, but God does. He holds that time in

His hand and has promised that He will go with us through death's dark shadowland (Psalm 23). The light beyond that valley is filled with the radiance of the exalted Christ and is reflected by His saints, who are in His unveiled presence. While we sorrow for them, there are no tears in heaven for us. This is so because the love and the presence of Christ fills them as it will soon fill us. Is it not a wonder that as He comes to feed us His body and blood, as He comes to strengthen us for the journey that remains, the church triumphant is with Him?

> One body we, one body who partake,
> One Church united in communion blest,
> One name we bear, one bread of life we break,
> With all Thy saints on earth and saints at rest.[39]

The following three topics are wonderful aspects of the Lord's Supper that flow from words and phrases of Jesus and St. Paul as the gift was first celebrated and commended to us. They are truths that can enrich our understanding of this mystery and encourage its presence in weekly worship.

Thanksgiving (*Eucharist*)

And He took bread, gave thanks, and broke it. (Luke 22:19)

Early in the second century, the word *eucharist* was already commonly used for the Lord's Supper. This was centuries before the idea of the Mass as the priest's unbloody sacrifice to God was common. *Eucharist* is also a word that comes from Jesus' institution of the Last Supper on Maundy Thursday. It is simply the transliteration of the Greek word *thanksgiving* from Jesus' own giving of thanks.

Luther understood the usage of *eucharist* in a positive way, so he wanted people to say, "I want to go to the Eucharist," and mean, "I want to go . . . to that office at which one thanks and praises God in his sacrament, as it appears the ancients intended that it should be done."[40] Liturgical scholar Frank Senn observes: "Luther believed that it was a result of such an understanding that the mood of praise and thanksgiving pervaded the mass from beginning to end: as, for example, in the Gloria, the Alleluia, the . . . Nicene Creed, the preface, the Sanctus, the Benedictus, and the Agnus Dei."[41]

The Lutheran Confessions also describe the Eucharist in the best of terms as they quote Cyprian, a bishop of Carthage in the third century who was martyred under the Emperor Valerian. The Confessions state:

> There are also statements about thanksgiving, like that very beautiful statement of Cyprian concerning those who receive the sacrament in godly fashion: He says, "In returning thanks to the Giver for such an abundant blessing, piety divides its thanks between what has been given and what has been forgiven." That is, piety focuses on what has been given and what has been forgiven; it compares the greatness of God's blessings with the greatness of our ills, our sin and our death, and it gives thanks. From this the term "Eucharist" arose in the church.[42]

When Christ instituted the Supper, He gave thanks. When Jesus concluded the Last Supper and went out singing hymns to the Mount of Olives, He gave thanks again, for the psalms appointed for the Passover observance were prayers and hymns of thanksgiving (Psalms 114–118). What our Lord accomplished on the next day is reason for eternal thanksgiving. By the sacrifice of His body and the shedding of His blood, the holy Lamb of God finished our redemption. The eternal reach of that reason for thanksgiving was seen in the early morning light of the third day, for it was impossible for death to keep its hold on Christ (Acts 2:24). That note of gladness and praise is unmistakable as the Holy Spirit was poured out at Pentecost. The reason for thankful hearts was the risen Christ, whom the Holy Spirit brought to His Church in Word and Sacrament, in the apostles' doctrine, and in the breaking of the bread (Acts 2:42–47). According to Sasse, "[t]his coming of the Lord in the Real Presence makes the Lord's Day a day of unspeakable joy, a day of praise and thanksgiving."[43]

It is the true bodily presence of the risen Lord Jesus Christ that is the Eucharist. He comes to make a happy exchange. He comes to give us peace with God, God's objective peace, a peace outside of us, a peace purchased with the blood of the cross. "The peace of the Lord be with you always," the pastor speaks after the consecration of the elements. "Amen," respond the people, which is to say, "Yes, it is so. God is present and has given us peace." "Take and drink," Jesus invites, and thirsty souls drink of His blood for the remission of sins. With gifts received, with joy restored, there is nothing else for us do but give thanks.

> O Lord, we praise you, bless you, and adore you,
> In thanksgiving bow before you.
> Here with your body and your blood you nourish
> Our weak souls that they may flourish.
> O Lord, have mercy!
> May your body, Lord, born of Mary,
> That our sins and sorrows did carry,
> And your blood for us plead
> In all trial, fear, and need:
> O Lord, have mercy![44]

Understanding the word *eucharist* and the eternal reasons this Meal brings for thanksgiving can encourage God's people to receive the Sacrament frequently and joyfully. Understanding the words "This do in remembrance of Me" can help us in a similar way.

In Remembrance of Me

Take, eat; this is My body which is broken for you; do this in remembrance of Me. (1 Corinthians 11:24)

This cup is the new covenant in My blood. This do, as often as you drink it, in remembrance of Me. (1 Corinthians 11:25)

The simplest meaning of the words "This do in remembrance of Me" in English is not what this phrase means in Paul's letter to the church at Corinth. The modern word *remembrance* generally means the recollection of something or someone who is absent. Such a remembrance would primarily be an exercise of mental effort in one's private corner. Such a remembrance applied to the Sacrament would include nostalgic contemplation of Jesus' past actions because He isn't present when He is being remembered. This view of remembrance or memorial as the real purpose of the Lord's Supper would make it into a human work, which is what the Sacrament was considered under the sacrifice of the Mass. Luther taught repeatedly that remembrance "does not consist of meditating on [Jesus'] suffering, with which some have sought to serve God as with a good work."[45]

In the Jewish world, remembrance was not understood as a mere mental activity. When the penitent thief said to Jesus, "Lord, remember me when You come into Your kingdom" (Luke 23:42), he did not expect Jesus merely to think about him. The remembering he had in mind was full of power and presence and action to help him, which is exactly what he received. Jesus responded: "Assuredly, I say to you, today you will be with Me in Paradise" (Luke 23:43). This type of remembering is found also in the Benedictus of Zechariah and the Magnificat of Mary in Luke 1. Mary sang: "He has helped His servant Israel, In remembrance of His mercy, As He spoke to our fathers, To Abraham and to his seed forever" (Luke 1:54–55). Zechariah sang that God "has raised up a horn of salvation for us . . . To perform the mercy promised to our fathers And to remember His holy covenant, The oath which He swore to our Father Abraham" (Luke 1:69, 72–73). God remembers His mercy and His holy covenant and is present in the flesh of Christ with action and power to help.

In looking at the context of the Lord's Supper as Paul commended its celebration in Corinth, we see that immediately following and linked with the remembrance is the proclamation of the Lord's death (1 Corinthians 11:25–26). In another text, Jesus' own words link remembering and proclaiming as Mary anoints His body for burial (Mark 14:9): "Assuredly, I say to you, wherever this gospel is preached throughout the whole world, what this woman did will also be told as a memorial to her."

Therefore Luther interpreted "This do in remembrance of Me" in accordance with Paul's words: "You proclaim the Lord's death until He comes" (1 Corinthians 11:26 ESV). Luther understood remembrance not as a mental act but as a sermon that testified of God's redemptive work, not man's work. For Luther it was as if Christ had said, "As oft as you do this sacrament you shall preach of me."[46] In another place, Luther writes: " 'Do this in remembrance of Me (Luke 22:19; 1 Cor. 11:24); that is, they are to proclaim His death (1 Cor. 11:26), preach penitence, the remission of sins, and eternal life. Then they are not to receive in vain the grace bequeathed by the testament but to make use of it against lusts."[47]

Lutheran theologian Martin Chemnitz speaks of a remembrance that would be in perfect harmony with that type of proclamation:

> But what kind of remembrance is it? It is the kind in which for the restoration of your fallen and lost nature I (1) have assumed "body and blood," that is, human nature, (2) have given My assumed body into death and shed My blood as a ransom . . . for you, and (3) offer for

you to receive in the Supper this body which has been given and this blood which has been shed, in order that this memory of Me, which is faith, may by this eating be more and more aroused, preserved, and confirmed in you.[48]

Notice here the equating of remembrance and faith! This is a crucial and comforting connection. This remembrance is not speculation about the divine majesty or love of a God who is absent and merely wants us to think about Him. This remembrance is faith, that is, receiving in faith the Lord who is present, bestowing His body and blood for the remission of our sins. This remembrance involves God's own remembering of His mercy and the new testament, which Jesus purchased with His blood and bestows with His blood. This remembrance carries with it the same power and presence and action to help us as when Jesus said to the thief on the cross, "Assuredly, I say to you, today you will be with Me in Paradise" (Luke 23:43).

"This do in remembrance of Me" are the words of Him who is bodily present in our midst to feed us, the God-man Jesus Christ. "This do in remembrance of Me," Christ says, meaning you are to proclaim His death and resurrection and repentance and forgiveness of sins in His name. "This do in remembrance of Me," Christ says, meaning you are to receive in faith what He is now present in the flesh to give you in Holy Communion. C. F. W. Walther echoed this thought and the confidence it gives to approach the altar: "By . . . 'Do this in remembrance of Me,' Christ means to say: 'Do it in faith.' Surely, He does not mean to say: 'Think of Me when you partake of My body and blood. Do not forget Me altogether!' Whoever thinks that Christ merely admonished His disciples not to consign Him to oblivion does not know the Savior."[49] When the depth of this remembrance is understood, the Lutheran practice of singing the Nunc Dimittis after Holy Communion is certainly fitting. God graciously remembers Jesus' cleansing blood even as we receive it in the remembrance of faith. He indeed makes us ready to depart this life in peace.

The Lutheran Confessions provide a helpful summation of what this remembrance is.

> Such use of the sacrament, in which faith gives life to terrified hearts, is the New Testament worship, because the New Testament involves spiritual impulses: being put to death and being made alive. Christ instituted the sacrament for this use when he commanded [1 Cor. 11:24], "Do this in remembrance of me." For to remember Christ is not an empty celebration or a show nor something instituted for the sake of an example, the way plays celebrate the memory of Hercules or Ulysses. It is rather to remember Christ's benefits and to receive them by faith so that we are made alive through them.[50]

> Unaided reason cannot see
> What eager faith embraces,
> But this consoling supper, Lord,
> Each restless doubt displaces.
> Your wondrous ways are not confined
> Within the limits of my mind;
> Your promise wholly triumphs.[51]

As noted above, Luther closely connected the remembrance of Holy Communion with the proclamation of the death of Christ. There is a sense in which a congregation's reception of this gift in faith is the greatest Gospel sermon that can be proclaimed.

Proclaiming Christ's Death until He Comes

> For as often as you eat this bread and drink this cup, you proclaim the Lord's death till He comes. (1 Corinthians 11:26)

There is a mission word in this verse, the word *proclaim*. It is the same word used throughout Acts as the apostles proclaimed Christ and the Word of God in different cities and regions. It is plural, literally, "you all proclaim." It indicates that the whole congregation is testifying to the death of Christ through the reception of Holy Communion.

Walther described the Sacrament as "the pulpit of the laity."[52] Gregory Lockwood writes concerning this description: "By their whole action in gathering for the Sacrament, hearing the Words of Institution, and eating and drinking the sacramental elements, members of the Christian community proclaim 'Jesus Christ and Him crucified' . . . for their sins."[53]

This has been true for the church down through the centuries. The faithful practice of closed Communion does not take away from this proclamation, but in fact the unity in doctrine it supports is the essence of this joint proclamation. It is a wondrous benefit that occurs completely as a gift of God, even as He gives us the gift of gifts in the Lord's Supper. Jesus, who stood physically on the earth and preached, now also preaches through His body, the church. In this Sacrament, He preaches primarily through mouths that are eating and drinking rather than through mouths that are talking. And no purer Gospel could be proclaimed than the proclamation God has set in place in this Meal.

As the text states, what is proclaimed in this way is the death of Christ. Some might ask, "Why not proclaim the resurrection of Christ? Won't proclaiming His death take away from the joy or the thanksgiving of this feast?" Not at all! It is the risen Christ who brings us this heavenly feast that proclaims His death. He comes into our midst from heaven where this same proclamation is made, "Worthy is the Lamb who was slain" (Revelation 5:12). Jesus' resurrection casts a brilliant light on His cross. In fact, it is the risen Christ Himself who is present to serve us as the Holy Spirit inspires this proclamation of His death.

This benefit has important mission implications. Mission philosophies that see every Sunday closed Communion as a barrier to spreading the Gospel would seem to contradict God's own revelation of what takes place in the celebration of this treasure. Clear and caring confession is needed, but there is clear witness that the Lord's Supper faithfully celebrated does not impede the true mission of Jesus Christ in bringing life to a dying world. Noting again Walther's description of the Sacrament as the "pulpit of the laity," we see also a mission benefit in recovering weekly Communion. The pastor's sermon from the pulpit may on some Sundays proclaim the Gospel more clearly and fully than on others. The proclamation of the laity from their pulpit is by God's doing pure Gospel. Is it not a wonder that even as we receive forgiveness of sins we are proclaiming the death of Him who is present to bestow that forgiveness? We receive grace upon grace from the God of grace and warm encouragement to provide the laity the opportunity to commune when they come for weekly worship.

Till He Comes

When the Lord's Supper is received by the congregation, together they proclaim the Lord's death till He comes. Each Communion service is proclamation to the world that the crucified and risen Lord will return in glory. Each Communion service is anticipation within the church of the Last Day as "[a]t every Eucharist the divine acquittal is pronounced that will be heard at the last day."[54] Already now there is no condemnation for those who are in Christ Jesus (Romans 8:1). The reason Jesus comes to feed us His body and blood is to keep us in Him, to take what is ours and to give us what is His. He comes to give us the very wedding garment we need to stand in the judgment. The Holy One of God comes to give you His holiness.

This Sacrament reaches back into the past. It also reaches into the future by virtue of its contact with the eternal High Priest (Hebrews 6:20). The Lord's Supper reaches over the span of nearly twenty centuries between Jesus' crucifixion and today by feeding us the body given into death and the blood shed on Calvary. It also reaches over the span of time from today to the Last Day, for the Judge of that day stands in our midst now. He comes *for us* to make a blessed exchange.

The apostle Peter asks, "Where is the promise of His coming?" (2 Peter 3:4). Surely it is in the preached Word of Jesus and His apostles and is now also in the preached Word of His pastors. But it is also in the Lord's Supper: "For as often as you eat this bread and drink this cup, you proclaim the Lord's death till He comes" (1 Corinthians 11:26). The most ancient liturgical prayer has a double meaning. That prayer is *maranatha*, which means "Our Lord come" or "Come, Lord Jesus." Since the early years of the church, it has belonged to the Communion liturgy. It is a prayer for the coming of the Risen One into His assembled congregation. At the same time, it is a prayer for His coming at the end of time—a coming that is prefigured now as He comes to His church in worship.[55] Because Christ comes to us now with forgiveness, life, and salvation, we are perfectly prepared for His coming again at the last.

> For Thy consoling Supper, Lord,
> Be praised throughout all ages!
> Preserve it, for in every place
> The world against it rages.
> Grant that this Sacrament may be
> A blessed comfort unto me
> When living and when dying.[56]

The death of Jesus that the Lord's Supper proclaims was bodily death. He was dead and buried. On the third day, He rose bodily from the grave as the first fruits of them that sleep. The future He has prepared for us includes eternal pleasure for our glorified bodies. The food He feeds us with now benefits the whole person—soul and body.

Food for Soul and Body

> He makes me to lie down in green pastures; He leads me beside the still waters. He restores my soul; He leads me in the paths of righteousness For His name's sake. (Psalm 23:2–3)

Gustaf Wingren writes: "The Lord's Supper is repeated, for it is the food and drink of the desert journey. But baptism is not repeated, for it is the crossing of the red Sea, which only took place once for all."[57] As God miraculously sustained Israel with manna during the wilderness wanderings, so He sustains us with the heavenly food of Christ's body and blood in the desert wanderings of our life. The manna couldn't be stored, except the day before the Sabbath when God provided enough for two days. The Lord's Supper cannot be stored either. Far from being a once-in-a-lifetime event like Baptism, the Lutheran Confessions call it our daily food and sustenance.

> Therefore, it is appropriately called food of the soul, for it nourishes and strengthens the new creature. For in the first instance, we are born anew through baptism. However, our human flesh and blood . . . have not lost their old skin. There are so many hindrances and attacks of the devil and the world that we often grow weary and faint and at times even stumble. Therefore the Lord's Supper is given as a daily food and sustenance so that our faith may be refreshed and strengthened and that it may not succumb in the struggle but become stronger and stronger.[58]

God created food and gave it for man to eat. When man used God's gift of food to bring sin and death, God gave a new food to bring new life. God gave Christ Himself, the bread of heaven, the Word made flesh. And just as all food comes from the death of living things, so now the bread of life comes from the death of Christ and His sacrifice on the cross.

> Without food, we would starve to death. We have to eat to fuel our physical life; otherwise, we grow weak and waste away. The only food that can sustain our bodies comes from the death of other living things. Whether we are nourishing ourselves from a bloody steak or ripped up plants in a vegetarian casserole, there can be no life, even on the physical level, apart from the sacrifice of other life. What is true for physical life is true for spiritual life—we can only live if there has been a sacrifice. And we can only live if we have continual nourishment.[59]

But such nourishment is not only for our souls. It has been rightly said that man does not consist of body and soul but that man *is* body and soul. We belong to God both body and soul. We eagerly wait for the Savior who, as we hear in the rite of committal at a graveside, will transform our lowly body so it may be conformed to His glorious body according to the working by which He is able even to subdue all things to Himself (Philippians 3:20–21). Luther said that "[t]he mouth, the throat, the body, which eats Christ's body, will also have its benefit in that it will live forever and arise on the Last Day to eternal salvation."[60] Luther also wrote:

> [I]t is a glory and praise of his inexpressible grace and mercy that he concerns himself so profoundly with us poor sinners and shows us such gracious love and goodness, not content to be everywhere in and around, above and beside us, but even giving us his own body as nourishment, in order that with such a pledge he may assure and promise us that our body too shall live forever, because it partakes here on earth of everlasting and living food.[61]

Modern Christianity is prone to forget that we belong to Christ, not only according to the spirit but also according to the body. This Paul makes explicit in writing to the saints at Corinth: "Do you not know that your bodies are members of Christ?" (1 Corinthians 6:15). As we confess in the Apostles' Creed, "I believe in . . . the resurrection of the body and the life everlasting." When we receive the Lord's Supper, the heavenly food Christ serves us benefits the whole person—body and soul. The fullness of those benefits will not be completely known by us until the Last Day when our Lord returns. Meanwhile, in the Lord's Supper, "Christ is present in a way that happens nowhere else. In Holy Communion God builds the bridge between heaven and earth so that no separation can exist between physical and spiritual need. In bread and wine, the body and blood of Jesus Christ are present to heal the deeper sickness of the soul, ultimately transforming earthly bodies into eternal ones."[62]

> The body of God's Lamb we eat
> A priestly food and priestly meat.
> On sin-parched lips the chalice pours
> His quenching blood that life restores.[63]

One dismissal for those communing states: "The body and blood of our Lord Jesus Christ strengthen and preserve you in body and soul to life everlasting." He who knows our bodily struggles and who knows the threats against our souls comes in His feast of love to benefit us in both body and soul. As He so loves us, so He gives us love for one another.

The Love of Christ, Love for the Neighbor

> By this we know love, because He laid down His life for us. And we also ought to lay down our lives for the brethren. (1 John 3:16)

God is love. Love moved the Father to give His only begotten Son. Love moved the Word made flesh to the cross with all its shame and rejection and death. Love is the fruit of the Holy Spirit. The Greek word for God's love for us is *agape*. In Scripture, this is a word of action, a word of doing, not principally a feeling. To love someone is to do for them what God has given you to do for them. It is a word of vocation. Thus Christ's love for us is seen in His journey to Jerusalem and His assent to heal us by His wounds, to save us by His suffering and bloody death.

Did Christ's love in action ever run contrary to His feelings? His agonized cry in Gethsemane answers *yes*: "Father, if You are willing, remove this cup from Me." Did anything, even Jesus' exceeding sorrow and agony, keep Him from giving us perfect love? His continued prayer in Gethsemane answers *no*: "Nevertheless, not My will, but Yours, be done" (Luke 22:42 ESV).

The moment we are born, love of self is the deadly enemy of love for our neighbor. As Luther said, our hearts are by nature curved in on themselves. This self-love proceeds from the sin of unbelief, for we do not fear and love and trust in God above all things. Therefore we do not love our neighbor as ourselves.

Love is from God (1 John 4:7). God's love for us is revealed in the sending of His Son so we might live through Him (1 John 4:9). That is why God gave us a Sacrament of love wherein Christ comes to us. He comes with the intense love of a bridegroom for his bride. Christ comes to give her all that He is and has, presenting her before Him without spot or blemish. Therefore nourished by the banquet He has prepared, His bride prays:

> We give thanks to you, almighty God, that you have refreshed us through this salutary gift, and we implore you that of your mercy you would strengthen us through the same in faith toward you and in fervent love toward one another; through Jesus Christ, your Son, our

Lord, who lives and reigns with You and the Holy Spirit, one God, now and forever. Amen.[64]

This love for the neighbor cannot be spiritualized into general feelings of love as we hear in popular songs. This love cannot be removed from our vocation in life and the concrete relationships God has given us. Who can calculate the pain and suffering caused by human hearts grabbing for the love of someone (including self) or of something while turning from God's revealed love for us and His will for us to love our neighbor in thought, word, and deed? Abortion, euthanasia, sexual immorality, unhappy marriages, broken homes, corporate greed, lazy workers, neglect of children, disobedience to parents, lack of doctrinal study by pastors, greed, gossip, omission of proportionate gifts for the work of Christ's church, churches in strife, churches at peace with false doctrine, forsaking weekly worship, not praying for the needs of our neighbor, and charity not given to the poor all proceed from self-love.[65]

Concerning this concrete love for our neighbor, the Lutheran Confessions state that "we never love as much as we should. Indeed, we do not love at all until our hearts truly realize that the forgiveness of sins has been given to us."[66] In other words, our love doesn't cause God's forgiveness of us but flows from it. And such forgiveness is what Jesus comes to bestow in Holy Communion.

Of the relationship between the Lord's Supper and love evidenced in sharing the misfortunes of the fellowship, Luther wrote:

> Here your heart must go out in love and learn that this is a sacrament of love. As love and support are given you, you in turn must render love and support to Christ in his needy ones. You must feel with sorrow all the dishonor done to Christ in his holy Word, all the misery of Christendom, all the unjust suffering of the innocent,

with which the world is everywhere filled to overflowing. You must fight, work, pray, and—if you cannot do more—have heartfelt sympathy. See, this is what it means to bear in your turn the misfortune and adversity of Christ and his saints. Here the saying of Paul is fulfilled, "Bear one another's burdens, and so fulfil the law of Christ" [Gal. 6:2].[67]

For Luther, concern for doctrine, for injury done to Christ in His holy Word, is at the heart of the love we are to give Christ in His needy ones. In other words, we don't love our neighbor by compromising the truth of God's written Word. Love is not doing what feels loving to us or to society but doing and acting in keeping with God's holy Word.

Believing the love that God has for us (1 John 4:16), God grant us love for our neighbor, a love that walks according to His commandments (2 John 6). It is important to note that this love does not originate from within us but that it comes from outside of us. As Harold Senkbeil writes:

> [T]his love is more than skin deep. The love which prompts us to thankful service to others is not our own. It is the very love of Christ Himself, continually extended and dispensed to us in the proclamation of His Word and the administration of His Sacraments. Every deed of kindness, each work of love which you and I do for our fellow man is not our own. It is the work which Jesus Christ does, using us as His instruments. St. Paul describes it this way: *I have been crucified with Christ and I no longer live, but Christ lives in me. The life I live in the body, I live by faith in the Son of God, who loved me and gave himself for me* (Gal. 2:20).[68]

> May God bestow on us his grace and favor
> To please him with our behavior
> And live together here in love and union
> Nor repent this blest communion.

O Lord, have mercy!
Let not your good Spirit forsake us,
But that heav'nly-minded he make us;
Give your Church, Lord, to see
Days of peace and unity.
O Lord, have mercy![69]

Discussion Questions

1. What is the highest way to worship God?

2. List the benefits of the eating and drinking of the Lord's Supper as enumerated in *Luther's Small Catechism*.

3. Describe your reaction to the examination questions on pp. 186–88 that are related to the Ten Commandments. How would these questions help you to prepare for reception of the Lord's Supper?

4. Describe the "blessed exchange" that Luther indicates occurs in the Lord's Supper. What becomes yours? What becomes Christ's?

5. Explain the relationship between the Holy of Holies in the Old Testament and the presence of the risen Christ in Holy Communion in the New Testament.

6. Discuss what it means that the altar (the Lord's Supper) is the closest meeting point between us and our loved ones who have died in the faith.

7. How is the word *eucharist* especially appropriate as another name for Holy Communion? How do the Lutheran Confessions describe the word?

8. How did Luther interpret the phrase "This do in remembrance of Me"?

9. Martin Chemnitz, C. F. W. Walther, and the Lutheran Confessions agree that "This do in remembrance of Me" means _____. Discuss the difference between the following:

- Jesus saying, "Think about Me. Remember what I did for you in the past. Don't forget Me as you do this meal for Me."
- Jesus saying, "Receive My body and blood in faith, believing that I am present in this Meal for you and doing just as I promised I would do."
10. What does C. F. W. Walther mean when he describes the Lord's Supper as "the pulpit of the laity"? Discuss.
11. In what sense does Jesus "preach" in the Sacrament? Discuss the implications of the fact that after Pentecost, in the early church, and in Reformation churches, the pulpit of the laity was present with the same frequency as the pulpit from which the pastor preached.
12. Describe the scriptural teaching of "love." Describe some the actions that proceed from self-love. What is the relationship between the Lord's Supper and love given to the neighbor? How does self-love elevate other concerns over the truth of God's words?

O Lord open my lips, And my mouth shall show forth
Your praise. (Psalm 51:15)

chapter eight
These Things Matter

Through years of conversations with pastors and with laity concerning the recovery of weekly Communion, some topics have arisen with regularity. In this chapter, the following topics are addressed: the liturgy, the sermon, closed Communion, preparation for Communion, as well as practical notes on the distribution of and the disposing of the elements.

The Liturgy

Martin Luther said that the service in common use at the time of the Reformation traced its way back to genuine Christian beginnings, as did the office of preaching. He acknowledged that both had become corrupted, however. In harmony with the Gospel that the Reformation was then recovering, he concluded: "As we do not on that account abolish the office of preaching, but aim to restore it again to its right and proper place, so it is not our intention to do away with the service, but to restore it again to its rightful use."[1]

What, then, is the rightful use of the sermon and the liturgy? What is it that Luther sought to restore? At the foundation of that understanding is the certainty that the worship of God is not something man created from his imagination. The worship of God in a specific place with special care and the best of materials is clearly revealed in the Old Testament (Exodus 25–31, 45–40; 1 Kings 6–8; 1 Chronicles 28–29). According to William Schmelder, "[w]hat should be especially noted is that the concept did not originate with man—making a house and inviting God to occupy it—but with the directive of God to build, because He wishes to be present in the midst of His people."[2]

The tabernacle of God's presence and the temple where He dwelt are now fulfilled in the body of Jesus Christ. The physical rituals of sacrifice through which God interacted with His Old Testament people have been fulfilled by the advent of Christ. "We are not Israelites longing for the first advent of Christ, nor do we worship God with animal sacrifices at the temple in Jerusalem. Rather, through the Word and Meal of Christ, we are involved in the liturgy performed together with the angels in the heavenly sanctuary," writes John Kleinig.[3] This is how the Lord is now present on this earth *for us*. The rightful use of the liturgy and sermon will flow from the recognition of what Christ is present to do and our response to His giving.

It is important to note that the liturgy is composed of phrases and images and verses taken directly from Scripture. That is, it is biblical, saying back to God what He has said to us in His written Word. William Schmelder writes:

> But the liturgy is scriptural in a second and, in a sense, more important manner. That is, the liturgy proclaims that which is central in the Bible: that man is justified by grace for Christ's sake through faith. What we do

together in worship, and that includes hymns and prayers as well, must be in conformity with what Scripture teaches, and must highlight the central teaching of Scriptures.[4]

The LCMS possesses a treasure that expresses this truth in the introduction to its hymnal *Lutheran Worship*:

> The rhythm of our worship is from him to us, and then from us back to him. He gives his gifts, and together we receive and extol them. We build one another up as we speak to one another in psalms, hymns, and spiritual songs. Our Lord gives us his body to eat and his blood to drink. Finally his blessing moves us out into our calling, where his gifts have their fruition. How best to do this we may learn from his Word and from the way his Word has prompted his worship through the centuries. We are heirs of an astonishingly rich tradition.[5]

The right understanding of the liturgy recognizes that it

- is not mere rites and ceremonies;
- is not unintelligible (though it must be taught and learned);
- is not a matter of entertainment and experimentation;
- is not able to be appreciated by the unbelieving world;
- is not composed of disconnected ideas about God;
- is not a German form but largely biblical and transcultural

On the other hand, the right understanding of the liturgy recognizes that it

- is rooted in Old Testament worship that is fulfilled in Christ;
- is communion with the risen Lord who is present to teach us and to feed us His true body and true blood;
- is otherworldly and transcends human culture;
- is a confession of the faith;
- is a matter of life and death;

- is the place of closest contact with those who have died in the faith;
- is not completed with the final "Amen" but continues in daily vocation and life.

Wilhelm Loehe, a German pastor who exercised great influence on the early years of the LCMS through the missionaries he sent to the United States, said that we should not be afraid to teach the liturgy: "It is taught like the catechism; it can become mere lip service, just as the catechism can, but it does not need to be."[6]

In my youth, Sunday worship was taken from the hymnal and made use of the creeds and ancient prayers. When Matins was used, we sang what Luther called the clearest confession of faith in song: the Te Deum Laudamus. My parents insisted that not a week pass without worship, even when we were traveling. I memorized[7] the Third Commandment and its meaning, along with all the chief parts of Luther's Small Catechism. This was all good and right, but the Lord's Supper was served only four times a year when I was young, and as I grew older, the practice increased only to once a month. The doctrinal teachings of that day didn't state as clearly that Luther and the reformers celebrated the Lord's Supper every Sunday, that it was not an appendage or an occasional extra.

Coupled with the occasional presence of the Sacrament was a lack of understanding concerning the true presence of the risen Christ to teach us and to feed us. As a child and young man, I had the sense of gathering in God's house to hear God's Word as it was read and preached. This was to be done reverently and respectfully. But I understood that as hearing about what Jesus once did and less as His presence in our midst to work His New Testament miracles in that very service. I didn't understand that it was the Word Incarnate who was the real preacher. And I didn't understand that the Word made flesh was the real celebrant in the occasional offering of Holy Communion. In other words, Christ-centered worship meant words about what He had done in the past or the help His Word could give with problems in the present. But Christ-centered worship did not mean words spoken by and gifts given by the risen Christ Himself, who now came among His gathered people.

Such worship is unlike anything else in the world; it is otherworldly yet full of meaning for daily life in this world. Richard Eyer writes:

> Worshiping God as He has called us to worship Him does not come naturally to us. By nature we worship self, not God. By nature we hide from God as did Adam and Eve in the Garden of Eden. Learning to worship God is an act of God's grace performed on us by the Holy Spirit. As parents and as members of the body of Christ, the church, we need to teach our children how to worship God and not leave it up to the tastes, trends, and inclinations of human nature.[8]

Worship always has liturgy, that is, worship always takes some form. Understanding who is present, what God is doing, and receiving His gifts in faith will determine whether it is God's form or man's form. Worship through the ages has not changed from generation to generation based upon the whims of the current culture. What change has occurred through the centuries has been gradual change in particulars, not change in substance. Eyer notes that "[t]here is no such thing as worship without liturgy, for liturgy is ritual, and human beings always follow ritual. Ritual, liturgy, is merely the habit of form. The only question is whether that ritual will be given us by God or made up by us according to our tastes. Liturgy conveys the essence and meaning of our worship of God."[9]

Early in my service as a pastor, I sometimes felt a need to change something in the liturgy in an attempt to make it more relevant. Another pastor who was aware of this asked me if I understood why the church had used a consistent liturgy through the centuries. At the time, I had to admit that I did not know much about the theology of worship. This pastor asked me if it wouldn't be better to understand what God had given us before attempting to modify it. It was a fair and loving question that inspired me to study and understand much of what is expressed here. I also believe that it is a question that goes hand in hand with recovering the opportunity to receive the Lord's Supper when we come for weekly worship.

The Sermon

In the introduction to this book, I noted that recovering weekly Communion does not elevate the Sacrament over the sermon, a frequently expressed concern. It may be helpful to remember that Luther did not see weekly Communion as a threat to the sermon. Rather, "[Luther] restored preaching to balance the offering of Word and Sacrament to God's gathered guests, retaining the celebration of the Sacrament of the Altar as a weekly, and in some locales, as a daily practice. This was not a reformation as much as a restoration of Holy Communion to God's gathered guests."[10] The following thoughts on the sermon are included to help understand this balance in recovering weekly Communion.

"And He began to say to them, 'Today this Scripture is fulfilled in your hearing' " (Luke 4:21). Jesus spoke these words in the synagogue of his hometown of Nazareth. He had quoted Isaiah's prophecy that the Messiah would preach the Gospel to the poor and proclaim release to the captives and recovery of sight to the blind, to set free those broken in pieces, and to proclaim the year of the Lord's favor (Isaiah 61). Then Jesus said: "Today this Scripture is fulfilled in your hearing." The tense of the word *fulfilled* means it is done and it continues as done. In other words, Jesus claimed to be the Messiah and claimed that His preached Word did what it says.

The Messiah did not come to proclaim earthly success and political power. The Messiah did come to proclaim release from sins and the binding up of the brokenhearted. When Jesus is present and preaching, there is release from sin and its binding and broken consequences. Everything depends upon Him, His presence, His proclamation. That's how the day of God's favor, the kingdom of God, comes to us—through our ears from Him.

That is why it is essential to understand the presence of Christ in the proclaimed Word and administered Sacraments. When Jesus sent out His apostles, He said to them, "He who hears you hears Me, he who rejects you rejects Me, and he who rejects Me rejects Him who sent Me" (Luke 10:16). The work of the office to which this text applies is "to preach the gospel, to forgive sin, to judge doctrine and reject doctrine that is contrary to the gospel, and to exclude from the Christian community the ungodly whose ungodly life is manifest—not with human power but with God's Word alone."[11] Speaking of called ministers and Jesus' words in Luke 10:16, the Lutheran Confessions also say:

> [T]hey represent the person of Christ on account of the call of the church and do not represent their own persons, as Christ himself testifies [Luke 10:16], "Whoever listens to you listens to me." When they offer the Word of Christ or the sacraments, they offer them in the stead and place of Christ. The words of Christ teach us this so that we are not offended by the unworthiness of ministers.[12]

In the Divine Service, then, the hearers do not come simply to hear a preacher. They come to meet with the risen Christ, who comes to teach them and to feed them. As William Schmelder writes:

> The preacher acts in Christ's stead, as he does at Holy Baptism where Christ is the true Baptizer, at confession where the word of absolution is as valid and certain in

heaven also as if Christ our dear Lord dealt with us Himself, at the Eucharist where Christ is the true Celebrant, the true Host who invites and gives His body and blood, so in the pulpit Christ is the true Preacher and the One being preached.[13]

In the sermon, Christ continues to proclaim the Good News to the poor and release for the captives. He is truly present, and He comes to make a blessed exchange. What He began to do and teach before His ascension (Acts 1:1), He continues to do now. He still brings the day of God's favor to the people in their ears, in the hearing of His Word, for faith comes by hearing (Romans 10:17). And as Jesus said, "He who hears you hears Me" (Luke 10:16).

Luther himself called the preached Word the living voice of the Gospel. To him, when the preacher stood in the pulpit, he was an oracle of God and revealer of the divine mysteries of the faith.[14] The bond between the mystery of the preached Word and the mystery of the visible Word, the Lord's Supper, was so strong for Luther that he could say: "The sermon ought to be nothing else than the proclamation of this testament. But who can hear it if nobody preaches it?"[15] This does not mean that one should mechanically refer to the Lord's Supper in each sermon or in the same way each week. A report is given of one woman who was asked if it was true that her pastor always referred to the Lord's Supper in the sermon.

[H]er response was as follows: "Yes, that's how we know he's almost over." In this case, while the pastor intended for his proclamation to invite hearers to God's gracious work in the Sacrament of the Altar, his formulaic and stereotypical approach invited one parishioner to look at her watch instead. For her, these words were a signal that the sermon was over, not that the feast would begin. . . . Evangelical proclamation is not the formulaic repetition of Law and Gospel vocables at certain points in the sermon, but a living proclamation of God's gracious work among his people that, like the text itself, varies in vocables from Sunday to Sunday.[16]

What Luther did mean is that "the sermon was to present Christ's suffering, death and resurrection as a present reality offered through faith alone, not as a long-past example to be followed by those who feared the law."[17] According to Gustaf Wingren, "[p]reaching is not just talk about a Christ of the past, but is a mouth through which the Christ of the present offers us life today."[18]

The breaking of the bread with the Emmaus disciples was the place in which the risen Christ was recognized on the day of His resurrection. Today, Jesus leads us to recognize His presence and receive Him as we eat His body and drink His blood. Christ's teaching and His feeding go hand in hand. On the day of His resurrection, the teaching came first and set hearts to burning. So today in the Divine Service, the Word comes before the Sacrament. In other words, preaching makes sense out of what is happening as Christ comes to serve His people. The proclamation of Christ is not disconnected from the life-giving provision He is present to bestow. He is present in the readings, recounting God's mighty acts of salvation. The sermon is a summation of the Scripture readings and an extension of the Gospel. The sermon stands under the Creed, confessing the faith that is stated therein. The sermon serves as the turning point to the feast that Christ has come to serve.

The sermon is not simply a lecture about Jesus or the Christian life; rather, it is Jesus speaking to His people to give them life. It is not a classroom exercise in education, though it will teach. It is not a pep rally, though it may excite. It is not an attempt to rile people up, though the Law always accuses and agitates. It is not a psychotherapy session aimed at soothing emotions, though the Gospel always comforts. It is not simply a history lesson, though it will be grounded in history. It is primarily the proclamation of Christ as revealed in the text, Christ who is now present in the midst of His gathered people.

> The sermon will therefore encourage and invite the hearers to receive right now what Jesus is present to bestow. That is, not only will the sermon trumpet our Lord's completed work at the cross and open tomb and not only will it trumpet the truth that this blessed release from sin is "for you" (the hearers), but the sermon will also trumpet the presence of the risen Christ to bestow his healing forgiveness in that very service through his appointed means. The sermon will proclaim how the gap between the cross and us sinners is right now, today, bridged in the water of Baptism, in the sacrament of Christ's body and blood, in Holy Absolution, and in the proclamation of the Gospel. The sermon will not merely talk about Christ but speak the very word of Christ through which the Word made flesh is present.[19]

Timothy Quill writes: "To step into the pulpit with the understanding that we are to speak His Word and that His Word bestows what it says is an awesome thing."[20] Words are to be chosen with care because they have authority only if they are God's words. This calls for prayer by the pastor on behalf of the hearers. This calls for prayer by the hearers on behalf of their pastor. Former LCMS President A. L. Barry notes:

> The pastor's sermon must be textual, relevant, meaningful and clearly presented to the people of God . . . our pastors' sermons should reflect the high and holy calling in the Lord that our pastors have to shepherd the flock of God over whom they have been made overseers by the Holy Spirit (Acts 20:28). The people do not attend church to listen to the pastor simply amuse them, or give them a "pep talk", or a psychotherapy session in feeling

better about themselves. The people come to hear a word from God through their pastor's sermon.[21]

Jesus said that repentance and forgiveness of sins should be preached to all nations (Luke 24:47). God's terrible and textual Law is needed. It is true that we are beggars before God. Our sinful nature and the sins that emanate from it must be exposed. Sin, death, and hell are not necessarily felt needs, but they are real needs for which we have no answer.

God's life-giving Gospel is the answer. It is a Gospel so full that it includes not only the blood of Christ but also the anguish of hell that Christ suffered as He bore the full wrath of God as our substitute.[22] By a happy exchange, our gracious God makes us new and comes even now to create clean hearts within us. In the presence of Jesus, receiving His Word of release in faith, we are heirs of God and brothers of Christ.

In Luther's mind, the Gospel was not first a book but a sermon, a church was not a house of writing but a house of speaking, a mouth house. Therefore Holy Scripture existed not primarily to be read or studied, according to Luther, but to be preached. His pulpit became the battlefield of Christ, the center of the service.[23] The battle continues today. That is why the risen Christ continues to come into the midst of His gathered people to teach and feed them.

Preparation for Communion

Both the liturgy and the sermon as discussed previously are closely related to another frequently raised issue concerning weekly Communion: the proper preparation for the Sacrament.

> But let a man examine himself, and so let him eat of that bread and drink of that cup. For he who eats and drinks in an unworthy manner eats and drinks judgment to himself, not discerning the Lord's body. (1 Corinthians 11:28–29)

Who receives this Sacrament worthily?

Fasting and bodily preparation are certainly fine outward training. But that person is truly worthy and well prepared who has faith in these words: "Given and shed for you for the forgiveness of sins."

But anyone who does not believe these words or doubts them is unworthy and unprepared, for the words "for you" require all hearts to believe.[24]

This concern is proper, for the Lord's Supper is not a magical meal that benefits unbelieving hearts *ex opere operato* (simply by doing the deed). Without announcing for Communion, as was done in bygone days, and with the Lord's Supper available every Sunday, what does this mean for being worthy and well prepared to receive this gift? It means those without faith; those living in open impenitence, willfully clinging to sins; and those who have been expelled from the congregation should not be communed. In the Large Catechism and in various other writings, Luther stated these exclusions. His writings about those who denied the presence of the true body and blood of Christ, those who had a different confession, also made it clear that he did not consider them part of his communing congregation.

According to Ernest Bartels, Luther said that "those who commune together should all have the same faith and doctrine."[25] It is the communing congregation, the hearers of the correctly preached Word, that Luther is addressing in his statements in the Large Catechism concerning the Sacrament.[26] Luther's words about individual worthiness to commune must not be taken out of context. They do not imply that pastors and congregations should practice open Communion and welcome worshipers to the altar regardless of the public confession they make by their membership in a church body.

Luther expressed the following concerns for members of congregations who were confessing the same doctrine. He

attacked the errors of the papacy that drove people away from the
Lord's Supper. One of those errors was the universal requirement
of penance and annual communing at Easter.

> But suppose you say, "What if I feel that I am unfit?"
> Answer: This is my struggle as well, especially inherited
> from the old order under the pope when we tortured
> ourselves to become so perfectly pure that God might
> not find the least blemish in us. Because of this we
> became so timid that everyone was thrown into conster-
> nation, saying, "Alas, you are not worthy!" Then nature
> and reason begin to contrast our unworthiness with this
> great and precious blessing, and it appears like a dark
> lantern in contrast to the bright sun, or as manure in
> contrast to jewels; then because they see this, such peo-
> ple will not go to the sacrament and wait until they are
> prepared, until one week passes into another and one
> half-year into yet another. If you choose to fix your eye
> on how good and pure you are, to wait until nothing
> torments you, you will never go.[27]

> We must never regard the sacrament as a harmful thing
> from which we should flee, but as a pure, wholesome,
> soothing medicine that aids you and gives life in both
> soul and body. For where the soul is healed, the body is
> helped as well. Why, then, do we act as if the sacrament
> were a poison that would kill us if we ate of it?[28]

Luther then addressed the matter of our feelings about
worthiness.

> [T]hose who feel their weakness, who are anxious to be
> rid of it and desire help, should regard and use the sacra-
> ment as a precious antidote against the poison in their
> systems. . . . If you are burdened and feel your weakness,
> go joyfully to the sacrament and let yourself be
> refreshed, comforted, and strengthened. For if you wait
> until you are rid of your burden in order to come to the

sacrament purely and worthily, you will have to stay
away from it forever. . . . .Therefore the only ones who
are unworthy are those who do not feel their burdens
nor admit to being sinners.[29]

In other words, if you feel that you are unworthy, you feel correctly. Go joyfully to the Sacrament, and let yourself be helped.
Luther went on to discuss the case of those who cannot feel this
need and do not hunger and thirst for the Sacrament. He directs
them to see if they are still made of flesh and blood and to review
what the Epistle to the Galatians says about the fruits of our sinful flesh. He continues:

For this reason, if you cannot feel the need, at least
believe the Scriptures. They will not lie to you, since they
know your flesh better than you yourself do. . . . [T]he
fact that we do not feel it is all the worse, for it is a sign
that ours is a leprous flesh, which feels nothing although
it rages with disease and gnaws away at itself. As we have
said, even if you are so utterly dead in sin, at least believe
the Scriptures, which pronounce this judgment upon
you. In short, the less you feel your sins and infirmities,
the more reason you have to go to the sacrament and
seek its help and remedy.[30]

In other words, if you don't feel unworthy, if you don't feel
the leprosy of your sin, you have even more reason to go to the
Sacrament and seek its help. This is truly an amazing combination of thoughts regarding our feelings and the reception of the
Lord's Supper! If we feel our weakness and burdens and infirmities, in effect, our unworthiness, we feel rightly. We should come
and let ourselves be helped. If we do not feel our sin and do not
hunger and thirst for the Sacrament, we should also come and
seek its help and remedy. For in such cases our condition is even
worse and more in need of God's help. The key in both instances
is that Luther places the witness of Scripture over the sentiment

of our minds or the emotions of our hearts. About the devil and his lies, Luther writes: "If you could see how many daggers, spears, and arrows are aimed at you every moment, you would be glad to come to the sacrament as often as you can."[31]

The Greek text in 1 Corinthians 11 does not speak of eating unworthily in a general way; rather, it speaks of it in a way of unbelief concerning what Christ gives there. It states that anyone who eats and drinks without discerning the body of the Son of God eats and drinks judgment on himself. That is the scriptural truth Luther was conveying about the bodily eating and drinking that takes place in the Sacrament. He concludes his final question concerning the Sacrament of the Altar in his Small Catechism in this manner: "But that person is truly worthy and well prepared who has faith in these words: "Given and shed for you for the forgiveness of sins."[32] For those Luther is addressing, for the hearers of the apostolic word in the congregation, faith in the treasure that God offers in these words is the sum total of a Christian's preparation.

More than fifty years later, another summary of worthiness was stated in the Formula of Concord. Again, it must be noted that this writing is meant to contend for the pure teaching of the Gospel and the administration of the Sacraments in conformity with the divine Word. This document was written to combat the threat of open Communion with those of other confessions and the harmful effect of errant teaching. Its gracious invitation is to those weak in faith who have been purely taught.

> The true and worthy guests, for whom this precious sacrament above all was instituted and established, are the Christians who are weak in faith, fragile and troubled, who are terrified in their hearts by the immensity and number of their sins and think that they are not worthy of this precious treasure and of the benefits of Christ because of their great impurity, who feel the

weakness of their faith and deplore it, and who desire with all their heart to serve God with a stronger, more resolute faith and pure obedience. As Christ says, "Come to me, all you that are weary and are carrying heavy burdens, and I will give you rest" [Matt. 11:28], and, "Those who are well have no need of a physician, but those who are sick" [Matt. 9:12]. . . . Moreover, this worthiness consists not in a greater or lesser weakness or strength of faith, but rather in the merit of Christ, which the troubled father with his weak faith (Mark 9[:24]) possessed, just as did Abraham, Paul and others who have a resolute, strong faith.[33]

Concerning worthiness to commune, it is important to state that the gift of private confession and absolution has often been linked with the gift of Holy Communion in the life of the church. The most notorious connection was the 1216 papal decree that all the faithful must confess their sins once a year at Easter and also must take the Lord's Supper at Easter. This type of legalism is not in keeping with these gracious gifts of Jesus. Because of such abuses under Rome's system of penance, Lutheran reaction often included an aversion to using the gift of Holy Absolution. This is a great loss because the focus of confession and absolution is on God's gift of absolution, not on the complete enumeration of sins. Therefore the Augsburg Confession states clearly: "Concerning confession it is taught that private absolution should be retained and not abolished. However, it is not necessary to enumerate all misdeeds and sins, since it is not possible to do so. Psalm 19[:12]: 'But who can detect their errors?' "[34] The Augsburg Confession also states:

Confession has not been abolished in our churches. For it is not customary to administer the body of Christ except to those who have been previously examined and absolved. The people are also most diligently taught concerning faith in the word of absolution, about which there was a great silence before now. People are taught to make the most of absolution because it is the voice of God and is pronounced following the command of God. The power of the keys is praised and remembered for bringing such great consolation to terrified consciences, both because God requires faith so that we believe such absolution as God's own voice resounding from heaven and because this faith truly obtains and receives the forgiveness of sins.[35]

The sixteenth-century reformers sought to reclaim this Gospel gift that was centered on absolution. Luther once said that an evangelical minister cannot open his mouth without pronouncing absolution. There is no doubt that while Luther stood firmly against any attempt to require confession, he nonetheless highly treasured it and used it as a consoling and strengthening gift of God and instructed others for such use.

In the seventeenth century, private confession developed an obligatory nature in the Lutheran Church, and this had a negative effect on the frequency of offering the Lord's Supper. As Toivo Harjunpaa observes: "The pastor became more like a judge, or a strict schoolmaster, than a sympathetic shepherd of souls . . . the number of communion Sundays began to drop considerably from what it had been in the days of the reformers. The gulf between the clergy and the laity became wider."[36]

Confession and absolution is really a return to our Baptism, a dying and rising to life again. Making it an obligation necessary for the reception of the Lord's Supper is not in keeping with its nature as a gracious gift of God. In the nineteenth century, Walther, speaking of absolution, said that Christ "has ordained a peculiar office, the incumbents of which have nothing else to do than to keep on saying to men what Christ said to the paralytic" in Luke 5:21 and Matthew 9:8, that is, "Your sins are forgiven."

Walther concludes that "[w]e are to proclaim this truth to all our fellow-men."[37]

Aversion to receiving the gift of absolution is not unrelated to a lack of hunger and thirst for the Sacrament of the Altar. Self-examination of personal sin is foundational to both, and this is not our most cherished undertaking. As Ted Kober observes, "[l]eft to our own vices, we slip into believing that our own sins are not as bad as others. Self-justification leads to a myriad of other sins, not the least of which is judging."[38] Such self-justification also leads to excusing ourselves, conflict in relationships, anxiety, and a host of other sinful reactions.

Our sinful hearts are such that they can swing from confident pride to crushing despair, from carefree pleasure-seeking to anxious depression, from worldly idolatry to spiritual apathy, from foolish boldness to fearful inactivity. Our sinful hearts run away from the Lord, who lovingly pursues us with the truth about ourselves and the treasures of His forgiving love. Harold Senkbeil writes:

> It's fairly easy to say the words *I am a sinner*. It is quite another thing to confess our sin; that is, to lay it out openly before God in all of its ugliness. That's why we tend to hide our sin. Like Adam and Eve, we hide from God in shame. *"I was afraid,"* Adam said, *"because I was naked; and so I hid myself."* But God is not ashamed of the nakedness of our sin. Remember, Jesus Christ joyfully embraced our shame on the cross so that He could remove it forever. And so there is no shame in sin confessed, no matter how ugly it may be. The only real shame is in trying to live with all that ugliness inside.[39]

Confession and absolution is not a substitute for the Sacrament of the Altar nor is it in competition with the Sacrament of the Altar. It is also not an obligation that makes one worthy to receive the Sacrament of the Altar. It is grace upon grace from the

God of grace. It is God's good and beautiful and healing gift of forgiveness spoken to us personally. As *Luther's Small Catechism* asks: "What is Confession? Confession has two parts. First, that we confess our sins, and second, that we receive absolution, that is, forgiveness, from the pastor as from God Himself, not doubting, but firmly believing that by it our sins are forgiven before God in heaven."[40] Hermann Sasse says: "Against the foolish objection that already before the Communion we receive forgiveness in the absolution Luther has already said what is necessary. We cannot receive forgiveness often enough and should receive it in all kinds of ways, for we remain sinners until we die, even though in faith we are righteous."[41]

As expressed earlier, Luther took seriously the recognition of our sinfulness. The Christian questions and answers in the Small Catechism were prepared for assistance in self-examination for Holy Communion.[42] These questions do not allow room for extenuating circumstances as an excuse for sin. Those who have been instructed in the Small Catechism also know how to consider God's Law. But what should be done if one has not set aside time for such questions or for thoughtful prayer about the Sacrament? If one is able to be present in the Divine Service, can one yet be prepared to commune?

The sermon should certainly be central to such preparation, for therein God's Law is at work to uncover our sin, to shake comfortableness in our own goodness and our own strength, giving nothing and demanding total love and fear and trust in God. Therein God's Gospel is also at work as total gift, asking nothing and giving the undeserved love of God through the merits of Christ. Luther writes: "He is truly worthy and well prepared who has faith in these words."[43] Because faith comes by hearing and hearing through the speaking of Christ (Romans 10:17), the sermon is intimately connected to Communion and our preparation for it. The risen Christ has come into our midst to teach us of Himself, to set our hearts burning, and to feed us with His very body and very blood. Preparation for receiving His Meal cannot be separated from hearing His Word.

Just as the Lutheran Confessions clearly state, "Luther consistently regarded the minister of the word and sacraments as speaking and acting in the place of Christ, especially where the forgiveness of sins is being proclaimed."[44] For that reason, he also found certainty and delight in an act of preparing for Holy Communion that we might not normally consider as preparation. This act occurs in the liturgy as the Pax Domini, "the peace of the Lord."

The Pax Domini was the greeting of the risen Christ to His fearful, hiding disciples on the day of His resurrection: "Peace be with you!" (Luke 24:36). As the risen Christ comes into our midst and prepares to serve us His body and blood, the liturgy leads the pastor to say, "The peace of the Lord be with you always." This is to be said facing the people, and Luther regarded it as "a public absolution of the sins of the communicants, the true voice of the gospel announcing remission of sins, and therefore the one and most worthy preparation for the Lord's Table, if faith holds to these words as coming from the mouth of Christ himself."[45]

That is certainly not what we have judged the one and most worthy preparation for Holy Communion. By rejoicing in it, Luther was not disavowing the importance of personal introspection and examination. What he was directing us to do at the heart of our preparation is to examine also what Christ is present in our midst to do. Our unworthiness consists of what we examine within. Our worthiness consists of what we receive from without, bestowed upon us by God's grace.

The following meditation by sixteenth-century theologian Johann Gerhard on preparing for reception of the Sacrament was republished in the April 7, 1891, issue of *The Lutheran Witness*.[46] As these early Lutherans in what was later to become the English

District of the LCMS read it more than one hundred years ago, it is here included in its entirety for your reading.

Serious Preparation before Receiving the Lord's Supper

No common meal, no royal banquet, but the most holy mystery of the body and blood of Christ is placed before us for our consideration. A preparation worthy the feast is therefore most certainly required of us, so as not to find death instead of life, judgment in place of mercy.

The most holy Patriarch, Gen. 18, 2 was conspicuous for the strength of his faith; yet how does he tremble, how fearful is he when once upon a time the Son of God appeared to him in human form and made known His intention of destroying Sodom! Here is the Lamb of God set before us not to look at, but to taste and eat. When Ussiah rashly approached the ark of the covenant, he was at once smitten with leprosy by the Lord, 2 Chron. 26, 16: hence what wonder that he eats and drinks damnation to himself, I Cor. 11, 29 who eats of this bread and drinks of this wine unworthily? Here indeed is the ark of the covenant, prefigured by that old one. The apostle teaches the true preparation in a word: "Let a man," says he, "examine himself and so let him eat of that bread and drink of that cup," 1 Cor. 11, 28. But since every examination of divine things must be done according to the rule of the Holy Scriptures, so also, for the same reason, this one which St. Paul requires.

Let us therefore in the first place consider our weakness. What is man? Dust and ashes, Gen. 18,27: Out of earth we are born, of the earth, we live, to earth we return. What is man? Stinking seed, a vessel of corruption, food for worms. Man is born to labor, not to honor. Man born of woman, and hence with guilt, John 14, 1 lives but a short time and therefore in fear; filled with many sorrows, and therefore in tears; filled indeed with many sorrows, because they at once touch his body and his soul. Man knows not his beginning, he knows not his end. As a summer plant we live but a short time, yet his short life has pains and labor by no means short.

Let us in the second place consider our unworthiness. In respect to the Creator every creature is indeed only a shadow, Ps. 39, 7, a dream, yea, nothing, therefore man also. But for more and graver reasons is man unworthy: for with sins he has offended his Creator. By nature and in essence God is just: therefore His nature and essence are provoked by sins. What are we stubbles against that consuming fire! Deut. 4, 24. How shall our detestable works stand? How shall our iniquities which Thou hast set before Thee, and our secret sins which Thou hast set in the light of Thy countenance? Ps. 90.8. God is infinite and always the same, of infinite justice and of infinite anger; as in all His works, so also in His anger, justice and punishments is God great and admirable. He who spared not His own Son, will He spare the work of His hands? He who spared not the most holy, will He spare the unprofitable servant? So odious is sin in God's sight that He punishes it in the most beloved, as such is patent in the case of Lucifer, the chief of angels.

But our examination must not be confined to ourselves alone, but extend also to this bread of blessing, which is the communion of the body of Christ; then the true fountain of grace and the inexhaustible source of mercy will appear; surely the Lord can not neglect us whom He makes partakers of His flesh: for who ever yet hated his own flesh? Eph. 5, 29. This holy banquet will change our souls; this most heavenly banquet will make us children of God, until we are at length made partakers of the future felicity "where we shall comprehend God wholly and alone and be wholly like God;" what we have here in faith and in mystery we shall there possess in fruition and openly. And our very bodies will attain to this dignity that in them we may see God face to face, 1 Cor. 13, 12, which even now are the temples of the Holy Spirit and are sanctified and enlivened by the body and blood of Christ dwelling in us. This most holy medicine heals all wounds of sin: this enlivening flesh overcomes every mortal sin: this is the most sacred seal of the divine promise which we may produce at the judgment bar of God: this pledge given us, we may confidently glory in our eternal life. If Christ's body and blood is given us, then surely also all benefits acquired by that most holy body and that blessed blood: how can He who has given us the greater, deny us the lesser? "He that delivered up his own son for us, how shall he not with him also freely give us all things?" Rom. 8, 32.

The bride may therefore rejoice; for the time is near when she will be called to the marriage of the Lamb, Rev. 19, 7. Let her clothe herself in her richest apparel; let her put on her wedding garment, lest she be found naked, Matth. 22, 12. That garment is the righteousness of the Bridegroom which we put on in baptism: far from being the wedding garment, our righteousness is but as a filthy rag, Isa. 64, 6. Let us therefore beware of bringing to this most solemn marriage the most abominable and filthy garments of our works; may God clothe us, that we may not be found naked, 2 Cor. 5, 3.

Note that Gerhard directs the start of examination of ourselves not to sins (deeds and misdeeds) but to original sin, that which infects us, the death that hangs over us, our wasting away in this fleeting life. That is a crucial starting point, for it is the fountain from which all our sins and troubles flow. But notice also, like Luther in referring us to the Pax Domini as part of our preparation, Gerhard directs us to examine Christ, who is present in that service to unite Himself with us. Examination includes sorrow, for the sin that infects us goes over our heads. But examination also includes delight, for our Savior's love overrules our sin. As Gerhard says: "The Bride may therefore rejoice!" As we read in Revelation: "Let us be glad and rejoice and give Him glory, for the marriage of the Lamb has come, and His wife has made herself ready" (19:7).

There is no substitute foundation for the examination of ourselves and our Savior than God's revelation. Instruction in His holy Word through preaching and through the study of the Small Catechism are foundational to this examination. To that end, confirmation should never be viewed as graduation. To that end, the Small Catechism should not be viewed as a block of material to be learned so we are worthy to commune. Rather, the Small Catechism is a prayer book or a handbook that teaches us how to confess our sins and how to pray. While instruction for confirmation should not be limited to the eighth grade, such a focused period of instruction as has historically preceded confirmation should not be discarded. The concern during this period should not be the memorization of material but the learning by heart of the treasures of God's own giving for use in all of life. Luther's own approach to the age at which children can commune was earlier than has been our practice in the United States.[47]

Closed Communion

Let a man so consider us as servants of Christ and stewards of the mysteries of God. (1 Corinthians 4:1)

In her earliest centuries, the church received God's Word and Sacrament each week while showing careful concern for those who communed. All were invited to hear the Word, but not all were invited to receive the Sacrament. Numerous conversations about recovering weekly Communion in our day have also shown the need for recovering an understanding of the scriptural and loving nature of closed Communion. Because of its loving nature, closed Communion should not at all discourage the recovery of weekly Communion.

Closed Communion is not a statement that we are better than someone else on some scale of religious goodness. Nor is it a denial that there are true Christians in other confessions of the faith. Rather, it is the loving statement that we are in the same distress as everyone else, dying sinners in a dying world, and that our only hope is Jesus and His words of life (John 14:24; 15:7). Closed Communion is the historic practice of the church. Only as the truthfulness of Scripture came to be questioned and denied in such a broad manner in the twentieth century has open Communion become prevalent.

When Luther wrote his Table of Duties in the Small Catechism, the first two offices that he set forth were pastors and hearers. Among other things, a pastor is to be the husband of one wife and able to teach (1 Timothy 3:2–4). He is not to be a recent convert (1 Timothy 3:6). He must hold firmly to the trustworthy message as it has been taught so he is able to encourage and refute with sound doctrine (Titus 1:9). Among other things, hearers are to share all good things with their pastors (Galatians 6:6–7), consider pastors worthy of double honor (1 Timothy 5:17–18), hold them in the highest regard in love because of their work (1 Thessalonians 5:12–13), and obey them as men who must give an account (Hebrews 13:17).[48]

The account that a pastor must give is directly related to the preaching and teaching he does for his hearers, the congregation through whom Christ has called him to serve as pastor. As St. Paul wrote to the young pastor Timothy: "Take heed to yourself and to the doctrine. Continue in them, for in doing this you will save both yourself and those who hear you" (1 Timothy 4:16). Those who hear the preached Word from their pastor are also those who receive the visible Word, the Lord's Supper, from their pastor. In this gift Christ also is speaking to His church.

Just like after Pentecost, preaching the apostles' doctrine goes hand in hand with administering the Lord's Supper. The Lutheran Confessions clearly state: "The church is the assembly of saints in which the gospel is taught purely and the sacraments are administered rightly."[49] To administer the Lord's Supper to those living in open, unrepentant sin would not be in conformity with the divine Word. To administer the Lord's Supper to those who publicly deny the apostles' doctrine would not be in conformity with the divine Word. To administer the Lord's Supper to those who do not discern the body and blood of Christ in the Sacrament would not be in conformity with the divine Word. According to Ernest Bartels, "[i]n 1523 Luther wrote a letter to a church at Frankfurt am Main warning them not to commune other Protestants who denied the sacramental union of Christ's body and blood in the Lord's Supper. He wrote that it terrified him to hear that both those who accepted the doctrine of the sacramental union and those who denied it were allowed to receive 'one and the same Sacrament' at a Lutheran altar."[50]

Salvation of the hearers, which is directly linked to the Word that is taught, cannot be separated from the Sacrament that is to be administered in conformity with that Word. Therefore open Communion is not in keeping with the vocation to which Christ calls pastors. This aspect of a pastor's vocation is clearly seen in the Lutheran Confessions. Even as the Augsburg Confession extols the Lord's Supper and states that no novelty has been introduced, it also bears positive witness to the pastor's responsibility to invite or forbid reception of the Sacrament.[51]

Raymond Hartwig highlights the specific responsibility of the pastor in this regard by explaining the Latin rendering of Article V of the Augsburg Confession. This article sets forth the ministry of teaching the Gospel and administering the Sacraments: "Here the Latin word . . . is used with its meaning of 'offering with the hand,' this versus another word that might have been used . . . meaning to 'administer' in only general terms. Our Lutheran fathers understood the careful nature of the Office of the Ministry."[52] The directions or rubrics in the *Lutheran Worship Altar Book* also express a similar understanding of the pastoral office and admission to the Lord's Supper: "Since the administration of the Lord's body is the decisive act of admission to the sacrament, the presiding minister, as the responsible minister of the sacrament, distributes the body of the Lord. The assisting minister(s) may distribute the blood."[53]

As a steward of the mysteries of Christ (1 Corinthians 4:1), a pastor should not administer the Sacrament to someone who is living in continuous, open, unrepentant sin. To commune such individuals as unworthy communicants (1 Corinthians 11:28–29) would be to aid them in receiving God's judgment. Nor should a pastor administer Communion to someone who belongs to a church body whose public teachings have departed from the apostles' doctrine. This would violate confessional unity (Acts 2:42).[54] To separate devotion to the Lord's Supper from devotion to the apostles' doctrine is contrary to the leading of the Holy Spirit after Pentecost.

Individual Christians represent the confession of the church body to which they have promised their loyalty. Even as communing at an altar is a mark of the confession of the faith, so also church membership is a mark of the confession of the faith. Paul McCain points out that "[t]he Sacrament of Holy Communion is not simply a personal, individual act. The celebration of Holy Communion is also a public act of confession. In other words, it testifies to our unity in the 'teaching of the Apostles' (cf. Acts 2:42). When you receive the sacrament at a church's altar, you are giving public testimony that you agree with that church's doctrinal position."[55] This truth needs careful and patient explanation in the face of American individualism and the modern consumer-oriented movement among denominations. Jeffrey

Gibbs makes the telling point that the connection between the individual communicant and other members of the body communing is carried in the word *participation* in 1 Corinthians 10:16. He adds:

> To speak of "individuals" communing with their Lord in the Eucharist can lead to a serious misunderstanding. For the participation in Christ's body and blood through eating and drinking, necessarily involves the individual with those whom he or she is communing. This Paul explicitly states in verse 17—"Because there is one bread we the many are one body, for we all share from the one bread."[56]

When teachings of church bodies depart from Scripture, there is danger to one's life in Christ. This affects Communion fellowship. While there may be an emergency or crisis circumstance in which pastoral discretion is called for, such a circumstance would be a loving exception to the scriptural and historic practice of closed Communion followed each week in the Divine Service.

The phrase "close Communion" came into Lutheran usage from Baptist debates concerning admission to Communion. The term appeared in Lutheran publications from 1900 to 1911, then fell out of sight until recent decades.[57] Its original Lutheran usage meant Communion overseen by the pastor and offered to those who confessed the faith taught at that altar, which continues the historic practice of the church. In recent decades, some have shifted the meaning of *close* to "nearness" or "similar," thus using the phrase "close Communion" to mean something different from pastoral oversight and unity of confession by those communing. Therefore many pastors and congregations use the phrase "closed Communion" to identify the historic practice.[58] Use of "close Communion" may still indicate the loving historic practice of the church in a congregation if its meaning has not been shifted. This ambiguity caused by recent efforts to redefine the meaning of *close* is why the phrase "closed Communion" has been used in this discussion.

In their faithful practice of closed Communion, pastors and congregations should be encouraged to do so humbly and with heartfelt prayer that the divisions that separate Christians may be healed on the basis of God's Word. They should also be encouraged to do so joyfully, for it is a deeply loving act that has been practiced since the earliest centuries of church history. It is a practice that expresses love for God and His church, a practice adopted by Luther and the reformers. Closed Communion was practiced also by Walther and the founding fathers of the LCMS. Despite the confessional chaos and widespread agreements of disagreement in our time, closed Communion will remain a deeply loving practice until our Lord's return.

Closed Communion does not indicate that a Lutheran congregation wants to bar fellow saints from the blessings of the Sacrament. Nor do Lutherans want to be separatists or set themselves as judges of others. The practice of closed Communion is prompted by love and is born of the heartfelt conviction, on the basis of Scripture, that we must follow Christ's command. This means refusing the Sacrament to those whose belief is unknown to us. It is not loving, in the scriptural sense, to allow a person to do something spiritually harmful. Closed Communion also means that if one is a member of a church body that in its teachings deviates from the teaching of Scripture, the error and problem cannot be minimized by opening the altar to any and all Christians who err in the faith or belong to churches, even those with the name Lutheran, that tolerate and permit error.[59]

Because of its loving nature, the practice of closed Communion should not be an impediment to efforts at recovering the opportunity for every Sunday Communion. Timothy Maschke addresses the concern of what visitors might think if they cannot attend Communion. He writes:

Although a valid concern, the elimination of the Lord's Supper for the sake of visitors misses the purpose of the Sacrament. Normally, guests at one's home do not set the meal schedule or determine the menu. Holy Communion is for the faith-full. It is a statement of what is important for Lutheran believers. Lutheran congregations need to consider how to celebrate the Lord's Supper in ways that clearly express hospitality to the stranger while maintaining the biblical and Lutheran practice of close(d) Communion.[60]

As members inform guests of this practice, as pastors express it to those gathered for worship, it is good to remember that with which we started: Closed Communion is not a statement that we are better than someone else on some scale of religious goodness. Nor is it a denial that there are true Christians in other confessions of the faith. Rather, it is the loving statement that we are in the same situation as everyone else, dying sinners in a dying world, and that our only hope is Jesus and His words of life (John 14:24; 15:7). To downplay or set aside teachings of the Word of God for an outward show of unity would not be in keeping with the loving practice of Jesus or the apostles or Luther or Walther.

Bulletin announcements concerning Communion practice, as well as verbal announcements, should be clearly and caringly done. Following are three helpful examples.

Our congregation is a member of The Lutheran Church —Missouri Synod, a family of congregations who pledge themselves to teach and to believe the same teachings. We believe that we are given a great responsibility to commune only those persons who are members of our confessional fellowship. We want to express our sincere welcome to our guests and assure them that for their spiritual welfare we practice closed Communion.

Guests desiring to learn more about our beliefs are asked to speak with our pastor.[61]

Right from the beginning the Early Church practiced closed Communion. The Lord's Supper was only received in the context of common devotion to the Apostles' Doctrine (Acts 2:42). Closed Communion remains a loving and God-pleasing practice today. It is for this reason that the churches of The Lutheran Church—Missouri Synod have committed themselves to observe this practice. Guests and visitors who desire to commune are kindly asked to speak with the pastor before the service.[62]

Our practice of closed Communion is the historic practice of the church. It is prompted by love, both for God's Word and for God's people. It does not deny that members of other denominations are Christians. Rather, it bows the knee to the Bible's witness that doctrinal unity is central to the common reception of this sacrament. Members of sister LCMS congregations who are communing regularly in their home congregations, and members of our foreign partner churches are invited to commune. Other guests are invited to speak with the pastor after the service about communing with us in the future. We give thanks for your presence and pray that you are blessed by the Word of God that the risen Christ comes among us to speak.[63]

Distributing and Disposing of the Elements

In the same manner He also took the cup after supper, saying, "This cup is the new covenant in My blood." (1 Corinthians 11:25)

Each record of Jesus' institution of the Supper identifies the cup in the singular (Matthew 26; Mark 14; Luke 22; 1 Corinthians 11). This singular cup conveys meaning concerning Holy

Communion as the Sacrament of union with one another.[64] The Lutheran Confessions always refer to a singular cup when quoting Christ's institution and when making other teaching points concerning the Sacrament. This merits careful consideration in our highly individualized, me-first age. Hurt feelings, misunderstandings, and self-centeredness all tend to cloud a full expression of the unity Christ gives us. The unity conveyed by the one cup Jesus used and also that His church used for more than nineteen centuries is not without significance.

The historical novelty of individual glasses came into use in Protestant congregations after grape juice replaced the use of wine. Such a transition from wine to grape juice was especially prominent during Prohibition because it was difficult for Protestants to justify using a banned substance for a religious act that symbolized Jesus' blood. But without the alcoholic content of the wine, there was concern about the spread of infection with the common cup.[65] Lutheran congregations continued to use wine, but they did copy the practice of placing the wine in individual glasses. Thus it was not a scriptural or confessional reason that caused this change in practice; rather, it was an action that imitated the example of American Protestantism and also proceeded from heightened but errant concerns for hygiene among members of LCMS congregations.

Regarding the concern for hygiene, a helpful article in Lee Maxwell's *Altar Guild Manual* states:

> The use of the chalice (or "common cup") used to be universal in Lutheranism but in the last century its use has become infrequent. One of the reasons for replacing it with "individual glasses" was hygiene. People believe (mistakenly) that germs are easily transmitted by using the chalice. However, the combination of the noble metal of the chalice (such as gold or silver) and the alcohol content of the wine makes the possibility for germs to be transmitted almost nonexistent.[66]

The manual then quotes other articles concerning infectious diseases, including AIDS, and the scientific research related to such diseases and the use of the chalice in serving the Lord's Supper. No link has been detected between the transmission of disease and the use of the common chalice. One article relates: "It is through hands that most disease is transmitted . . . And how many hands touch the 'little glasses?' "[67] The article also helps us see the caring concern at work when God's people are not denied the opportunity to receive from the common cup, even when the alternative use of individual cups is also provided in a congregation.

Lutherans are reminded that Luther restored the cup when Roman Catholics had all but eliminated it from the peoples' Communion. He did it because his loyalty was to the command of Christ in the Bible. The use of the common cup was normative until the nineteenth century and was eliminated in those churches in which Communion was not understood to be the body and blood of Christ.[68] The relatively recent adoption of individual cups by LCMS congregations did not indicate agreement with the denial of the body and blood of Christ by others. It occurred more because of the pressure in the surrounding religious culture.

The concerns expressed here must not be interpreted as a prohibition of the use of the individual cups nor a denial that the Lord's Supper is present because they are used. Rather, the concerns expressed are intended to encourage that God's people not be denied the opportunity to receive Christ's blood from the common chalice in the same fashion as their brothers and sisters in the faith have received it through the ages. The underlying thought would be that though some may not wish to receive from the common chalice, others would not be prohibited from doing so.

Norbert Mueller and George Krause, in their book *Pastoral Theology*, summarize this issue, indicating that the common chalice is present and reverently treated even when there are compelling reasons for individual cups to be present: "Communion from the chalice is the historic practice of the evangelical Lutheran church and, while not scripturally mandated, is generally encouraged. The use of individual cups is a 20th century innovation. When there are compelling reasons for the use of individual cups, they should be treated with the same humility and reverence as the chalice and its contents."[69]

There has also been careful concern expressed by our forefathers concerning the disposal of the remaining elements when Holy Communion is finished. The reformers were clear that in any use outside of that given by Christ, the elements were not to be regarded as the Sacrament, such as in processions, reservations, displays for adoration, and so on. But the reformers were equally clear about the reverent treatment of consecrated elements. Wolferinus, a pastor in Eisleben, was in the habit of storing hosts consecrated but not consumed at one celebration along with unconsecrated hosts. Luther's letter to him indicates that all the consecrated elements should be consumed so the Sacrament is not divided. He writes:

> Therefore see to it that if anything is left over of the Sacrament, either some communicants or the priest himself and his assistant receive it, so that it is not only a curate or someone else who drinks what is left over in the chalice, but that he gives it to the others who were also participants in the Body (of Christ), so that you do not appear to divide the Sacrament by a bad example or to treat the sacramental action irreverently.[70]

When Adam Besserer, a young clergyman in Weida, Naumburg, carelessly mixed consecrated and unconsecrated hosts, he was suspended from his duties and placed under arrest pending a ruling from Wittenberg. Luther's written opinion declared that the pastor was guilty not only of negligence but also of despising

God and man by publicly treating consecrated and unconsecrated hosts alike. His judgment was that the pastor should be released from prison but expelled from the churches.[71]

It is important to note that the reformers did not fix a mathematical point at which the real presence began and at which it ended. Their counsel for reverent treatment of consecrated elements, however, did not end with the last communicant who came forward to receive the Sacrament. Rather, their counsel focused on the consumption of all those elements that had been consecrated. Understanding Luther's concerns in the above cases, C. F. W. Walther expresses similar care: "If something remains of the consecrated elements, the wine should be drunk by the communicants, the elders, etc., perhaps in the sacristy. By no means is it to be mixed again with unconsecrated wine."[72] If remaining elements are to be taken to the sick, they are kept separate from unconsecrated elements, treated reverently, and consecrated again as they are served to the sick. This reverent treatment, of course, multiplies the work significantly when individual glasses are used. Just as with the chalice, individual glasses should be rinsed separately. The water used to rinse the vessels should be poured onto the ground or into the piscina, a sink with direct drainage to the ground.[73] Such reverent care should apply whether individual glasses are made of glass or plastic.

Why do such things as the liturgy, the sermon, preparation for Communion, closed Communion, and even proper distribution and disposal of the elements matter so much? Why did Luther counsel that a pastor be removed from the church for mishandling the elements after Communion? In the big picture of daily life and the needs of people, doesn't this depict majoring in minors? In truth, these are not minor things. As one considers the witness of Scripture, church history, and the statements in the Lutheran Confessions concerning the presence of the Lord's Supper, it is seen to be at the center of the life of the church. This does not mean the Supper as opposed to or in competition with the sermon. Rather, the single serving of two treasures that the Holy Spirit led the church to be devoted to after Pentecost is the focus. Concern for matters connected with our risen Lord's service to us in Word and Sacrament is not majoring in minors, for here heaven touches earth. Here Christ comes to serve us for the life of the world. Here is reason for joyful and reverent care in all matters.

Discussion Questions

1. Concerning the liturgy, name two ways that it is scriptural. Discuss whether worshiping God as He has called us to worship Him comes naturally to us.

2. Concerning the sermon, discuss the relevance of Jesus' words, "He who hears you, hears Me." What did Luther call the preached Word? Explain what is meant by the statement "Preaching makes sense out of what is happening as Christ comes to serve His people." Discuss the difference between understanding the sermon as speech about Jesus or speech by Jesus to His flock. Why is such a difference important?

3. Does the Lord's Supper benefit people regardless of faith *ex opera operato*? According to Luther, if we feel unworthy of the Lord's Supper, we feel correctly. But what if we cannot feel the need? What does Luther place over our feelings?

4. What place does the sermon have in preparation for the Sacrament? What did Luther regard as the most worthy preparation for the Lord's Table? Discuss.

5. What is the most notorious linkage of private confession and Holy Communion? Was this a proper linkage? What did Luther and the Lutheran Confessions have to say about private confession and absolution? Is confession and absolution a substitute for the Lord's Supper? Is it an obligation for the Lord's Supper? Discuss.

6. Discuss the historic use of the practice of closed Communion. How would you respond to those who say closed Communion is a statement of superiority in the faith? Is the reception of Holy Communion a personal, individualistic act? How would you respond to those who say closed Communion is an impediment to the recovery of every Sunday Communion?

7. When did grape juice begin to replace wine in Protestant churches? What change in practice accompanied the switch to grape guice? What reasons were behind these changes in practice, even in Lutheran congregations? Were such changes necessary? What happened to the clergyman in Weida who mixed consecrated and unconsecrated hosts? Discuss. The reformers reverent treatment of consecrated elements focused on . . .

Let us hold fast the confession of our hope without wavering, for He who promised is faithful. And let us consider one another in order to stir up love and good works, not forsaking the assembling of ourselves together, as is the manner of some, but exhorting one another, and so much the more as you see the Day approaching. (Hebrews 10:23–25)

CHAPTER NINE

Into the Future

The Twenty-first Century

Christ's real presence to teach His gathered people and to feed them with His true body and true blood has always been accused by Satan, assaulted by the world, and assessed as of no importance by our sinful nature. Therefore it has also been at the center of the struggle within the church. This century and all centuries until the Lord returns will witness the same.

Revelation 13 speaks of two beasts that will threaten the church until Christ returns. The beast from the sea (Revelation 13:1–10) represents external threats—that is, all political, social, educational, and individual opposition to Christ and His Word. The beast from the earth (Revelation 13:11–18) represents internal seduction from within the church herself. This beast pictures religion that functions in the name of Christianity but has evolved into a false religion.[1]

The external threats to the church—the beast from the sea—will remain widespread. We live in a culture of death. Viewing death for others as one of life's answers for ourselves is now part of the fabric of our nation. Under the banner of "quality of life," we have instead harvested an unspeakable quantity of death. Abortion is now being joined by euthanasia of the aged and infirm and unwanted. This false philosophy will continue to threaten God's people in the future. It is ironic that the more men see death as the answer, the more they will reject the one death that is the answer for sinful man—the death of Christ, the death we proclaim in the Lord's Supper.

Another external threat to the church that will not evaporate is the pseudoscientific theory of evolution. Millions believe that they happened by chance and that God is not the creator of man in His image. Schools, universities, and the media routinely teach this theory to children and adults as if it were true, though it cannot be proven scientifically either by controlled experimentation or by field observation. In this worldview, death is seen as a good thing that betters the changeable human nature and fosters evolution by cutting off the weak and undesirable. In this worldview, God's promise of life through the death of His Son on the cross cannot exist. A human nature that can change from monkey to man can have no solidarity with the man that is God in the flesh, the Second Adam who unites us with God according to our own kind, made in His image (Genesis 1–2). Either we are who we are and sin has fatally marred that existence, requiring God's intervention and forgiveness, or sin is a matter of clinical self-improvement in the vein of Christian Science and Scientology.

Therefore the presence of the risen Christ in the Divine Service to serve us His life-giving gifts, including the heavenly food by which He imparts forgiveness of sins, life, and salvation, cannot exist in the world of evolution and the cult of death. Under the evolutionary worldview, if consistently believed, the only way in which God can be present with us is through some kind of symbolic or pantheistic manner. Most Christians who embrace the theory of evolution embrace a theoretical system modified to include God and Christ in some way. This, however, is a form of fence-sitting that ignores the basic premise of evolutionary theory. The premise is that we ourselves, along with everything that we call true, can be changed or even snuffed out by natural forces that wield the two swords of mutation and death as good things. As the caskets of our loved ones are lowered into the earth and as we await the resurrection of all flesh, does the idea of death as good not seem preposterous? In short, modern man's incorrect worldview about who we are and how we got here and where we are going will continue to cause barriers to the reception of God's gifts of life in this dying world.

External threats against the church will also continue to come from rapidly decaying morals in modern culture. The breakup of the family, the celebration of sexual immorality, the epidemic of cohabitation outside of marriage, the forceful promotion of same-sex relationships are all accelerating as this new century begins. He who created male and female for the one-flesh relationship of marriage has said, "Marriage should be honored by all, and the marriage bed kept pure, for God will judge the adulterer and all the sexually immoral" (Hebrews 13:4 NIV). Like St. Paul, those who speak this truth in love will be considered the enemy (Galatians 4:16). In the brokenness of life, men will continue to rationalize their choices and continue to reject the healing that Christ brings in His Sacred Meal.

In the face of these external threats, the church of Christ is not called to transform the world. She is called to speak the truth in love. She is called to love her enemies and pray for those who persecute her. She is called to obey God rather than men. Her pastors are called to preach the Word of God in season and out of season. The church is called to faithfully persevere in suffering as the risen Christ comes to give Himself to her in His Word and Sacrament for the life of the world.

Perhaps surprisingly to us, the greatest threats against the church have historically come from the beast from the earth, that is, from within the church. As we have seen, C. F. W. Walther identified the chief cause for the disintegration of the Lutheran Church after Luther's death as the failure of its people and leaders to cling to the pure doctrine proclaimed by the reformer. Walther held that the leaders of the fledgling Lutheran Church did not openly teach false doctrine. Their intention was certainly to cling to justification by grace for Christ's sake through faith. But for the sake of pursuing other objectives, they showed less and less enthusiasm to fight against errors in doctrine and practice. This brought the Lutheran Church to the brink of destruction.

When any other objectives, even otherwise good objectives, such as life issues, mission issues, patriotic issues, even family issues, separate Jesus from His words or make doctrine and its practice a secondary priority, Christ's church will be spiritually harmed. The caring churchly beast does not initially attack the faith openly. Rather, his serious spiritual work is accomplished by energetic misdirection and substitution.

Walther made it crystal clear that proclaiming the pure doctrine also meant identifying and reproving false doctrine. He wrote: "He who insists on pure doctrine but does not refute the contrary false doctrine . . . is not a faithful steward of God's mysteries (1 Cor. 4:1) . . . no faithful shepherd of the sheep entrusted to him."[2] Walther quotes Luther, who wrote: "A teacher who is silent about errors and yet wants to be a correct teacher is worse than a manifest heretic and is doing more damage by his hypocrisy than a heretic. He is not to be trusted."[3] As I once heard it expressed, a person who loves flowers and wants to see them grow must also hate weeds and see to their demise.

Lack of concern for pure doctrine will increasingly threaten the faith. Key watchwords of U.S. culture are *tolerance* and *inclusiveness*. Key visions of U.S. civil religion include outward harmony and practical results. Friendliness is viewed as faithfulness. Bigger is viewed as better. Religious words and actions that confess what Jesus says and does are not easily tolerated by our culture or by the external church that has married our culture. As was the case in third-century persecutions, naming Jesus is permissible and not viewed as inherently offensive. But naming Jesus as God in the flesh, the one who cannot be separated from His words (John 14:23–24; 12:48) and through whom alone life and salvation come into our dying world is highly offensive. Naming Jesus as truly present among us to give us His very body to eat and His very blood to drink is also viewed as foolishness.

In the face of this beast's activity, we are to teach everything that Christ has mandated (Matthew 28:20). As in past history, speaking the truth concerning His Word and His gifts may lead to charges of being loveless or unconcerned for the salvation of souls. Speaking of those who deny the bodily presence of Christ in the Lord's Supper, Luther said that they do as follows:

> [A]ccuse us today of being quarrelsome, harsh, and intractable, because, as they say, we shatter love and harmony among the churches on account of the single doctrine about the Sacrament. They say that we should not make so much of this little doctrine . . . . To this argument of theirs we reply with Paul: "A little yeast leavens the whole lump" In philosophy a tiny error in the beginning is very great at the end. Thus in theology a tiny error overthrows the whole teaching. Therefore doctrine and life should be distinguished as sharply as possible. Doctrine belongs to God, not to us; and we are called

only as its ministers. Therefore we cannot give up or change even one dot of it (Matt. 5:18).[4]

Threats from inside the church will also come from the confusion of faith and feeling. In fact, there is perhaps no greater danger to remaining in the faith than our feelings—feelings that are pulled and pushed by the devil, the world, and our sinful nature. One seminary professor expressed this truth by saying that the Holy Spirit has never promised to make His home in our adrenal glands. Faith and feelings are two different things! Sometimes, by God's doing, our feelings may respond in step with the revealed Word of God. But by nature they do not, even when we may feel strong and sincere in religious purpose. Harold Senkbeil cites Luther on this subject:

> [W]e must clearly point out the inherent instability of a theology based on feeling. Luther found from his own experience that feelings can't be trusted because they always undermine the message of the objective Word: "If you are not ready to believe that the Word is worth more than all you see or feel, then reason has blinded faith. So the resurrection of the dead is something that must be believed. I do not feel the resurrection of Christ but the Word affirms it. I feel sin but the Word says that it is forgiven to those who believe. I see that Christians die like other men, but the Word tells me that they shall rise again. So we must not be guided by our own feelings but by the Word."[5]

Walther clearly taught the same truth: "[T]he blessedness of Christians does not consist in pleasant feelings, but in their assurance that in spite of the bitterest feelings imaginable they are accepted with God and in their dying hour will be received into heaven."[6] Consider, for example, what Walther taught those studying to be pastors: "When a parishioner comes to you complaining of his inability to believe, you must tell him that you are not surprised at his statement; for no man can; he would be a marvel if he could. And you must instruct him to do nothing but listen to the Word of God, and God will give him faith."[7] And concerning the Word of God that the parishioners need to hear, Walther wrote:

> A preacher must be able to preach a sermon on faith without ever using the term faith. It is not important that he din the word "faith" into the ears of his audience, but it is necessary for him to frame his address so as to arouse in every poor sinner the desire to lay the burden of his sins at the feet of the Lord Jesus Christ and say to Him: "Thou art mine, and I am Thine." Here is where Luther reveals his true greatness. He rarely appeals to his hearers to believe, but he preaches concerning the work of Christ, salvation by grace, and the riches of God's mercy in Jesus Christ.[8]

Those are the very riches Christ is present to bestow as He comes to teach and feed His people in the Divine Service. Each week as we gather together in His name, the risen Christ comes *for us*, inviting us to lay the burdens of our sins at His feet. We may not feel our need to be in His presence in worship, but those feelings are wrong. Dean Wenthe insightfully asks whether the greatest threat to the people of God and the priesthood of all believers today might be an assault on the necessity of the church's own marks, that is, Word and Sacrament. He writes: "The radical individualism and interiorizing of the life of the Church at the expense of Israel's history, the incarnation of Christ, and the means of grace have exacted a great price. Cut off from the flesh and blood of Israel and of Christ the individual easily fills even Biblical phrases with culturally generated content."[9]

This glorification and trust in feelings has greatly affected worship. Richard Eyer points out that "we have turned worship into a subjective experience that depends for its worth on us and our feelings rather than the activity of God."[10] This is the greatest of spiritual threats because "the link between God and the believer is never the believer's own feelings, but the Person of Jesus Christ, God's Son, who comes to us in his gospel."[11]

The Christian faith, however, is fixed and not subject to change. We are to contend for the faith once for all given to the saints (Jude 1:3). It is the same body of truth to be held for all believers for all time, for there is only one Lord, one faith, one Baptism (Ephesians 4:5). It is faith in Jesus Christ (Philippians 3:9), who is both its author and finisher (Hebrews 12:2). It is faith that cannot be judged by our feelings, for we live by faith and not by sight (2 Corinthians 5:7).

It is the faith once given that Jesus continues to give as He comes to teach and feed us. He was handed over by Judas (Mark 14:10), the Sanhedrin (Mark 15:1), and Pilate (Luke 23:25) so he could hand over to us the life purchased by His death on the cross. This life comes only through His Word, for in these last days God has spoken to us through His Son through whom He made the universe (Hebrews 1:2). This life comes only through His body and blood because only He is the Word made flesh (John 1:14).

Conclusion

As Jesus comes into the midst of His gathered people today, we speak not of His omnipresence but of His saving presence. This is His true presence in concrete, specific means to which He has connected His promise. This is His presence *for us*. Jesus comes to speak to us His Word and to feed us with His Sacrament. It has been the intention of this book to extol the place of this single serving of two treasures in weekly worship.

To extol the place of the Sacrament of the Altar is not to do so in isolation from the Word or at the expense of the Word. As has been made clear, they are joined by Christ in the Words of Institution. They are also joined by the Holy Spirit, who led the church after Pentecost in equal devotion to both Word and Sacrament. Just as the breaking of bread in Acts 20:7 included in it the message of Paul that preceded, so extolling the Sacrament of the Altar today cannot be divorced from the sermon that precedes it. Thus Harold Senkbeil extols the reality of Christ's presence with His church in His Word and Sacrament when he states:

> The value of the sacrament of the altar can hardly be overstated for anyone who wants to know where God is at work in this world. From his Father's right hand in glory, Jesus continues to distribute to people of every age the very same body and blood with which he earned their salvation. Here again time and space are removed, and we join with the saints of all time in common celebration of the testament established once and for all at the cross outside Jerusalem. In his holy supper, Jesus gives us reality, not symbol.[12]

This means that weekly worship is not a mundane matter of "going to church." It is the magnificent moment of meeting with the risen Christ as His bride to receive His love. It is a moment intimately related to the table fellowship that Jesus came to restore with fallen man, a fellowship with God that man lost by grabbing for food that wasn't his. The Son of Man acted to restore that fellowship by His bloody, sacrificial death on the cross. There, in the miracle of the ages, the Word made flesh finished our redemption. There, under the damning wrath of God against our sin, the Lamb of God took away the sin of the world.

As Jesus came to give His church life in this dying world, He didn't pit His Word against His Meal or elevate one over the other. On the night of His betrayal, He was the preacher and the host at the table in the Upper Room. On the evening of His resurrection, He first taught His disciples and was then recognized by them in the breaking of the bread (Luke 24:31, 35). Jesus comes to serve us now just as He did after Pentecost. The church's equal devotion to the apostles' doctrine and the breaking of bread (Acts 2:42) was not accidental or incidental. This is how the Holy Spirit brought the life of Jesus Christ to the infant church. Word and Sacrament were not and are not liturgy-dividing competitors. Word and Sacrament were and are life-giving complements. They are the single serving in two treasures of the risen Lord as He comes among His gathered people.

In the early church, God's people continued to draw their life from Christ's presence in the weekly Eucharist. Some gave their lives as martyrs rather than give up the weekly meeting with Christ to receive Word and Sacrament. It was not until the church became acceptable and fashionable in the politics and culture of the fourth century that a decline in lay Communion could be seen. The decline that set in at the time of Constantine and the Arian controversies continued through twelve centuries. In those centuries, abuses in teaching were introduced that redefined the Lord's Supper from a communal meal for the forgiveness of the living to a sacrificial act performed by a priest to benefit the dead. The abuse of indulgences that became wedded to the performance of the Mass was one of the initial concerns of Martin Luther at the time of the Reformation.

In seeking to restore the worship of Scripture and the early church, the Lutheran Confessions proclaim the celebration of the Lord's Supper every Lord's Day and on other days when it is desired. Next to the article of justification by grace through faith, the recovery of the scriptural understanding and practice of Holy Communion was at the heart of the Reformation.

With the Counter-Reformation that followed Luther's death, with military defeats and doctrinal compromises, with the Thirty Years' War and the forced Prussian Union in later centuries, with the devastating effects of Pietism and Rationalism, the practice of every Sunday Communion was not consistently recovered in a widespread manner. The recovery trumpeted with high esteem in the Lutheran Confessions and championed by Luther met with various forms of resistance.

In the early history of the LCMS, there was frequent Communion in a few of the founding congregations. By the early twentieth century, however, the frequency in most LCMS congregations mirrored that of American Protestantism in general with Communion offered four to six times a year. The scriptural, historic, and confessional place of the Lord's Supper was not without witness in the earliest period of LCMS history, however, as the following quote of C. F. W. Walther's brother-in-law and colleague shows:

> On the basis of Acts 2:42 and I Cor. 11 and according to the example of the ancient Church, the Lutheran Church regards the Communion Service as the most glorious and important of all public services. . . . She therefore distinguishes between the Main Service and Minor Services. A divine service becomes the Main Service not by virtue of the significance of the Sunday or the holy Day, nor because of the season of the year, nor through liturgical elaboration, but, as given by the Scriptural relation of Word and Sacrament, by virtue of the fact that the action of the Sacrament of the Body and Blood of Christ immediately follows upon the proclamation of the Word of the Gospel, and thus represents the seal of the Word, the aim and conclusion of the Service. All other services, in which the action of the Sacrament is not intended from the outset, become Minor Services.[13]

As Timothy Maschke likewise summarizes

> [t]he Chief Divine Service (*'Hauptgottesdienst'*) is a service of Word *and* Sacrament. The early church and the

Lutheran reformers celebrated Holy Communion every Sunday . . . . A later Reformed tradition separated the Service of Communion from the Service of the Word, so weekly Communion was not the norm for Lutheran congregations for several generations. To end the worship service without the Sacrament terminates the movement from God's gracious words to God's gracious action in the Lord's Supper.[14]

The heart and center of this book is the loving encouragement that God's people not be denied the opportunity to receive the main service when they come for regular weekly worship. The minor services have a beautiful place for daily prayer, and encouragement is offered here for their increased use as well. But as God's sheep come for their one regular weekly gathering with the risen Christ and His church, their need for the heavenly food of His body and blood is no less than the need of their brothers and sisters after Pentecost and in the early church and in the church of the Reformation.

In the LCMS the opportunity to commune increased from quarterly to monthly through the 1950s and 1960s. At the end of the twentieth century, the majority of LCMS congregations offered the Lord's Supper in some combination of twice a month. Additionally, the survey noted in chapter 6 of this book indicates that there is growth in the recognition of the scriptural, historic, and confessional witness to every Sunday Communion. These encouraging signs do not indicate experimentation with a new program designed to achieve visible results. These signs will not cause excitement in the wider religious scene in the United States. To generic religion and to the workaday business world, this product cannot be marketed. Rather, these signs in our midst indicate a recognition of and intitial recovery of God's treasures in the scriptural, confessional, and historic practice of making the Lord's Supper available to the Lord's people on the Lord's Day.

The watchword in this recovery must continue to be *opportunity*. The Lord's Supper is the Gospel, not the Law. In fact, as Luther said, it is the sum and substance of the Gospel! We are not advocating that people be made to commune. In harmony with the scriptural, historic, and confessional witness, we are encouraging that they not be denied the opportunity to commune when they come for regular weekly worship.

Nearly twenty years ago that young man asked me the right question: "Pastor, if the Lord's Supper is everything that the Bible and the catechism say it is, then why don't we have the opportunity to receive it when we come for worship each week?" This is the kind of question Luther longed to hear in the church as he instructed pastors that "we should preach in such a way that the people . . . just plain compel us pastors to administer the sacrament to them."[15] God bless the preaching of God's pastors and the hearing of God's people in this way. There is nothing in the Scriptures or the history of the church or in the Lutheran Confessions that would give a negative answer to the question I was asked so many years ago. That is, there has never been a point at which the church has said we will stop offering God's people the Sacrament along with the Word in weekly worship for these scriptural and doctrinal reasons. Rather, the reasons for the loss of weekly Communion in the history of the church were negative, threatening, impoverishing reasons.

What Christ initially handed over to His church in love during Holy Week was His bodily presence both in teaching and feeding them. What the Holy Spirit led the early church to receive at Pentecost was the true presence of the living Christ teaching and feeding them. The Holy Spirit brought the risen Christ to His gathered people to release them from the binding effects of sin and death and the devil for the life of the world. What the Reformation sought to recover regarding the Lord's Supper was the healing, releasing presence of the risen Christ received by the laity.

Nothing is more unshakable than the love of Jesus Christ. In the Divine Service, His love is so certain, so clearly, so concretely given that the heavenly Bridegroom gives His bride His very body to eat and His very blood to drink. The Bridegroom who came in the flesh to redeem us, the risen God-man, continues to come into our midst *for us.* He comes as the preacher. His proclamation gives what it says. He comes as host of the Meal. He feeds us with heavenly food as we participate with angels and archangels and all the company of heaven in the heavenly liturgy.

Having Him, we have all we need. Receiving Him, His Bride may therefore rejoice! Resting in Him, His Bride may also depart in peace!

> Lord, now lettest Thou Thy servant
> depart in peace according to Thy word,
> For mine eyes have seen Thy Salvation:
> which Thou hast prepared before the face of all people,
> a Light to lighten the Gentiles
> and the Glory of Thy people Israel.
> Glory be to the Father and to the Son and to the Holy Ghost;
> As it was in the beginning, is now, and ever shall be,
> world without end. Amen.[16]

Discussion Questions

1. What does the beast from the sea picture (Revelation 13:1–10)? What does the beast from the earth picture (Revelation 13:11–18)?
2. What are some of the threats from the beast from the sea and from the beast from the earth? From which beast has the church historically faced the greatest threats? Discuss.

3. What did C. F. W. Walther and Luther write about those who do not refute false doctrine?

4. Discuss Luther's comments about those who deny the bodily presence of Christ in the Lord's Supper by making charges against those who confess it. Discuss the relationship between faith and feelings.

5. Discuss Dean Wenthe's thoughts concerning the great threat of individualizing and interiorizing the faith.

6. Discuss the statement: Weekly worship is no mundane matter of "going to church." What does it mean that Word and Sacrament are not liturgy-dividing competitors?

7. What must remain the watchword in recovering the opportunity for people to commune when they come for regular weekly worship? Discuss.

8. Concerning the Sacrament, how did Luther say pastors should preach? Discuss.

9. As one reviews the history of the church, what can be said about the reasons for the loss of weekly Communion?

For More Information

In addition to the books and articles noted in the footnotes and bibliography of this text, the LCMS Commission on Worship offers resources to aid in understanding the liturgy and the place of the Lord's Supper in weekly worship. By going to the Web site www.lcms.org and searching out the area of worship, a rich store of articles can be found under the topics "The Lord's Supper," "Worship/Theology," or "Corporate Worship." The Commission on Worship also offers bulletin inserts entitled "Kids in the Divine Service," as well as periodic inserts in the *Reporter* that address areas of interest to those involved with planning, leading, or learning more about worship.

A helpful twelve-part video series entitled *Liturgy: Yesterday, Today, Tomorrow* by Arthur Just is available from Lutheran Visuals, 10466 Plano Road, Dallas, TX 75238 (1-800/527-3211). This video series includes discussion questions and is a wonderful foundational tool to help congregations understand and rejoice in Lutheran worship.

Notes

INTRODUCTION

1. *Luther's Small Catechism*, 237.

2. Mueller and Kraus, *Pastoral Theology*, 97.

3. LCMS, *Convention Proceedings: 59th Regular Convention*, 113.

4. Commission on Worship, *Reflections on Contemporary/Alternative Worship*, 2 *(emphasis added)*.

5. Schoessow, "Holy Communion," 232.

6. Barry, *Unchanging Truth*. This pamphlet is available through Concordia Publishing House.

7. Lewis, *Screwtape Letters*, 25.

8. Eyer, *They Will See His Face*, 10–11.

9. Vajta, *Luther on Worship*, 87.

10. Luther, "That These Words of Christ," LW 37:68.

11. Senkbeil, *Dying to Live*, 104. For a Scripture-rich and straightforward discussion of this foundational truth, see Senkbeil's entire book, especially chapter 6.

12. Ap X, 4 (K-W, 185).

13. Pittelko and Precht, *Guide to Introducing Lutheran Worship*, 25.

14. Grime and Herl, *Hymnal Supplement 98 Handbook*, 24.

15. Commission on Worship, *Lutheran Worship*, 331:4.

CHAPTER ONE

1. FC SD VII, 44 (K-W, 600).

2. FC SD VII, 52–53 (K-W, 602).

3. LC V, 4 (K-W, 467).

4. Just, *Luke 9:51–24:53*, 831.

5. Krauth, *Conservative Reformation*, 787.

6. Krauth, *Conservative Reformation*, 780.

7. Krauth, *Conservative Reformation*, 780.

8. *Luther's Small Catechism*, 30–31.

9. LC V, 2 (K-W, 467).

10. LC V, 6–7 (K-W, 467).

11. Kolb, *Christian Faith*, 228–29.

12. Lindemann, *Till He Come*, 59.

13. Luther, "Treatise on the New Testament," LW 35:84.

14. Luther, "Adoration of the Sacrament," LW 36:277.

15. FC SD VII, 75 (K-W, 606).

16. Walther, *Pastoral Theology*, 133.

17. Luther, "Sacrament of the Body and Blood of Christ," LW 36:337–38.

18. *Luther's Small Catechism*, 235. See also LC V, 15–19 (K-W, 468), and FC SD VII, 88 (K-W, 608).

19. *Luther's Small Catechism*, 237.

20. Luther, "That These Words of Christ," LW 37:117.

21. LC V, 12–14 (K-W, 468).

22. Krauth, *Conservative Reformation*, 655.

23. Franzmann, *Word of the Lord Grows*, 195–96.

24. The Greek text reads "the prayers," not "prayer." The Greek word translated as *devoting* can be translated as "to continue steadfast" or "to faithfully [obstinately] persist" in something or "to adhere with strength."

25. Bruce, *Book of the Acts*, 79.

26. Just, *Luke 9:51–24:53*, 829.

27. Hoerber, *Concordia Self-Study Bible*, 1659, 1697.

28. Franzmann, *Concordia Self-Study Commentary*, 108.

29. *Luther's Small Catechism*, 232.

30. Ap XXII, 7 (K-W, 246).

31. Marshall, *Acts of the Apostles*, 83.

32. Lenski, *Interpretation of the Acts of the Apostles*, 117.

33. Senkbeil, *Dying to Live*, 120–21.

34. Just, *Luke 1:1–9:50*, 231–41. Just's "Excursus on Jesus' Table Fellowship" is the foundation for the following discussion.

35. LaVerdiere, *Eucharist in the New Testament*, 97.

36. Hoerber, *Reading the New Testament for Understanding*, 60.

37. Just, *Luke 1:1–9:50*, 236 (*Just's emphasis*).

38. Just, *Luke 1:1–9:50*, 237.

39. Just, *Luke 1:1–9:50*, 388 (*Just's emphasis*).

40. See Just, *Luke 9:51–24:53*, 574–77, for a full discussion of this beatitude.

41. Just, *Luke 9:51–24:53*, 1012 (*Just's emphasis*).

42. Just, *Ongoing Feast*, 240, 243.

43. Just, *9:51–24:53*, 1019.

44. Stephenson, *Lord's Supper*, 52.

45. Stephenson, *Lord's Supper*, 12. See especially Stephenson's discussion of how some were martyred rather than deny this confession (12–13).

46. See Collver, "Real Presence," 142–59, for a discussion of the history of this term and the confusion in how it is sometimes used today.

47. Lockwood, *1 Corinthians*, 341 (*Lockwood's emphasis*).

48. Luther "That These Words of Christ," LW 37:142.

49. Kolb, *Speaking the Gospel Today*, 230.

50. Brege, "Learning of Old Testament Sacrificial Concepts," 4.3. See also Brege's helpful article "Eucharistic Overtones Created by Sacrificial Concepts in the Epistle to the Hebrews," *Concordia Theological Quarterly* 66, no. 1 (January 2003): 61–81.

51. Brege, "Learning of Old Testament Sacrificial Concepts," 4.11. See Brege's dissertation for an explanation of how St. Paul linked the peace offering to the celebration of the Lord's Supper in 1 Corinthians 10 (4.11–13) and how the other Old Testament sacrifices included meal or table fellowship with God.

52. Kleinig, *Leviticus*, 94. See also Kleinig's discussion of the fulfillment of the peace offering by Christ in the Lord's Supper (94–96).

53. See Plass, *What Luther Says*, 1:147, especially paragraph 435.

54. Walther, *Gnadenjahr*, 209ff. Quoted in Marquart, "Word as Life," 52.

55. Just, *Luke 9:51–24:53*, 827.

56. Just, *Luke 9:51-24:53*, 827–28 (*Just's emphasis*).

57. Lindemann, *Till He Come*, 31.

58. Lockwood, *1 Corinthians*, 380.

59. Lockwood, *1 Corinthians*, 383.

60. Lindemann, *Till He Come*, 29.

61. Lockwood, *1 Corinthians*, 389.

62. Weinrich, "Lutheran Reformation and the Early Church," 5.

63. Lindemann, *Till He Come,* 32.

64. Brighton, *Revelation*, 61–62.

65. From *God's Gift to You* by Gaylin R. Schmeling, page 23 © 2001 Northwestern Publishing House, Wauwatosa, WI. Used with permission.

66. Lathrop, *Holy Things*, 53.

CHAPTER TWO

1. Lindemann, *Till He Come*, 52–53.

2. AC XXIV, 34–41 (K-W, 71–73).

3. MacKenzie, "Lutheran Reformers' Understanding," 20–21.

4. Weinrich, "Lutheran Reformation and the Early Church," 2–3.

5. Frend, *Rise of Christianity*, 29.

6. Robertson, *Redating the New Testament*, 327.

7. Kretzmann, *Christian Art*, 243.

8. The connection between the opportunity to commune in the regular weekly service and the practice of closed Communion will be more thoroughly discussed in chapter 8.

9. Ray C. Petry, ed., *A History of Christianity* (Grand Rapids: Baker, 1962), 1:14.

10. Kretzmann, *Christian Art*, 241.

11. Willimon, *Word, Water, Wine, and Bread*, 16.

12. Cullmann, *Christ and Time*, 11.

13. Cullmann, *Christ and Time*, 13.

14. Willimon, *Word, Water, Wine, and Bread*, 34.

15. Metzger, *History of the Liturgy*, 77–78.

16. Lindemann, *Till He Come*, 42.

17. González, *Church History*, 26.

18. Baue, *Spiritual Society*, 103.

19. Hippolytus, *Apostolic Tradition*, 25.

20. Willimon, *Word, Water, Wine, and Bread*, 34–35.

21. Willimon, *Word, Water, Wine, and Bread*, 37.

22. Bainton, *Church of Our Fathers*, 34–35.

23. González, *Story of Christianity*, 1:87.

24. González, *Story of Christianity*, 1:87.

25. Luther "That These Words of Christ," LW 37:122. Luther is quoting *Letter 53*, 2, in *Patrologia, Series Latina*, ed. by J. P. Migne (Paris, 1844–1904), 3:856. It is also found in *The Ante-Nicene Fathers*, ed. Alexander Roberts and James Donaldson (Buffalo, 1885–1896), 5:337.

26. González, *Story of Christianity*, 1:96.

27. González, *Story of Christianity*, 1:99.

28. Dix, *Shape of the Liturgy*, 17.

29. Dix, *Shape of the Liturgy*, 17.

BLESSINGS OF WEEKLY COMMUNION

30. Veith, *God at Work*, 127.

31. Wiest, "Evangelical Impetus for Evangelization," www.lsfmissiology.org/Essays/1999%20Professional.pdf.

32. González, *Story of Christianity*, 1:125.

33. Church Growth Committee, *For the Sake of Christ's Commission*. See especially pp. 8–13 for a helpful discussion of the relationship between mission and worship.

34. González, *Story of Christianity*, 1:95, 99.

35. González, *Story of Christianity*, 1:100.

36. Cullmann and Leenhardt, *Essays on the Lord's Supper*, 10.

37. *Ichthus* is the Greek word for fish. The Greek letters are also the first letters for the words in the phrase "Jesus Christ, God's Son, Savior." It was the most common representation of Jesus Christ from the second through the fourth centuries. Its historical use did not picture Christianity in general so much as it pictured Jesus *for us*, present among His gathered people in Word and Sacrament.

38. Schmeling, *God's Gift to You*, 87.

39. Dix, *Shape of the Liturgy*, 19.

40. González, *Story of Christianity*, 1:104.

41. González, *Story of Christianity*, 1:106.

42. Lathrop, *Holy Things*, 39.

43. Bainton, *Church of Our Fathers*, 39–40.

44. Kretzmann, *Christian Art*, 349.

45. Kretzmann, *Christian Art*, 353.

46. González, *Story of Christianity*, 1:158.

47. Scaer, *Christology*, 102.

48. Kelly, *Early Christian Creeds*, 237–38.

49. Kelly, *Early Christian Creeds*, 329. See Kelly's full discussion on pp. 296–331.

50. Senn, *Christian Liturgy*, 535.

51. Senn, *Christian Liturgy*, 535.

52. Noll, *Turning Points*, 63.

53. González, *Story of Christianity*, 1:136.

54. Noll, *Turning Points*, 62.

55. Taft, "Frequency of the Eucharist," 18. Taft is citing a sermon by Chrysostom, *Heb. 10 hom. 17,4*, in *Patrologia, Series Graeca*, ed. J. P. Migne (Paris, 1857–1866), 63:131.

56. Jungmann, *Early Liturgy*, 197.
57. Jungmann, *Early Liturgy*, 197–98.
58. Jungmann, *Mass of the Roman Rite*, 2:362–63.
59. Jungmann, *Mass of the Roman Rite*, 363.
60. Kretzmann, *Christian Art*, 247.
61. Senn, *Christian Liturgy*, 157.
62. González, *Story of Christianity*, 1:217, 232.
63. González, *Story of Christianity*, 1:218.
64. Metzger, *History of the Liturgy*, 84–85.
65. Tappert, "Meaning and Practice in the Middle Ages," 76.
66. Metzger, *History of the Liturgy*.
67. Metzger, *History of the Liturgy*, 98.
68. Dix, *Shape of the Liturgy*, 130.
69. Metzger, *History of the Liturgy*, 99.

CHAPTER THREE

1. Noll, *Turning Points*, 114.
2. Noll, *Turning Points*, 84.
3. Noll, *Scandal of the Evangelical Mind*, 44.
4. González, *Story of Christianity*, 1:241.
5. González, *Church History*, 43.
6. Klauser, *Short History of the Western Liturgy*, 103.
7. See González, *Story of Christianity*, 1:247
8. Ramer, "Liturgical Influence of Gregory the Great," 5.
9. Ramer, "Liturgical Influence of Gregory the Great," 6. See also González, *Story of Christianity*, 1:247.
10. MacKenzie, "Lutheran Reformers' Understanding," 26.
11. Ap XXIV, 6 (K-W, 258–59).
12. Ap XXIV, 94 (K-W, 276).
13. Willimon, *Word, Water, Wine, and Bread*, 48.
14. Lindemann, *Till He Comes*, 51.
15. Noll, *Turning Points*, 116.
16. Tappert, "Meaning and Practice in the Middle Ages," 82–83.
17. Tappert, "Meaning and Practice in the Middle Ages," 83.
18. Tappert, "Meaning and Practice in the Middle Ages," 83.

19. Willimon, *Word, Water, Wine, and Bread*, 49.

20. Noll, *Turning Points*, 100.

21. Klauser, *Short History of the Western Liturgy*, 103.

22. Willimon, *Word, Water, Wine, and Bread*, 53.

23. Bartels, *Take Eat, Take Drink*, 113. See his discussion of the private or silent Mass.

24. Willimon, *Word, Water, Wine, and Bread*, 53.

25. Willimon, *Word, Water, Wine, and Bread*, 53–54.

26. Metzger, *History of the Liturgy*, 126–28.

27. Metzger, *History of the Liturgy*, 137.

28. González, *Story of Christianity*, 1:234.

29. Noll, *Turning Points*, 108.

30. Noll, *Turning Points*, 120.

31. Noll, *Turning Points*, 119.

32. Noll, *Turning Points*, 121.

33. Clouse et al., *Two Kingdoms*, 148.

34. Clouse et al., *Two Kingdoms*, 148.

35. Lueker, *Lutheran Cyclopedia*, 348.

36. AC V, 1–2 (German text; K-W, 40).

37. González, *Story of Christianity*, 1:275.

38. Noll, *Turning Points*, 102.

39. Lueker, *Lutheran Cyclopedia*, 182.

40. See Lockwood, *1 Corinthians*, 516–44, for a helpful excursus on "The Ordination of Women."

41. O'Brien, *Medieval Church*, 67.

42. White, *Brief History of Christian Worship*, 99.

43. Senn, *Christian Liturgy*, 223.

44. Senn, *Christian Liturgy*, 223.

45. Senn, *Christian Liturgy*, 225.

46. White, *Brief History of Christian Worship*, 88.

47. Bartels, *Take Eat, Take Drink*, 114.

48. Senn, *Christian Liturgy*, 225.

49. White, *Brief History of Christian Worship*, 88, 90.

50. Willimon, *Word, Water, Wine, and Bread*, 57.

51. Tappert, "Meaning and Practice in the Middle Ages," 82–83.

NOTES: CHAPTER 3, PAGES 82–97

52. Bartels, *Take Eat, Take Drink*, 115. See Bartels's helpful discussion of related matters on pp. 113–15.

53. Klauser, *Short History of the Western Liturgy*, 106–7.

54. Willimon, *Word, Water, Wine, and Bread*, 57–58.

55. Vauchez, *Laity in the Middle Ages*, 121.

56. AC XXVII, 48 (Latin text; K-W, 89).

57. AC XXI, 1–2 (German text; K-W, 58).

58. Vauchez, *Laity in the Middle Ages*, 237–38.

59. SA II, II, 1 (K-W, 301).

60. SA II, II, 5 (K-W, 302).

61. SA II, II, 12 (K-W, 303).

62. SA II, II, 6 (K-W, 302).

63. SA II, II, 3 (K-W, 302).

64. The teaching of indulgences is still present in the Roman Catholic Church. In November 1998, Pope John Paul II issued a papal bull entitled "The Mystery of the Incarnation," which offered plenary indulgences (a full pardon for sins as opposed to a shortening of time spent in purgatory) during the Jubilee Year of 2000 for private devotions (such as the rosary), private service (such as visiting the sick), or private sacrifice (such as fasting or giving up smoking for a time).

65. Bainton, *Church of Our Fathers*, 120.

66. Aland, *Martin Luther's 95 Theses* (2004), 56.

67. Aland, *Martin Luther's 95 Theses* (2004), 57.

68. Aland, *Martin Luther's 95 Theses* (2004), 58.

69. Senn, *Christian Liturgy*, 258.

70. Bainton, *Church of Our Fathers*, 121.

71. Vauchez, *Laity in the Middle Ages*, 238–40.

72. Clouse et al., *Two Kingdoms*, 225–26.

73. Bartels, *Take Eat, Take Drink*, 127.

74. González, *Church History*, 64.

75. See Bartels, *Take Eat, Take Drink*, 126–28, for an interesting discussion of varied Hussite beliefs and the protracted struggles after Hus's death.

76. Schwiebert, *Luther and His Times*, 27–28.

77. Noll, *Turning Points*, 133.

78. González, *Church History*, 66.

CHAPTER FOUR

1. Clouse et al., *Two Kingdoms*, 237.

2. Kalb, *Theology of Worship*, 18, quoting from Vajta, *Luther on Worship*.

3. Teigen, "Luther and the Consecration," 321.

4. Kleinig, "Lutheran Liturgies," 126.

5. Senn, *Christian Liturgy*, 267–68.

6. Senn, *Christian Liturgy*, 271. See the same page for a discussion of this two-pronged attack.

7. Luther, "Babylonian Captivity of the Church," LW 36:51.

8. AC XXIV, 21–23 (German text; K-W, 68, 70).

9. Luther, "Order of Mass and Communion," LW 53:20.

10. Senn, "Reform of the Mass," 39.

11. Nagel, "Luther's Liturgical Reform," 24.

12. Schwiebert, *Luther and His Times*, 704.

13. Bruzek, "Five-Word Faith," 108.

14. Schwiebert, *Luther and His Times*, 701.

15. See Eyer, *They Will See His Face*, 101–11.

16. Luther, "Concerning the Order of Public Worship," LW 53:11.

17. Kretzmann, *Christian Art*, 278.

18. Tappert, "Meaning and Practice in the Reformation," 99.

19. White, *Christian Worship in North America*, 35.

20. White, *Christian Worship in North America*, 122.

21. Luther, "Letter to Lazarus Spengler," LW 49:206.

22. Luther, "Letter to Lazarus Spengler," LW 49:207.

23. Luther, "On the Councils and the Church," LW 41:148–66.

24. Luther, "On the Councils and the Church," LW 41:154.

25. Commission on Worship, *Lutheran Worship: Agenda*, 212–13.

26. Stephenson, "Holy Eucharist," 158.

27. AC XXV, 1–2 (German text; K-W, 72).

28. Luther, "Order of Mass and Communion," LW 53:34.

29. Senn, *Christian Liturgy*, 352.

30. Tappert, "Meaning and Practice in the Reformation," 98.

31. Tappert, "Meaning and Practice in the Reformation," 102.

32. Arand, *Testing the Boundaries*, 106.

33. Ferry, "What Did It Mean to Be Lutheran?" 7.

34. Ferry, "What Did It Mean to Be Lutheran?" 8.

35. Olson, "Matthias Flacius," 90.

36. Bruzek, "Five-Word Faith," 88–89. This dissertation provides a readable discussion of this crucial struggle.

37. Senn, *Christian Liturgy*, 326.

38. FC SD X (K-W, 635–40).

39. Clouse, *Church in the Age of Orthodoxy*, 40–41.

40. Arand, *Testing the Boundaries*, 107.

41. Arand, *Testing the Boundaries*, 108, quoting Walther, *Stern und Kern*, 39.

42. Arand, *Testing the Boundaries*, 108.

43. "Editors' Introduction to the Formula of Concord," K-W, 484.

44. Arand, *Testing the Boundaries*, 108.

45. Bruzek, "Five-Word Faith," 110.

46. Bruzek, "Five-Word Faith," 110.

47. Bruzek, "Five-Word Faith," 136.

48. Arand, *Testing the Boundaries*, 111. I have summarized points that he presents more completely.

49. Strauss, *Luther's House of Learning*, 268.

50. Strauss, *Luther's House of Learning*, 271–87.

51. Asch, *Thirty Years War*, 37.

52. Asch, *Thirty Years War*, 24.

53. Asch, *Thirty Years War*, 78.

54. González, *Church History*, 77.

55. Senn, *Christian Liturgy*, 495.

56. Asch, *Thirty Years War*, 177–78.

57. Stoeffler, *Rise of Evangelical Pietism*, 181.

58. Senn, *Christian Liturgy*, 495–96.

59. Senn, *Christian Liturgy*, 496.

60. Senn, *Christian Liturgy*, 496 (*emphasis added*).

61. Loescher, *Complete Timotheus Verinus*, 12–20, esp. 19.

62. Stoeffler, *Rise of Evangelical Pietism*, 13–22.

63. Feuerhahn, "Roots and Fruits of German Pietism," 60.

64. Pless, "Liturgy and Pietism," 151.

65. Stoeffler, *Rise of Evangelical Pietism*, 22. See also p. 20.

66. Pless, "Liturgy and Pietism," 145.

67. Pinson, *Pietism*, 41, 45.

68. Gerhard, *Comprehensive Explanation*, 222–23.

69. McCain, "Orthodox Lutheran Response to Pietism," 79–80.

70. Pless, "Liturgy and Pietism," 149–50.

71. Lueker, *Lutheran Cyclopedia*, 882.

72. Webber, *Studies in the Liturgy*, 44–45.

73. Wolf, *Lutherans in North America*, 2.

74. Wolf, *Lutherans in North America*, 3–5.

75. Wolf, *Lutherans in North America*, 6–7.

76. Noll, *History of Christianity*, 37.

77. Bainton, *Church of Our Fathers*, 202.

78. Noll, *History of Christianity*, 48.

CHAPTER FIVE

1. Northwick, "Development of the Missouri Synod," 13.

2. Vajta, "Worship and Sacramental Life," 129.

3. Sasse, "Holy Supper," 485. See Sasse's *This Is My Body* and *We Confess: The Sacraments* for a wealth of scriptural, historical, and confessional witness to the place of the Sacrament in worship.

4. Stiller, *Johann Sebastian Bach*, 132.

5. Stiller, *Johann Sebastian Bach*, 136.

6. Vajta, "Worship and Sacramental Life," 128.

7. Vajta, "Worship and Sacramental Life," 129.

8. Tappert, "Orthodoxism, Pietism, and Rationalism," 71.

9. Tappert, "Orthodoxism, Pietism, and Rationalism," 42.

10. Senn, *Christian Liturgy*, 541

11. White, *Brief History of Christian Worship*, 143–44.

12. Tappert, "Meaning and Practice in Europe since the Reformation," 122.

13. Baue, *Spiritual Society*, 165.

14. Noll, *History of Christianity*, 134. citing Marcus Cunliffe.

15. Noll, *History of Christianity*, 97.

16. Noll, *History of Christianity*, 104.

17. Wolf, *Lutherans in North America*, 21.

18. Pless, "Liturgy and Pietism," 151–52.

19. *Luther's Small Catechism*, 39–42.

20. *Luther's Small Catechism*, 43.

21. Arand, *Testing the Boundaries*, 25.

22. Deitz, "Lord's Supper in American Lutheranism," 142.

23. Arand, *Testing the Boundaries*, 25.

24. Deitz, "Lord's Supper in American Lutheranism," 139–40.

25. Kemerer, "Early American Lutheran Liturgies," 2:86–69.

26. The use of the formula "Christ says" prior to the Verba was considered Calvinistic by confessional Lutherans and was specifically condemned in the 1846 document "Proposals for the Constitution of the LCMS"; see Article V.14.

27. DeVries, "Prussian Union," 135–36.

28. Kalb, *Theology of Worship*, IX.

29. Gustafson, *Lutherans in Crisis*, 107.

30. Tappert, "Meaning and Practice in Europe since the Reformation," 123–24.

31. Kleinig, "Lutheran Liturgies," 143–44.

32. Harms, "Ninety-Five Theses," 67–68.

33. Harms, "Ninety-Five Theses," 67–68.

34. Meyer, *Moving Frontiers*, 97.

35. Briese, "Wilhelm Loehe," 32.

36. Deitz, "Lord's Supper in American Lutheranism," 146.

37. Arand, *Testing the Boundaries*, 34.

38. Rast, "Catholicity in Missourian Orthodoxy," 64.

39. Gustafson, *Lutherans in Crisis*, 109.

40. Kalb, *Theology of Worship*, x.

41. Nelson, *Lutherans in North America*, 157.

42. Saleska, "Frederich Conrad Dieterich Wyneken," 55.

43. Saleska, "Frederich Conrad Dieterich Wyneken," 55–56. The Jesuits, an order of Roman Catholic missionary priests, were formed as part of the Counter-Reformation. They took special vows of allegiance to the pope, and during the Counter-Reformation, the reconversion of many Protestants was attributed to their efforts—sometimes by force.

44. Saleska, "Frederich Conrad Dieterich Wyneken," 56.

45. Arand, *Testing the Boundaries*, 91.

46. Walther, *Pastoral Theology*, 82.

47. Fuerbringer, *80 Eventful Years*, 157.

48. Zetto, "Aspects of Theology," 114.

49. These final two aspects will be examined in chapter 6.

50. The LCMS published the first English translation of its constitution in 1924.

51. LCMS, *Statistical Yearbook*, 239.

52. SC Preface, 22 (K-W, 350).

53. Zetto, "Aspects of Theology," 7–8.

54. Zetto, "Aspects of Theology," 157.

55. "The Altar Is Neglected," *The Lutheran Witness* 48, no. 3 (1929): 39.

56. See articles in *The Lutheran Witness* 49, no. 4 (February 18, 1930): 54, 59.

CHAPTER SIX

1. See "What Do We Call This Story?" *Reporter* (October 1999), specifically in the Commission on Worship insert (vol. 4, no. 4), p. 3.

2. *Luther's Small Catechism*, 12.

3. *Luther's Small Catechism*, 31.

4. See pp. 167–73 for more specifics.

5. See pp. 252–54 for a brief discussion of the use of the common cup.

6. See pp. 244–51 for a brief discussion of closed Communion.

7. LC V, 68 (K-W, 474).

8. See pp. 190–219 for some of these treasures.

9. SC Preface, 22 (K-W, 350).

10. Billington, *Protestant Crusade*, 1.

11. Billington, *Protestant Crusade*, 11–16.

12. Billington, *Protestant Crusade*, 18–19.

13. Billington, *Protestant Crusade*, 20, 23.

14. Billington, *Protestant Crusade*, 44.

15. Ellis, *American Catholicism*, 62–67.

16. Ellis, *American Catholicism*, 83.

17. Marty, *Invitation to American Catholic History*, 120.

18. See González, *Story of Christianity*, 2:243.

19. Ellis, *Documents of American Catholic History*, 2:483–85.

20. "Editae Saepe 176," encyclical of Pope Pius X on St. Charles Borromeo, May 26, 1910. "Pastors and Preachers," the pope writes, "should take every possibility to urge the people to cultivate the practice of frequently receiving Holy Communion. In this they are following the

example of the early church . . . and finally the teaching of the Council of Trent. The last mentioned would have the faithful receive Communion in every mass, not only spiritually, but sacramentally" (Pope Pius X, in *The Papal Encyclicals*, vol. 3, *1903–1939* [Wilmington, NC: McGrath, 1981], 123).

21. Luther, "Concerning Rebaptism," LW 40:233.

22. LCMS, *Statistical Yearbook*, 239.

23. Luther, "Confession Concerning Christ's Supper," LW 37:317.

24. Luther, "Open Letter to Those in Frankfurt on the Main," 337.

25. Luther, "Open Letter to Those in Frankfurt on the Main," 338.

26. Lee, *Against the Protestant Gnostics*, 103.

27. Lewis, *Screwtape Letters*, 20.

28. Lee, *Against the Protestant Gnostics*, 103.

29. White, *Brief History of Christian Worship*, 145.

30. White, *Brief History of Christian Worship*, 155, was used as the basis for these thoughts.

31. Lee, *Against the Protestant Gnostics*, 109.

32. Arand, *Testing the Boundaries*, 26.

33. Pless, "Liturgy and Pietism," 155.

34. Noll, *Scandal of the Evangelical Mind*, 93.

35. Marzolf, "C. F. W. Walther," 89–90.

36. Noll, *Scandal of the Evangelical Mind*, 67.

37. Lee, *Against the Protestant Gnostics*, 182.

CHAPTER SEVEN

1. LC V, 70 (K-W, 474).

2. Ap IV, 154 (K-W, 144).

3. *Luther's Small Catechism*, 31.

4. Plass, *What Luther Says*, 1293–320, entry nos. 4139, 4179, 4187, 4190, 4208, 4207, 4239.

5. These questions are taken from material developed for the Concordia Catechetical Academy; see Bender, *Lutheran Catechesis*, 35–61, for the complete list of questions.

6. Gerhard, *Sacred Meditations*, 12.

7. FC SD VII, 69–70 (K-W, 605).

8. *The Lutheran Hymnal* (St. Louis: Concordia, 1941), 315:6.

9. Sasse, *This Is My Body*, 326.

10. Sasse, *This Is My Body*, 325–26.

11. Eyer, *They Will See His Face*, 37.

12. Kleinig, *Leviticus*, 153.

13. Kleinig, *Leviticus*, 222.

14. Wingren, *Living Word*, 156.

15. Veith, *Spirituality of the Cross*, 51. This book is an excellent choice for help in understanding central treasures.

16. LC V, 66 (K-W, 473–74).

17. Commission on Worship, *Lutheran Worship*, 239:1.

18. See Baneck, "Sacramental Preaching," 100, 102, 161.

19. Veith, *Spirituality of the Cross,* 51.

20. Stephenson, "Holy Eucharist," 163, quoting WA 17/1:174.21–175.10.

21. Luther, "That These Words of Christ," LW 37:101.

22. Senkbeil, *Where in the World Is God?* 102.

23. Commission on Worship, *Lutheran Worship*, 250:3.

24. Commission on Worship, *Lutheran Worship*, 245:2.

25. Eyer, *They Will See His Face*, 36.

26. Kleinig, *Leviticus*, 11–12 (*Kleinig's emphasis*).

27. Eyer, *Holy People, Holy Lives*, 74.

28. Just, "Sacramental Practice," 121.

29. Keinig, *Leviticus,* 172.

30. Commission on Worship, *Hymnal Supplement 98*, 853:3–5.

31. Luther, "Blessed Sacrament of the Holy and True Body of Christ," LW 35:51.

32. Sasse, *This Is My Body*, 320.

33. Sasse, *This Is My Body*, 321–22. See Sasse's discussion of why partaking of the Sacrament constitutes the fellowship of the believers and why church fellowship has been altar fellowship and vice versa on pp. 321–22.

34. Sasse, *This Is My Body*, 323.

35. *The Lutheran Hymnal*, 478:1.

36. Schmeling, *God's Gift to You*, 92.

37. Eyer, *They Will See His Face*, 83.

38. Eyer, *They Will See His Face*, 83–84.

39. Commission on Worship, *Hymnal Supplement 98*, 856:3.

40. Luther, "Admonition Concerning the Sacrament," LW 38:123.

41. Senn, *Christian Liturgy*, 458.

42. Ap XXIV, 76 (K-W, 271–72).

43. Sasse, *This Is My Body*, 325.

44. Commission on Worship, *Lutheran Worship*, 238:1.

45. Luther, "Admonition Concerning the Sacrament," LW 38:116.

46. Vajta, *Luther on Worship*, 59, 60, 82, quoting WA 1:334; 6:373, 378; 12:181.

47. Luther, "Lectures on Hebrews," LW 29:214.

48. Chemnitz, *Lord's Supper*, 186–87.

49. C. F. W. Walther, *The Proper Distinction between Law and Gospel*, trans. W. H. T. Dau (St. Louis: Concordia, 1986), 353.

50. Ap XXIV, 71–72 (K-W, 271).

51. Commission on Worship, *Lutheran Worship*, 246:4.

52. Lockwood, *1 Corinthians*, 395, quoting Walther, *Ein Handbuch zur Täglichen Hausandacht*.

53. Lockwood, *1 Corinthians*, 395.

54. Wainwright, *Eucharist and Eschatology*, 83.

55. Cullmann, *Christ and Time*, 74.

56. *The Lutheran Hymnal*, 306:8.

57. Wingren, *Living Word*, 160.

58. LC V, 23–25 (K-W, 469).

59. Veith, *Spirituality of the Cross*, 53.

60. Luther, "That These Words of Christ," LW 37:134.

61. Luther, "That These Words of Christ," LW 37:71.

62. Richard Eyer, *Pastoral Care under the Cross* (St. Louis: Concordia, 1994), 68.

63. Commission on Worship, *Hymnal Supplement 98*, 853:6.

64. Commission on Worship, *Lutheran Worship*, p. 174.

65. Veith, *God at Work*, 134–37. This listing is my own, but it flows from Veith's helpful and enriching discussion of Christian vocation in all of life.

66. Ap IV, 110 (K-W, 139).

67. Luther, "Blessed Sacrament of the Holy and True Body of Christ," LW 35:54.

68. Senkbeil, *Dying to Live*, 162 *(Senkbeil's emphasis)*.

69. Commission on Worship, *Lutheran Worship*, 238:3.

4

CHAPTER EIGHT

1. Luther, "Concerning the Order of Public Worship," LW 53:11.
2. Schmelder, *Oh, Come, Let Us Worship*, 12.
3. Kleinig, *Leviticus*, 25. See his enlightening discussion of God's presence in the Old Testament rituals that God commanded and His presence now in Christ on pp. 20–30.
4. Schmelder, *Oh, Come, Let Us Worship*, 24.
5. Commission on Worship, *Lutheran Worship*, p. 6.
6. Stuckwisch, "Liturgical Theology of Johannes Konrad Wilhelm Löhe," 27.
7. See Bender, *Lutheran Catechesis*, 1–13, for a helpful discussion of the importance of memorizing or "learning by heart."
8. Eyer, *They Will See His Face*, 10.
9. Eyer, *They Will See His Face*, 117.
10. Maschke, *Gathered Guests*, 465.
11. AC XXVIII, 21 (German text; K-W, 94).
12. AC VII–VIII, 28 (German text; K-W, 178).
13. Schmelder, "Liturgical Preaching," 122–23.
14. Ferry, "Preaching on Preaching," 35.
15. Luther, "Treatise on Good Works," LW 44:56.
16. Schmitt, "Law and Gospel in Sermon and Service," 35. See his entire essay for a helpful discussion of avoiding both Law and Gospel negligence and Law and Gospel obsession.
17. Windh, "Early Christian Masses," 13.
18. Wingren, *Living Word*, 108.
19. Wieting, "Sacramental Preaching," 69.
20. Quill, "Law-Gospel Preaching," 47.
21. Barry, *Unchanging Feast*, 46.
22. Rossow, *Preaching the Creative Gospel Creatively*, 27. See especially chapter 1 for a helpful discussion of preaching the Gospel.
23. Windh, "Early Christian Masses," 13.
24. *Luther's Small Catechism*, 31.
25. Bartels, *Take Eat, Take Drink*, 146.
26. LC V, 31–35 (K-W, 470).
27. LC V, 55–57 (K-W, 472–73).
28. LC V, 68 (K-W, 474).
29. LC V, 70, 72–74 (K-W, 474).

30. LC V, 76–78 (K-W, 474–75).

31. LC V, 82 (K-W, 475).

32. *Luther's Small Catechism*, 31.

33. FC SD VII, 69–71 (K-W, 605–6).

34. AC XI, 1–2 (German text; K-W, 44).

35. AC XXV, 1–4 (Latin text; K-W, 73).

36. Harjunpaa, "Pastor's Communion," 158.

37. Walther, *Proper Distinction between Law and Gospel*, 176–77.

38. Kober, *Confession and Forgiveness*, 98. See chapter 10 for a direct discussion of examination of sin.

39. Senkbeil, *Dying to Live*, 87.

40. *Luther's Small Catechism*, 26.

41. Sasse, *We Confess: The Sacraments*, 109.

42. *Luther's Small Catechism*, 40–44.

43. *Luther's Small Catechism*, 31.

44. Senn, *Christian Liturgy*, 279.

45. Luther, "Order of Mass and Communion," LW 53:28–29.

46. This meditation can be found as part of a newer translation in Gerhard, *Sacred Meditations*.

47. For a helpful discussion of the Rite of Confirmation, see Precht, *Lutheran Worship*, 387–400.

48. *Luther's Small Catechism*, 35–36.

49. AC VII, 1 (Latin text; K-W, 43).

50. Bartels, *Take Eat, Take Drink*, 146.

51. AC XXIV, 36–37 (K-W, 70).

52. Hartwig, *Close Communion*, 15.

53. Commission on Worship, *Lutheran Worship Altar Book*, 31.

54. Commission on Theology and Church Relations, *Admission to the Lord's Supper*. For an overview of frequent misunderstandings and questions concerning admission to the Lord's Supper, see especially pp. 49–58.

55. McCain, *Communion Fellowship*, 12.

56. Gibbs, "Exegetical Case for Close(d) Communion," 153.

57. McCain, *Communion Fellowship*, 12.

58. See Grase, "Terms for Communion," 67. His entire paper is helpful reading.

59. McCain, *Communion Fellowship*, 9. This is patterned after a quote of

Donald Deffner in Commission on Theology and Church Relation, *Theology and Practice of the Lord's Supper* (St. Louis: The Lutheran Church—Missouri Synod, 1983), 22.

60. Maschke, *Gathered Guests*, 466.

61. McCain, *Communion Fellowship*, 10.

62. Wieting, *Lord, May Your Body and Your Blood*, 12.

63. Kenneth W. Wieting, parish bulletin announcement.

64. Stephenson, "Reflections on the Appropriate Vessels," 11.

65. Bartels, *Take Eat, Take Drink*, 194. Bartels discusses the fear of infection and the first use of individual glass cups.

66. Maxwell, *Altar Guild Manual*, 102.

67. Maxwell, *Altar Guild Manual*, 102, quoting "The Common Cup and Disease," in *The Bride of Christ*, vol. XII, no. 3.

68. Maxwell, *Altar Guild Manual*, 102–3.

69. Mueller and Kraus, *Pastoral Theology*, 105.

70. Stephenson, "Reflections on the Appropriate Vessels," 15.

71. Stephenson, "Reflections on the Appropriate Vessels," 16.

72. Walther, *Pastoral Theology*, 145.

73. Maxwell, *Altar Guild Manual*, 101.

CHAPTER NINE

1. See Brighton, *Revelation*, 348–65.

2. Walther, *Pastoral Theology*, 65.

3. Walther, *Pastoral Theology*, 65.

4. Luther, "Lectures on Galatians," LW 27:37.

5. From *Sanctification: Christ in Action* by Harold L. Senkbeil, pp. 116–17, © 1989 Northwestern Publishing House, Wauwatosa, WI. Used with permission. Senkbeil is quoting from Luther's March 31, 1529, sermon on 1 Corinthians 15:1ff.

6. Walther, *Proper Distinction between Law and Gospel*, 312.

7. Walther, *Proper Distinction between Law and Gospel*, 264.

8. Walther, *Pastoral Theology*, 260.

9. Wenthe, "God's Character," 230.

10. Eyer, *They Will See His Face*, 66.

11. From *Sanctification: Christ in Action* by Harold L. Senkbeil, pp. 12, © 1989 Northwestern Publishing House, Wauwatosa, WI. Used with permission.

12. From *Sanctification: Christ in Action* by Harold L. Senkbeil, pp. 164, © 1989 Northwestern Publishing House, Wauwatosa, WI. Used with permission.

13. Marquart, "Some Aspects of a Healthy Church Life," 51.

14. Maschke, *Gathered Guests*, 134 (*Maschke's emphasis*).

15. SC Preface, 22 (K-W, 350).

16. *The Lutheran Hymnal*, pp. 29–30.

Bibliography

Aland, Kurt, ed. *Martin Luther's 95 Theses*. St. Louis: Concordia, 1967. Reprint 2004.

Arand, Charles P. *Testing the Boundaries*. St. Louis: Concordia, 1995.

Asch, Ronald G. *The Thirty Years War*. New York: St. Martin's Press, 1997.

Bainton, Roland, *The Church of Our Fathers*. New York: Scribner's, 1941.

Banek, James. "Sacramental Preaching." D.Min. diss. project, Concordia Theological Seminary, 2001.

Barry, A. L. *The Unchanging Feast*. St. Louis: Office of the President, The Lutheran Church—Missouri Synod, 1995.

————. *Unchanging Truth in Changing Times*. St. Louis: Office of the President, The Lutheran Church—Missouri Synod, 2001.

Bartels, Ernest. *Take Eat, Take Drink*. St. Louis: Concordia, 2004.

Baue, Frederic W. *The Spiritual Society*. Wheaton, IL: Crossway, 2001.

Bender, Peter C. *Lutheran Catechesis*. Catechist Edition. Sussex, WI: Concordia Catechetical Academy, 1999.

Billington, Ray Allen. *The Protestant Crusade, 1800–1860*. New York: Rinehart, 1938.

Brege, Daniel J. "The Learning of Old Testament Sacrificial Concepts Will Enhance One's Appreciation for the Lord's Supper." D.Min. diss., Concordia Theological Seminary, 2002.

Briese, Russel John. "Wilhelm Loehe and the Rediscovery of the Sacrament of the Altar in Nineteenth Century Lutheranism." *Lutheran Forum* 30, no. 2 (1996): 31–34.

Brighton, Louis. *Revelation*. Concordia Commentary. St. Louis: Concordia, 1999.

Bruce, F. F. *The Book of the Acts*. New International Commentary on the New Testament. Grand Rapids: Eerdmans, 1988.

Bruzek, Scott Arthur. "A Five-Word Faith: The Eucharistic Theology of Martin Chemnitz' *Fundamenta Sacrae Doctrinae*." PhD. diss., Princeton Theological Seminary, 1995.

Carlen, Claudia, comp. *The Papal Encyclicals*. Vol. 3, *1903–1939*. Wilmington, NC: McGrath, 1981.

Chadwick, Henry. *The Early Church*. Pelican History of the Church 1. New York: Penguin, 1967.

Chemnitz, Martin. *The Lord's Supper.* Translated by J. A. O. Preus. St. Louis: Concordia, 1979.

Church Growth Study Committee, LCMS. *For the Sake of Christ's Commission.* St. Louis: Church Growth Study Committee of The Lutheran Church—Missouri Synod, 2001.

Clouse, Robert G. *The Church in the Age of Orthodoxy and the Enlightenment.* Church in History 5. St. Louis: Concordia, 1980.

————, Richard V. Pierard, and Edwin M. Yamauchi. *Two Kingdoms.* Chicago: Moody, 1993.

Collver, Albert B. "Real Presence: An Overview and History of the Term." *Concordia Journal* 28, no. 2 (April 2002): 142–59.

Commission on Theology and Church Relations, LCMS. *Admission to the Lord's Supper.* St. Louis: The Lutheran Church—Missouri Synod, 2000.

Commission on Worship, LCMS. *Hymnal Supplement 98.* St. Louis: Concordia, 1998.

————. *Lutheran Worship.* St. Louis: Concordia, 1982.

————. *Lutheran Worship Agenda.* St. Louis: Concordia, 1984.

————. *Lutheran Worship Altar Book.* St. Louis: Concordia, 1982.

————. *Reflections on Contemporary/Alternative Worship.* St. Louis: Commission on Worship of The Lutheran Church—Missouri Synod, 1998.

Cullmann, Oscar. *Christ and Time: The Primitive Christian Conception of Time and History.* Translated by Floyd Filson. Philadelphia: Westminster Press, 1964.

———— and F. J. Leenhardt. *Essays on the Lord's Supper.* Translated by J. G. Davies. Ecumenical Studies in Worship 1. Richmond: John Knox, 1958.

Deitz, Reginald W. "The Lord's Supper in American Lutheranism." In *Meaning and Practice of the Lord's Supper,* edited by Helmut T. Lehmann. Philadelphia: Muhlenberg, 1961.

DeVries, Kim. "The Prussian Union." *Concordia Historical Institute Quarterly* 49, no. 1: 131–40.

Dix, Gregory. *The Shape of the Liturgy.* London: Adam & Charles Black, 1945.

Ellis, John Tracy, ed. *Documents of American Catholic History.* Vol. 2, *1866–1966.* Wilmington, DE: M. Glazier, 1987.

————. *American Catholicism.* Chicago History of American Civilization. Chicago: University at Chicago Press, 1955.

Eyer, Richard C. *Holy People, Holy Lives.* St. Louis: Concordia , 2000.

————. *Pastoral Care under the Cross.* St. Louis: Concordia, 1994.

————. *They Will See His Face.* St. Louis: Concordia, 2002.

Ferry, Patrick. "Preaching on Preaching: *Postils*, the *Predigtampt* and the People." *Logia* 3, no. 4 (October 1994): 35.

———. "What Did It Mean to Be Lutheran in the Confessional Period (1530–80)?" Pages 1–24 in *What Does It Mean to Be Lutheran?* Edited by John A. Maxfield and Jennifer H. Maxfield. Pieper Lectures 4. St. Louis: Concordia Historical Institute, 2000.

Feuerhahn, Ronald. "The Roots and Fruits of German Pietism." Pages 50–74 in *Pietism and Lutheranism*. Edited by John A. Maxfield. Pieper Lectures 3. St. Louis: Concordia Historical Institute, 1999.

Franzmann, Martin. *Concordia Self-Study Commentary: New Testament*. St. Louis: Concordia, 1979.

———. *The Word of the Lord Grows*. St. Louis: Concordia, 1961.

Frend, W. H. C. *The Rise of Christianity*. Philadelphia: Fortress, 1984.

Fuerbringer, Ludwig Ernest. *80 Eventful Years*. St. Louis: Concordia, 1944.

Gerhard, Johann. *A Comprehensive Explanation of Holy Baptism and the Lord's Supper (1610)*. Translated by Elmer Hohle. Malone, TX: Repristination Press, 2000.

———. *Sacred Meditations*. Translated by C. W. Heisler. Decatur, IL: Repristination Press, 1998.

Gibbs, Jeffrey A. "An Exegetical Case for Close(d) Communion: 1 Corinthians 10:14–22; 11:17–34." *Concordia Journal* 21, no. 2 (April 1995): 148–63.

González, Justo L. *Church History: An Essential Guide*. Abingdon Essential Guides. Nashville: Abingdon, 1996.

———. *The Story of Christianity*. Vol. 1, *The Early Church to the Dawn of the Reformation*. Vol. 2, *The Reformation to the Present Day*. San Francisco: Harper & Row, 1984–1985.

Grase, Mark H. "Terms for Communion." M.Div. paper, Concordia Theological Seminary, 2002.

Grime, Paul, and Joseph Herl, eds. *Hymnal Supplement 98 Handbook*. St. Louis: Commission on Worship, The Lutheran Church—Missouri Synod, 1998.

Gustafson, David A. *Lutherans in Crisis*. Minneapolis: Fortress, 1993.

Harjunpaa, Toivo. "The Pastor's Communion." *Concordia Theological Quarterly* 52, nos. 2–3 (April-July 1988): 149–67.

Harms, Claus. "Ninety-Five Theses." In *Moving Frontiers,* edited by Carl S. Meyer. St. Louis: Concordia, 1964.

Hartwig, Raymond L. *Close Communion: Sharing God's Meal*. St. Louis: Concordia, 1995.

Hippolytus. *Apostolic Tradition*. Translated by Burton Scott Easton. Hamden, CT: Archon, 1962.

Hoerber, Robert, gen. ed. *Concordia Self-Study Bible*. St. Louis: Concordia, 1986.

———. *Reading the New Testament for Understanding*. St. Louis: Concordia, 1986.

Jungmann, Josef A. *The Early Liturgy*. Translated by Francis A. Brunner. University of Notre Dame Liturgical Studies 6. South Bend, IN: University of Notre Dame Press, 1959.

———. *The Mass of the Roman Rite*. Vol. 2. Translated by Francis A. Brunner. Westminster, MD: Christian Classics, 1986.

Just, Arthur A. Jr. *Luke 1:1–9:50*. Concordia Commentary. St. Louis: Concordia, 1996.

———. *Luke 9:51–24:53*. Concordia Commentary. St. Louis: Concordia, 1997.

———. *The Ongoing Feast*. Collegeville, MN: Liturgical Press, 1993.

———. "Sacramental Practice in a Post-Denominational America." In *Shepherd the Church: Essays in Honor of the Rev. Dr. Roger D. Pittelko*, edited by Frederic W. Baue et al. Fort Wayne, IN: Concordia Theological Seminary Press, 2002.

Kalb, Friedrich. *Theology of Worship in 17th-Century Lutheranism*. Translated by Henry P. A. Hamann. St. Louis: Concordia, 1965.

Kelly, J. N. D. *Early Christian Creeds*. London: Longmans, 1960.

Kemerer, D. M. "Early American Lutheran Liturgies." Pages 86–89 in vol. 4 of *Memoirs of the Lutheran Liturgical Association*. Pittsburgh: Lutheran Liturgical Association, 1986–1987.

Klauser, Theodor. *A Short History of the Western Liturgy*. Translated by John Halliburton. London: Oxford University Press, 1969.

Kleinig, John W. *Leviticus*. Concordia Commentary. St. Louis: Concordia, 2003.

Kleinig, Vernon. "Lutheran Liturgies from Martin Luther to Wilhelm Löhe." *Concordia Theological Quarterly* 62, no. 2 (April 1998): 125–44.

Kober, Ted. *Confession and Forgiveness*. St. Louis: Concordia, 2002.

Kolb, Robert, and Timothy J. Wengert, eds. *The Book of Concord*. Translated by Charles Arand et al. Minneapolis: Augsburg Fortress, 2000.

———. *The Christian Faith*. St. Louis: Concordia, 1993.

———. *Speaking the Gospel Today*. St. Louis: Concordia, 1984.

Krauth, Charles Porterfield. *The Conservative Reformation and Its Theology*. Reprint Minneapolis: Augsburg, 1978.

Kretzmann, P. E. *Christian Art*. St. Louis: Concordia, 1921.

Lang, Paul H. D. *What an Altar Guild Should Know*. St. Louis: Concordia, 1964.

Lathrop, Gordon. *Holy Things*. Minneapolis: Fortress, 1993.

LaVerdiere, Eugene. *The Eucharist in the New Testament and the Early Church*. Collegeville, MN: Liturgical Press, 1996.

Lee, Philip J. *Against the Protestant Gnostics*. New York: Oxford University Press, 1987.

Lenski, R. C. H. *The Interpretation of the Acts of the Apostles*. Minneapolis, Augsburg, 1961.

Lewis, C. S. *The Screwtape Letters*. New York: Macmillan, 1950.

Lindemann, Fred H. *Till He Come*. New York: Ernst Kaufmann, 1948.

Lockwood, Gregory. *1 Corinthians*. Concordia Commentary. St. Louis: Concordia, 2000.

Loescher, Valentin Ernst. *The Complete Timotheus Verinus*. Part Two. Translated by Robert J. Koester. Milwaukee: Northwestern, 1998.

Lueker, Erwin, ed. *Lutheran Cyclopedia*. St. Louis: Concordia, 1954.

Luther, Martin. "Admonition Concerning the Sacrament of the Body and Blood of Our Lord." Translated by Martin E. Lehmann. Vol. 38 of Luther's Works. Philadelphia: Fortress, 1971.

———. "The Adoration of the Sacrament." Translated by Abdel Ross Wentz. Vol. 36 of Luther's Works. Philadelphia: Fortress, 1959.

———. "The Babylonian Captivity of the Church." Translated by A. T. W. Steinhäuser. Revised by Frederick C. Ahrens and Abdel Ross Wentz. Vol. 36 of Luther's Works. Philadelphia: Muhlenberg, 1959.

———. "The Blessed Sacrament of the Holy and True Body of Christ, and the Brotherhoods." Translated by Jeremiah J. Schindel. Revised by E. Theodore Bachmann. Vol. 35 of Luther's Works. Philadelphia: Muhlenburg, 1960.

———. "Concerning Rebaptism." Translated by Conrad Bergendoff. Vol. 40 of Luther's Works. Philadelphia: Muhlenburg, 1958.

———. "Concerning the Order of Public Worship." Translated by Paul Zeller Strodach. Revised by Ulrich S. Leupold. Vol. 53 of Luther's Works. Philadelphia: Fortress, 1965.

———. "Confession Concerning Christ's Supper." Translated by Robert H. Fischer. Vol. 37 of Luther's Works. Philadelphia: Fortress, 1961.

———. "Lectures on Galatians." Translated by Jaroslav Pelikan. Vol. 27 of Luther's Works. St. Louis: Concordia, 1964.

———. "Lectures on Hebrews." Translated by Walter A. Hansen. Vol. 29 of Luther's Works. St. Louis: Concordia, 1968.

——. "Letter to Lazarus Spengler." Translated by Gottfried G. Krodel. Vol. 49 of Luther's Works. Philadelphia: Fortress, 1972.

——. "On the Councils and the Church." Translated by C. M. Jacobs. Revised by Harold J. Grimm. Vol. 31 of Luther's Works. Philadelphia: Fortress, 1966.

——. "An Open Letter to Those in Frankfurt on the Main, 1533." Translated by Jon D. Vieker. *Concordia Journal* 16, no. 2 (October 1990): 333–51.

——. "An Order of Mass and Communion for the Church at Wittenberg." Translated by Paul Zeller Strodach. Revised by Ulrich S. Leupold. Vol. 53 of Luther's Works. Philadelphia: Fortress, 1965.

——. "The Sacrament of the Body and Blood of Christ—Against the Fanatics." Translated by Frederick C. Ahrens. Vol. 36 of Luther's Works. Philadelphia: Fortress, 1959.

——. *Small Catechism with Explanation.* St. Louis: Concordia, 1986.

——. "That These Words of Christ, 'This Is My Body,' Etc., Still Stand Firm against the Fanatics." Translated by Robert H. Fischer. Vol. 37 of Luther's Works. Philadelphia: Fortress, 1961.

——. "Treatise on Good Works." Translated by W. A. Lambert. Revised by James Atkinson. Vol. 44 of Luther's Works. Philadelphia: Fortress, 1966.

——. "A Treatise on the New Testament, That Is the Holy Mass." Translated by Jeremiah J. Schindel. Revised by E. Theodore Bachmann. Vol. 35 of Luther's Works. Philadelphia: Fortress, 1960.

The Lutheran Church—Missouri Synod. *Convention Proceedings: 59th Regular Convention, The Lutheran Church—Missouri Synod.* St. Louis: Office of the Secretary, The Lutheran Church—Missouri Synod, 1995.

——. *Statistical Yearbook of The Lutheran Church—Missouri Synod for the Year 1950.* St. Louis: Concordia, 1951.

The Lutheran Hymnal. St. Louis: Concordia, 1941.

MacKenzie, Cameron A. "The Lutheran Reformers' Understanding of the Historical Deformation of the Church." In *Lutheran Catholicity*, edited by John A. Maxfield. Pieper Lectures 5. St. Louis: Concordia Historical Institute, 2001.

Marshall, I. Howard. *The Acts of the Apostles.* Tyndale New Testament Commentaries. Grand Rapids: Eerdmans, 1980.

Marty, Martin. *An Invitation to American Catholic History.* Chicago: Thomas More, 1986.

Marquart, Kurt. "Some Aspects of a Healthy Church Life." *Lutheran Synod Quarterly* 8, no. 3 (1968): 51.

——. "The Word as Life." *Lutheran Synod Quarterly* 8, no. 3 (1968).

Marzolf, Dennis W. "C. F. W. Walther: The Musician and Liturgiologist." In *C. F. W. Walther: The American Luther: Essays in Commemoration of the 100th Anniversary of Carl Walther's Death*. Mankato, MN: Walther Press, 1987.

Maschke, Timothy H. *Gathered Guests*. St. Louis: Concordia Academic Press, 2003.

Maxwell, Lee A. *The Altar Guild Manual*. St. Louis: Concordia, 1996.

McCain, Paul T. *Communion Fellowship*. Waverly, IA: International Foundation for Lutheran Confessional Research, 1992.

———. "An Orthodox Lutheran Response to Pietism: An Introduction to the Work of Valentin Loescher." Pages 75–92 in *Pietism and Lutheranism*, edited by John A. Maxfield. Pieper Lectures 3. St. Louis: Concordia Historical Institute, 1999.

Metzger, Marcel. *History of the Liturgy*. Translated by Madeleine Beaumont. Collegeville, MN: Liturgical Press, 1997.

Meyer, Carl S., ed. *Moving Frontiers*. St. Louis: Concordia, 1964.

Mueller, Norbert, and George Kraus. *Pastoral Theology*. St. Louis: Concordia, 1990.

Nagel, Norman. "Luther's Liturgical Reform." *Logia* VII, no. 2 (Eastertide 1998): 23–26.

Nelson, E. Clifford, ed. *The Lutherans in North America*. Philadelphia: Fortress, 1975.

Noll, Mark A. *A History of Christianity in the United States and Canada*. Grand Rapids: Eerdmans, 1992.

———. *The Scandal of the Evangelical Mind*. Grand Rapids: Eerdmans, 1994.

———. *Turning Points*. Grand Rapids: Baker, 1997.

Northwick, Byron. *The Development of the Missouri Synod: The Role of Education in the Preservation and Promotion of Lutheran Orthodoxy, 1839–1872*. PhD. diss., Kansas State University, 1987.

O'Brien, John M. *Medieval Church*. Totowa, NJ: Littlefield, Adams, 1968.

Olson, Oliver K. "Matthias Flacius." In *The Reformation Theologians*, edited by Carter Lindberg. Oxford: Blackwell, 2002.

Petry, Ray C., ed. *A History of Christianity*. Grand Rapids: Baker, 1962.

Pinson, Kappel. *Pietism as a Factor in the Rise of German Nationalism*. New York: Octagon, 1968.

Pittelko, Roger D., and Fred L. Precht, eds. *Guide to Introducing Lutheran Worship*. St. Louis: Concordia, 1981.

Plass, Ewald, comp. *What Luther Says*. 3 vols. St. Louis: Concordia, 1959.

Pless, John. "Liturgy and Pietism: Then and Now." Pages 144–64 in *Pietism and Lutheranism*, edited by John A. Maxfield. Pieper Lectures 3. St. Louis: Concordia Historical Institute, 1999.

Precht, Fred, ed. *Lutheran Worship: History and Practice*. St. Louis: Concordia, 1993.

Quill, Timothy. "Law-Gospel Preaching." *Logia* III, no. 4 (Reformation 1994): 45–50.

Ramer, A. L. "The Liturgical Influence of Gregory the Great." In vol. 5 of *Memoirs of the Lutheran Liturgical Association*. Pittsburgh: Lutheran Liturgical Association, 1986–1987.

Rast, Lawrence R. Jr. "Catholicity in Missourian Orthodoxy." Pages 51–82 in *Lutheran Catholicity*, edited by John A. Maxfield. Pieper Lectures 5. St. Louis: Concordia Historical Institute, 2001.

Robertson, J. A. T. *Redating the New Testament*. Philadelphia: Westminster, 1976.

Rossow, Francis C. *Preaching the Creative Gospel Creatively*. St. Louis: Concordia, 1983.

Saleska, E. J. "Frederich Conrad Dieterich Wyneken, 1810–1876." STM thesis, Concordia Seminary, 1946.

Sasse, Hermann. "The Holy Supper and the Future of the Church." Pages 479–88 in vol. 1 of *The Lonely Way*. St. Louis: Concordia, 2001.

———. "The Lord's Supper in the Life of the Church (1939)." In *Scripture and the Church: Selected Essays of Hermann Sasse*, edited by Jeffrey Kloha and Ronald R. Feuerhahn. St. Louis: Concordia Seminary, 1995.

———. *This Is My Body*. Adelaide: Lutheran Publishing House, 1977.

———. *We Confess: The Sacraments*. Translated by Norman Nagel. St. Louis: Concordia, 1985.

Scaer, David P. *Christology*. Confessional Lutheran Dogmatics 6. Fort Wayne, IN: International Foundation for Lutheran Confessional Research, 1989.

Schmelder, William J. "Liturgical Preaching." *Concordia Journal* 16, no. 2 (April 1990): 121–36.

———. *Oh, Come, Let Us Worship*. Leaders Guide. St. Louis: Concordia, 1981.

Schmeling, Gaylin R. *God's Gift to You*. Milwaukee: Northwestern, 2001.

Schmitt, David R. "Law and Gospel in Sermon and Service." In *Liturgical Preaching*, edited by Paul Grime and Dean Nadasdy. St. Louis: Concordia, 2001.

Schoessow, David. "Holy Communion: Should We Offer It More Frequently?" *Concordia Journal* 24, no. 3 (July 1998): 225–33.

Schwiebert, E. G. *Luther and His Times*. St. Louis: Concordia, 1950.

Senkbeil, Harold L. *Dying to Live*. St. Louis: Concordia, 1994.

———. *Sanctification: Christ in Action*. Milwaukee: Northwestern, 1989.

———. *Where in the World Is God?* Compiled by Beverly K. Yahnke. Milwaukee: Northwestern, 1999.

Senn, Frank C. *Christian Liturgy*. Minneapolis: Fortress, 1997.

———. "The Reform of the Mass: Evangelical, But Still Catholic." In *The Catholicity of the Reformation*, edited by Carl E. Braaten and Robert W. Jenson. Grand Rapids: Eerdmans, 1996.

Stephenson, John R. "The Holy Eucharist: At the Center or Periphery of the Church's Life in Luther's Thinking?" In *A Lively Legacy: Essays in Honor of Robert Preus*, edited by Kurt E. Marquart, John R. Stephenson and Bjarne E. Teigen. Fort Wayne, IN: Concordia Theological Seminary, 1985.

———. *The Lord's Supper*. Confessional Lutheran Dogmatics 12. St. Louis: Luther Academy, 2003.

———. "Reflections on the Appropriate Vessels for Consecrating and Distributing the Precious Blood of Christ." *Logia* IV, no. 1 (Epiphany 1995): 11–19.

Stiller, Günther. *Johann Sebastian Bach and Liturgical Life in Leipzig*. Translated by Herbert J. A. Bouman et al. Edited by Robin Leaver. St. Louis: Concordia, 1984.

Stoeffler, F. Ernest. *The Rise of Evangelical Pietism*. Leiden: E. J. Brill, 1965.

Strauss, Gerald. *Luther's House of Learning*. Baltimore: Johns Hopkins University Press, 1978.

Stuckwisch, D. Richard. "The Liturgical Theology of Johannes Konrad Wilhelm Löhe: Confessional Lutheran Liturgiologist." STM research paper, Concordia Theological Seminary, 1994.

Taft, Robert. "The Frequency of the Eucharist throughout History." Pages 13–24 in *Can We Always Celebrate the Eucharist?* edited by Mary Collins and David Power. New York: Seabury Press, 1982.

Tappert, Theodore G. "Meaning and Practice in Europe since the Reformation." Pages 113–31 in *Meaning and Practice of the Lord's Supper*, edited by Helmut T. Lehmann. Philadelphia: Muhlenberg, 1961.

———. "Meaning and Practice in the Middle Ages." Pages 75–84 in *Meaning and Practice of the Lord's Supper*, edited by Helmut T. Lehmann. Philadelphia: Muhlenberg, 1961.

———. "Meaning and Practice in the Reformation." Pages 85–109 in *Meaning and Practice of the Lord's Supper*, edited by Helmut T. Lehmann. Philadelphia: Muhlenberg, 1961.

———. "Orthodoxism, Pietism, and Rationalism (1580–1830)." Pages

36–88 in vol. 2 of *Christian Social Responsibility*, edited by Harold Letts. Philadelphia: Muhlenberg, 1957.

Teigen, Erling. "Luther and the Consecration." Pages 321–40 in *Mysteria De Essays in Honor of Kurt Marquart*, edited by Paul T. McCain and John R. Stephenson. Fort Wayne, IN: Concordia Theological Seminary Press, 1999.

Vajta, Vilmos, *Luther on Worship: An Interpretation*. Translated by U. S. Leupold. Philadelphia: Muhlenberg, 1958.

———, ed. "Worship and Sacramental Life." In *The Lutheran Church, Past and Present*. Minneapolis: Augsburg, 1977.

Vauchez, André. *The Laity in the Middle Ages*. South Bend, IN: University of Notre Dame Press, 1993.

Veith, Gene Edward Jr. *God at Work*. Wheaton, IL: Crossway, 2002.

———. *The Spirituality of the Cross*. St. Louis: Concordia, 1999.

Wainwright, Geoffrey. *Eucharist and Eschatology*. New York: Oxford University Press, 1981.

Walther, C. F. W. *Gnadenjahr*. St. Louis: Lutherischer Concordia, 1890.

———. *Law and Gospel*. Translated by W. H. T. Dau. St. Louis: Concordia, 1929.

———. *Pastoral Theology*. Translated by John M. Drickamer. New Haven, MO: Lutheran News, 1995.

Weinrich, William. "It Is Not Given to Women to Teach." Paper published by the Lutheran Church of Christ the King, Duluth, MN, 1991.

———. "The Lutheran Reformation and the Early Church." In *Lutheran Catholicity*, edited by John A. Maxfield. Pieper Lectures 5. St. Louis, Concordia Historical Institute, 2001.

Webber, F. R. *Studies in the Liturgy*. Erie, PA: Ashby, 1938.

Wenthe, Dean O. "God's Character and the Calling of God's People." Pages 209–33 in *Shepherd the Church: Essays in Honor of the Rev. Dr. Roger D. Pittelko*, edited by Frederic W. Baue et al. Fort Wayne, IN: Concordia Theological Seminary Press, 2002.

White, James F. *A Brief History of Christian Worship*. Nashville: Abingdon, 1993.

———. *Christian Worship in North America*. Collegeville, MN: Liturgical Press, 1997.

Wiest, Stephen. "The Evangelical Impetus for Evangelization." www.lsfmissiology.org/Essays/1999/2000.

Wieting, Kenneth W. *Lord, May Your Body and Your Blood Be for My Soul the Highest Good!* Self-published, 1990.

Wieting, Kenneth W. "Sacramental Preaching: The Lord's Supper." In *Litur-*

ed by Paul J. Grime and Dean W. Nadasdy. St.
2001.

Word, Water, Wine, and Bread. Valley Forge: Judson,

rid. "Early Christian Masses." PhD. thesis, University of
71.

taf. The Living Word. Philadelphia: Muhlenberg, 1949.

rd C. Lutherans in North America. LCA School of Religion Series.
adelphia: Lutheran Church Press, 1965.

. Jeffrey. "Aspects of Theology in the Liturgical Movement in The
Lutheran Church—Missouri Synod, 1930–1960." ThD. diss., Christ
Seminary-Seminex, 1982.